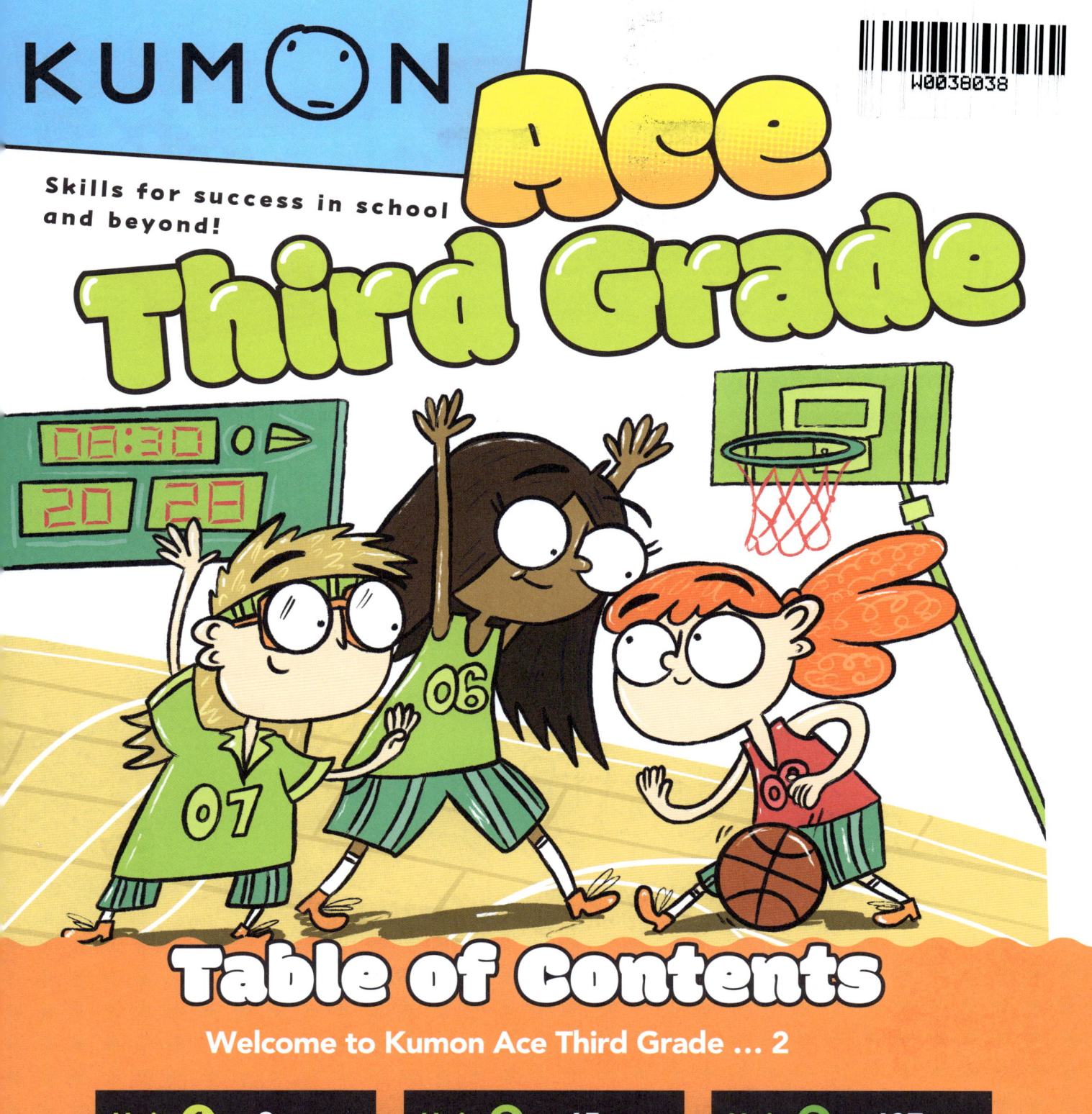

KUMON

Skills for success in school and beyond!

Ace Third Grade

W0038038

Table of Contents

Welcome to Kumon — Ace Third Grade

1 Write the date at the top of each page.

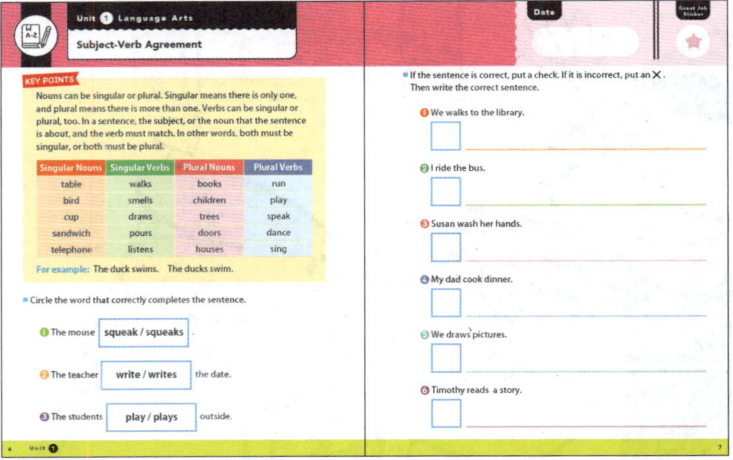

2 Read the directions and Key Points on each page. Then complete each activity.

3 When you complete a section, check your answers with the Answer Key in the back of the book. Try again if you got any wrong.

4 When you are done checking your answers, place a "Great Job" sticker on the top of the page!

Let's study!

⭐ When you have finished studying each unit, put a sticker on the sheet on page 319.

⭐ When you have finished all of the units, place the largest sticker at the bottom of the same sheet.

⭐ Then have your parent or guardian sign the Certificate of Achievement and present it to you!

Cut out the study posters and hang them up for further study!

Unit **1** Table of Contents

Use this page to keep track of your progress throughout the book. Place a check mark in the box when you have completed a section.

Language Arts

Reading

Math

Science

Social Studies

Technology

Nouns and Pronouns

KEY POINTS

Nouns are a person, place, thing, or idea.

Pronouns take the place of a noun. Some examples of pronouns are *he, she, they, it.*

Pronouns can be used in place of a noun to make a sentence more simple, or to add variety to a longer piece of writing.

For example:

Sarah went to the store. Sarah bought a watermelon. The watermelon weighed eight pounds!

Sarah went to the store. She bought a watermelon. It weighed eight pounds!

■ Match the noun with the correct pronoun.

Anna	●	●	they
Lee and Maude	●	●	it
Bicycle	●	●	she
Mike	●	●	he

■ Replace the nouns in red with pronouns. Rewrite the paragraph in the space below.

On Tuesday, I went over to Mindy's house. **Mindy** has a backyard. **Mindy and I** played outside. Mindy's family has a dog named Rover. **Rover** likes to play fetch in the backyard. **Mindy, Rover, and I** had a great time.

Subject-Verb Agreement

KEY POINTS

Nouns can be singular or plural. Singular means there is only one, and plural means there is more than one. Verbs can be singular or plural, too. In a sentence, the subject, or the noun that the sentence is about, and the verb must match. In other words, both must be singular, or both must be plural.

Singular Nouns	Singular Verbs	Plural Nouns	Plural Verbs
table	walks	books	run
bird	smells	children	play
cup	draws	trees	speak
sandwich	pours	doors	dance
telephone	listens	houses	sing

For example: The duck swims.   The ducks swim.

■ Circle the word that correctly completes the sentence.

❶ The mouse   **squeak / squeaks**   .

❷ The teacher   **write / writes**   the date.

❸ The students   **play / plays**   outside.

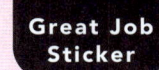

■ If the sentence is correct, put a check. If it is incorrect, put an ✕.
   Then write the correct sentence.

❶ We walks to the library.

❷ I ride the bus.

❸ Susan wash her hands.

❹ My dad cook dinner.

❺ We draws pictures.

❻ Timothy reads a story.

Comparative and Superlative Adjectives

KEY POINTS

Adjectives are words that describe a noun. Sometimes we can also use adjectives to compare two or more things. For example, *The tree is **tall**. That tree is **taller**!* While the first tree is tall, we now know that the second tree is even more tall than the first.

You can also use an adjective to show something that is the very most in its category. For example: *That tree is the **tallest**!* Now we know that the third tree is the most tall of all of the trees.

■ Write an adjective below each picture.

❶ **tall**   tall | taller | tallest

❷ **big** | |

❸ **long** | |

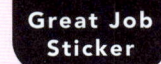

■ Next to each adjective, write the adjective that shows it is more than the first, and then the adjective that shows it is the most in its category.

❶ long | longer | longest |

❷ quiet | | |

❸ soft | | |

❹ happy | | |

❺ shiny | | |

❻ quick | | |

❼ slow | | |

❽ heavy | | |

Conjunctions

KEY POINTS

Conjunctions are words that bring together two or more ideas. Coordinating conjunctions are used when the ideas have the same importance. They include *and, but, or.*
For example: I went for a walk, *and* I saw my friend.

Subordinating conjunctions are used when one idea depends on another idea. They include *because, although, so.*
For example: I brought my library card *so* I can check out a book.

In the first example, the two actions are equally important. But in the second example, we can see that the person only brought their library card in order to get a book. Getting a book depends on having a library card.

■ Fill in an appropriate conjunction.

❶ I am working hard _____

I want to ace this test.

❷ I rode my bicycle, _____

it's not too far to walk.

❸ _____ I like ice cream,

I don't like sprinkles.

■ Write a sentence using the conjunction.

❶ Or

❷ Although

❸ But

❹ Because

❺ So

❻ And

Brain Break
Funny Fill-in!

■ Fill in words to complete the silly story.

On [_____], I went to [_____]
day of the week   noun, place

with [_____]. We wanted to
noun, person

[_____]. We took our [_____] and
verb   noun, object

[_____] with us. When we got there, it was
noun, object

[_____] [_____]. We stayed for
adverb   adjective

[_____]. It was a/an [_____] day!
amount of time   adjective

Mindfulness Break!

■ Use your finger to trace the rainbow and breathe in and out.

Breathe in · · ·

Breathe in · · ·

Breathe in · · ·

Breathe out · · ·

Breathe out · · ·

Breathe out · · ·

Start

Hold

Hold

Figurative Language: Similes

KEY POINTS

Similes are a type of figurative language that compares two things using the words "like" or "as."

Example: Her **hair** is as **golden** <u>as</u> the **sun**.
In the example, the girl's hair is being compared to the color of the sun.
Similes help the reader get a better picture of what a character or setting looks like in a story or poem.

■ Circle the noun being described in each simile. Draw a box around the comparing word. Underline the noun used as a comparison.

❶ The runner is fast like a cheetah on the track.

❷ Jamie was as strong as an ox.

❸ The teacher was as busy as a bee.

❹ She could swim like a fish.

■ **Fill in the blanks to complete the similes.**

1 My brother is wise like a(n) _____ .

2 The puppy was _____ like a(n) _____ .

3 JoJo was as smart as a(n) _____ .

4 Katherine was as _____ as a(n) _____ .

■ **Write your own similes. You can describe people, places, or things.**

1

_____

2

_____

3

_____

4

_____

Figurative Language: Metaphors

KEY POINTS

Metaphors are another type of figurative language used to compare two things. Metaphors do not use "like" or "as" for comparisons. They state that something is something else.

Example: The classroom was a zoo.

This example implies that the classroom was so wild it was like going to a zoo.

Metaphors make language fun and interesting. They can describe nouns in new ways that help readers better understand descriptions or comparisons.

■ Circle the noun being described in each metaphor. Underline each word being used as a comparison.

❶ He is a night owl.

❷ Laura is an angel.

❸ His head was always in the clouds.

❹ The tiger's teeth were knives.

■ Explain the metaphor in your own words.

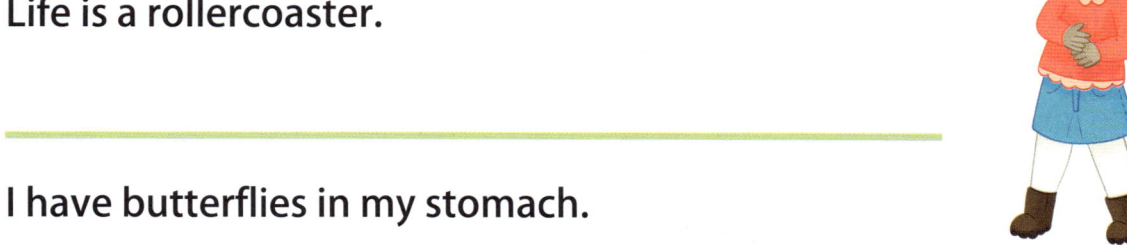

1 Life is a rollercoaster.

_____

2 I have butterflies in my stomach.

_____

3 The baby's cry was a siren sound.

_____

4 Paul's bedroom was a pigsty.

_____

■ Write your own metaphors. You can describe people, places, or things.

1

_____

2

_____

3

_____

4

_____

KEY POINTS

Poetry is a type of literature, or creative writing, that tries to make a reader imagine things differently and feel emotion. A poem does this through carefully written words and by arranging language for its meaning, sound, and rhythm. Some poems also use rhyming words, but not all poems have rhymes.

Nursery rhymes are a type of poem typically used to teach a lesson. Song lyrics can also be consider a type of poem.

For example:

Hickory dickory dock, the mouse ran up the clock.
The clock struck one, the mouse ran down, hickory dickory dock.
Hickory dickory dock, the mouse ran up the clock.
The clock struck two, the mouse said "Boo!" hickory dickory dock.
Hickory dickory dock, the mouse ran up the clock.
The clock struck three, the mouse said "Whee!" Hickory dickory dock.
Hickory dickory dock, the mouse ran up the clock.
The clock struck four, the mouse said "No more!" Hickory dickory dock.

■ Circle the rhyming words in the poem.

In the morning when I wake,
I look out my window to the lake.
To my surprise I see snowflakes.
I was not ready to see snow!

I jumped out of bed and dressed quickly,
in my wool coat that was quite prickly.
I ran outside to see the snow lay thickly
on the ground and all around the big brown hickory!

■ Read the poem and complete the rhymes.

Word Box

fro   regret   day   longer   measure   good-bye

Away to the ocean we go
to watch the waves roll to and _____.
They kiss the shore, and then return
to the depths that bring them in.

In the sand, we dig and play,
Building castles for the _____.
Collecting shells and other treasures,
filled with joy beyond _____.

Swimming through the dark blue water,
wishing to stay in a little _____.
Seagulls cry as they soar overhead,
and hermit crabs rest in sandy beds.

As the sun begins to set,
we pack our thing up with _____.
Stars appear in the dark blue sky
the ocean's dreams bid us _____.

KEY POINTS

Many poems use figurative language like similes and metaphors to create more vivid pictures with their words. Figurative language can be interpreted differently by different readers.

For example:

> Twinkle, twinkle little star,
> how I wonder what you are?
> Up above the world so high,
> like a diamond in the sky.

In this poem, the simile "like a diamond in the sky" means that the star twinkles and shines like a diamond does.

■ Underline the figurative language in the poem.

At the zoo, the lions roar like thunder,

monkeys swing playfully through the trees,

and zebras wear their stripes,

like puzzles in black and white.

Giraffes stand as tall as skyscrapers,

eating leaves from the tallest trees.

And elephants look like big grey ships,

Passing slowly through the sea.

■ Read the poem and explain the underlined simile or metaphor in your own words.

World of Wonders

The sky is a canvas, painted in blue,

In this world of wonders, there's magic for you.

In the forest, tall trees sway,

and the sun is a smile that brightens the day.

Bird song sounds like a violin,

clear and bright carried by the wind.

Flowers bloom in a colorful row,

like a cozy quilt made from a rainbow.

Look around and you will see,

magic in every flower, rock, and tree.

Ex.

_____

_____

Ex.

_____

_____

Ex.

_____

_____

Brain Break
Write your own poem!

■ Write your own poem. Use similes, metaphors, and rhyming words like
you learned in this section.

Mindfulness Break!

Be in the present moment. Write what you see, hear, feel, and smell right now.

■ Write a response for each sentence.

1 Right now I see…

_____

2 Right now I hear…

_____

3 Right now I feel…

_____

4 Right now I smell…

_____

Addition

■ Add.

1
```
  32
+ 28
────
  60
```

2
```
  44
+ 39
────
```

3
```
  17
+ 66
────
```

4
```
  59
+ 19
────
```

5
```
  267
+  17
─────
  284
```

6
```
  348
+  48
─────
```

7
```
  512
+  69
─────
```

8
```
  769
+  13
─────
```

9
```
  562
+ 333
─────
```

10
```
  435
+ 251
─────
```

11
```
  128
+ 671
─────
```

12
```
  835
+ 143
─────
```

13
```
  67
+ 15
────
```

14
```
  428
+  56
─────
```

15
```
  637
+  43
─────
```

16
```
  243
+ 234
─────
```

KEY POINTS

How to add 3-digit numbers with regrouping

Ex: 325 + 296

Step 1: Add the numbers in the ones column. Since 5 + 6 = 11, carry the 1 in the tens place over to the tens column. Finally, move the 1 in the ones column down below the answer line since 5 + 6 = 11.

Step 2: Add the numbers in the tens column including the 1 you carried over. Since 1 + 2 + 9 = 12, carry the 1 in the tens column over to the hundreds column and move the 2 down below the answer line.

Step 3: Add the hundreds column with the 1 you carried over.

```
  ¹              ¹ ¹            ¹ ¹
 325            325            325
+296           +296           +296
————           ————           ————
   1             21            621
```

■ **Add.**

1
```
 ¹ ¹
 248
+283
————
 531
```

2
```
 436
+198
————
```

3
```
 357
+379
————
```

4
```
 595
+185
————
```

5
```
 769
+139
————
```

6
```
 622
+278
————
```

7
```
 136
+396
————
```

8
```
 289
+434
————
```

Subtraction

■ Subtract.

①
$$\begin{array}{r} \overset{3}{\cancel{4}}\,\overset{12}{\cancel{2}} \\ -\ 1\ 8 \\ \hline 2\ 4 \end{array}$$

②
$$\begin{array}{r} 3\ 5 \\ -\ 1\ 6 \\ \hline \end{array}$$

③
$$\begin{array}{r} 7\ 4 \\ -\ 2\ 9 \\ \hline \end{array}$$

④
$$\begin{array}{r} 8\ 2 \\ -\ 3\ 7 \\ \hline \end{array}$$

⑤
$$\begin{array}{r} 1\,\overset{5}{\cancel{6}}\,\overset{13}{\cancel{3}} \\ -\ \ 1\ 5 \\ \hline 1\ 4\ 8 \end{array}$$

⑥
$$\begin{array}{r} 2\ 8\ 1 \\ -\ \ 2\ 4 \\ \hline \end{array}$$

⑦
$$\begin{array}{r} 6\ 4\ 6 \\ -\ \ 3\ 8 \\ \hline \end{array}$$

⑧
$$\begin{array}{r} 9\ 7\ 8 \\ -\ \ 1\ 9 \\ \hline \end{array}$$

⑨
$$\begin{array}{r} 3\ 7\ 6 \\ -1\ 2\ 3 \\ \hline \end{array}$$

⑩
$$\begin{array}{r} 5\ 3\ 1 \\ -3\ 1\ 0 \\ \hline \end{array}$$

⑪
$$\begin{array}{r} 7\ 0\ 6 \\ -4\ 0\ 5 \\ \hline \end{array}$$

⑫
$$\begin{array}{r} 6\ 9\ 7 \\ -6\ 7\ 1 \\ \hline \end{array}$$

⑬
$$\begin{array}{r} 6\ 3 \\ -2\ 7 \\ \hline \end{array}$$

⑭
$$\begin{array}{r} 2\ 6\ 1 \\ -\ \ 1\ 8 \\ \hline \end{array}$$

⑮
$$\begin{array}{r} 8\ 3\ 4 \\ -\ \ 2\ 6 \\ \hline \end{array}$$

⑯
$$\begin{array}{r} 4\ 6\ 3 \\ -1\ 2\ 4 \\ \hline \end{array}$$

KEY POINTS

How to subtract 3-digit numbers with regrouping

Ex: 453 − 165

Step 1: Start in the ones column. Since you cannot subtract 5 from 3, you need to borrow from the tens column. Regroup 10 from the tens column to the ones column to make the problem 13 − 5 = 8.

Step 2: Like in Step 1, you cannot subtract 6 from 4. Regroup 100 from the hundreds column to the tens column to make it 14 − 6 = 8. Move the 8 down below the answer line.

Step 3: Subtract the hundreds column with the new digits.

$$
\begin{array}{r}
\overset{4}{\cancel{4}}\,\overset{13}{\cancel{5}}3 \\
-165 \\
\hline
8
\end{array}
\qquad
\begin{array}{r}
\overset{3}{\cancel{4}}\,\overset{14}{\cancel{5}}\,\overset{13}{\cancel{3}} \\
-165 \\
\hline
88
\end{array}
\qquad
\begin{array}{r}
\overset{3}{\cancel{4}}\,\overset{14}{\cancel{5}}\,\overset{13}{\cancel{3}} \\
-165 \\
\hline
288
\end{array}
$$

■ Subtract.

1
$$
\begin{array}{r}
\overset{2}{\cancel{3}}\,\overset{13}{\cancel{4}}\,\overset{12}{\cancel{2}} \\
-158 \\
\hline
184
\end{array}
$$

2
$$
\begin{array}{r}
534 \\
-187 \\
\hline
\end{array}
$$

3
$$
\begin{array}{r}
623 \\
-356 \\
\hline
\end{array}
$$

4
$$
\begin{array}{r}
872 \\
-579 \\
\hline
\end{array}
$$

5
$$
\begin{array}{r}
\overset{3}{\cancel{4}}\,\overset{11}{\cancel{2}}\,\overset{18}{\cancel{8}} \\
-359 \\
\hline
69
\end{array}
$$

6
$$
\begin{array}{r}
261 \\
-198 \\
\hline
\end{array}
$$

7
$$
\begin{array}{r}
543 \\
-464 \\
\hline
\end{array}
$$

8
$$
\begin{array}{r}
735 \\
-678 \\
\hline
\end{array}
$$

Rounding to the Nearest Place Value

KEY POINTS

Rounding to the nearest ten
If the digit in the ones place is …

5 or greater: round up to the nearest ten.

$$1\underline{5} \rightarrow \boxed{20} \qquad 3\underline{8} \rightarrow \boxed{40}$$

4 or less: round down to the nearest ten.

$$7\underline{2} \rightarrow \boxed{70} \qquad 1\underline{4} \rightarrow \boxed{10}$$

■ **Round each number to the nearest ten.**

① 18 → ☐   ② 27 → ☐   ③ 55 → ☐

④ 12 → ☐   ⑤ 44 → ☐   ⑥ 61 → ☐

⑦ 33 → ☐   ⑧ 25 → ☐   ⑨ 93 → ☐

⑩ 76 → ☐   ⑪ 42 → ☐   ⑫ 86 → ☐

KEY POINTS

Rounding to the nearest hundred
If the digit in the tens place is ...

5 or greater: round up to the nearest hundred.

1 6̲3 → 200   4 5̲1 → 500

4 or less: round down to the nearest hundred.

1 3̲7 → 100   6 4̲9 → 600

■ Round each number to the nearest hundred.

❶ 184 → ⬜   ❷ 253 → ⬜   ❸ 671 → ⬜

❹ 127 → ⬜   ❺ 339 → ⬜   ❻ 845 → ⬜

❼ 461 → ⬜   ❽ 752 → ⬜   ❾ 938 → ⬜

❿ 729 → ⬜   ⓫ 684 → ⬜   ⓬ 539 → ⬜

Calculations with Estimation

■ Estimate the answer of these addition and subtraction problems by rounding each number to the nearest ten.

① $65 + 24$

↓   ↓

70   20

$$+\begin{array}{r} 70 \\ 20 \\ \hline \end{array}$$

② $53 - 28$

↓   ↓

50   30

$$-\begin{array}{r} 50 \\ 30 \\ \hline \end{array}$$

③ $42 + 35$

↓   ↓

$$+\begin{array}{r} \\ \\ \hline \end{array}$$

④ $67 + 31$

↓   ↓

$$+\begin{array}{r} \\ \\ \hline \end{array}$$

⑤ $83 - 19$

↓   ↓

$$-\begin{array}{r} \\ \\ \hline \end{array}$$

⑥ $76 - 61$

↓   ↓

$$-\begin{array}{r} \\ \\ \hline \end{array}$$

⑦ $37 + 24$

↓   ↓

$$+\begin{array}{r} \\ \\ \hline \end{array}$$

⑧ $46 - 17$

↓   ↓

$$-\begin{array}{r} \\ \\ \hline \end{array}$$

■ Estimate the answer of these addition and subtraction problems by rounding each number to the nearest hundred.

❶ 661 + 143

700   100

$$\begin{array}{r} 700 \\ +\ 100 \\ \hline \end{array}$$

❷ 428 − 192

400   200

$$\begin{array}{r} 400 \\ -\ 200 \\ \hline \end{array}$$

❸ 347 + 516

$$\begin{array}{r} \\ + \\ \hline \end{array}$$

❹ 165 + 716

$$\begin{array}{r} \\ + \\ \hline \end{array}$$

❺ 562 − 128

$$\begin{array}{r} \\ - \\ \hline \end{array}$$

❻ 317 − 188

$$\begin{array}{r} \\ - \\ \hline \end{array}$$

❼ 239 + 415

$$\begin{array}{r} \\ + \\ \hline \end{array}$$

❽ 916 − 497

$$\begin{array}{r} \\ - \\ \hline \end{array}$$

Word Problems

■ Answer the following word problems.

1 The librarian bought 174 storybooks and 286 picture books.
How many books did they buy in all?

Ans. _____ books

2 Ms. Lee spent $349 on a new computer and $329 on a new phone.
How much did she spend in all?

Ans. $ _____

3 There are 448 cows and 264 chickens on a farm.
How many animals are there in all?

Ans. _____ animals

4 Brad read 156 pages in a week and 165 pages the next week.
How many pages did he read in all?

Ans. _____ pages

■ Answer the following word problems.

1 Claire has 243 stickers. She gives her brother 125.
How many stickers does she have left?

Ans. _____ stickers

2 Of the 631 students at Eli's school, 147 had cavities.
How many students had no cavities?

Ans. _____ students

3 The cafeteria had 463 apples this morning.
They used 285 of them today. How many apples do they have left?

Ans. _____ apples

4 Lisa saved up 764 pennies. She used 389 pennies to buy some candy.
How many pennies does she have left?

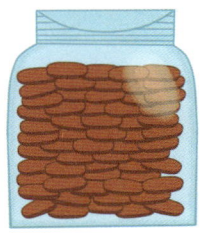

Ans. _____ pennies

■ The graphs and the chart show how students get to their school. Write a check mark (✓) on the one of these that represents different data than the other three.

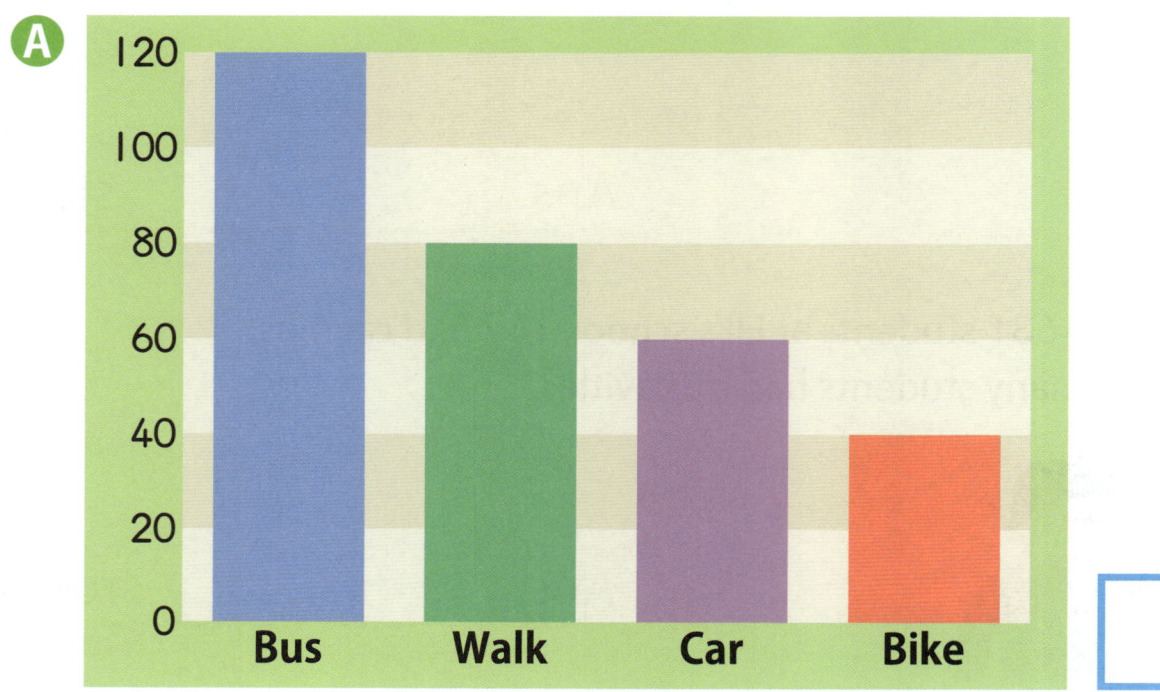

Ⓐ

| | Bus | Walk | Car | Bike |

Ⓑ * Each picture represents 20.

C

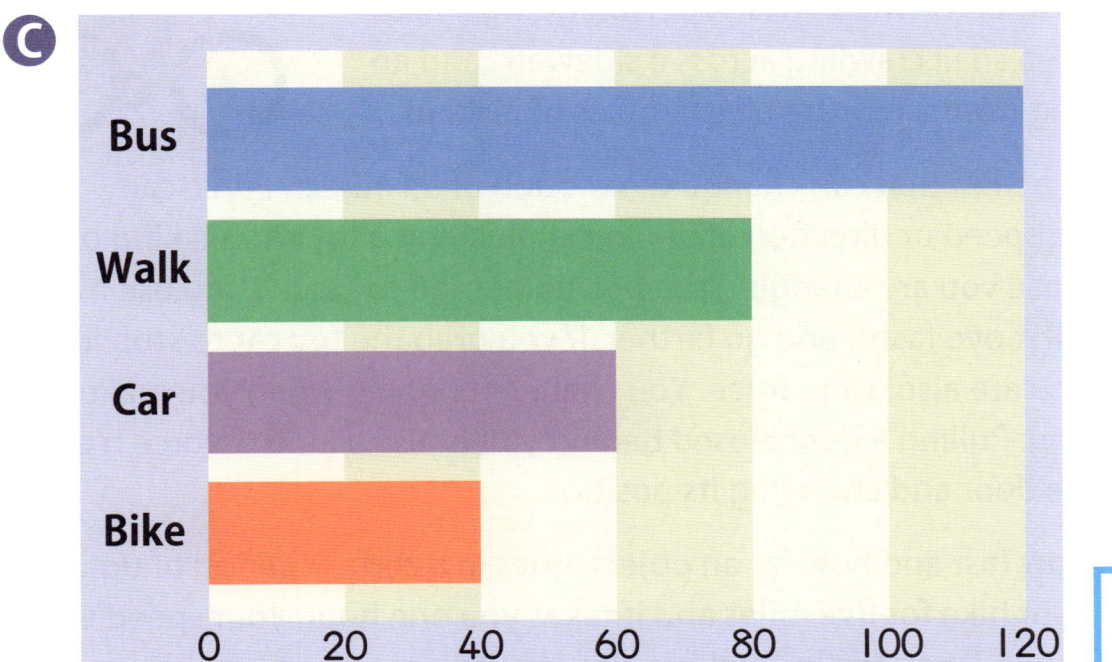

D

How they get to school	Number of students
Bus	120
Walk	80
Car	40
Bike	60

Forces and Motion

KEY POINTS

An object in motion is an object that is moving. Motion means the change in position of an object over time. An object's position is where it is. A person riding a bike down a hill, a snail crawling across a sidewalk, and an acorn falling from a tree are all examples of motion.

Force is an action that can change the motion of an object. Force can change the speed or direction of an object. Pushing a toy car is a kind of force because you are changing the position of the toy car. If you use more force, it will move faster and go farther. If you grab the toy car to stop it from moving, you are also using force. You change its speed when you make it stop moving. Pulling a door closed behind you is also a kind of force. You are moving the door and changing its position.

Speed is how fast and how far an object goes in a certain period of time. If you ride your bike for five miles and it takes you one hour, your speed is five miles per hour. If your little brother rides four miles in one hour, his speed is four miles per hour. Four miles per hour is slower than five miles per hour.

■ Answer the questions.

❶ What is needed to make an object move?

ⓐ **Speed**   ⓑ **Force**   ⓒ **Sunlight**

❷ What is something you do every day that uses force?

❸ How can force affect an object's speed?

■ Fill in the blanks with the correct words.

1 _____ is the change in an object's position over time.

2 How fast and how far an object goes in a period of time is its

_____ .

3 An action that changes the motion of an object is called a

_____ .

4 Pushing a toy car is a type of force because you change the

_____ of the car.

■ Circle the object that is going the fastest.

A train going 75 miles per hour.

A girl riding a bike going 5 miles per hour.

A race car going 100 miles per hour.

Balanced and Unbalanced Forces

KEY POINTS

Balanced forces can keep an object from moving or keep it going at the same speed and in the same direction. If you hold a block between your hands and push on it from both sides with equal force, the block will not move. That is because the block is getting equal force from opposite sides. When forces are balanced, objects that are in motion stay in motion. Objects that are at rest stay at rest.

If two teams play tug of war and they are both exactly as strong as each other, the rope will not move. The teams would be using equal force in opposite directions. However, one team usually has more force than the other, so they pull the rope towards them and win the game. This is an example of an unbalanced force. One of the teams uses more force than the other.

Unbalanced forces make things change their speed, direction, or position. A cat can use force to push a glass of water off of a table onto the floor. A person can use force to pick up a book. These are examples of unbalanced forces because they change an object's speed, direction, and position.

■ Fill in the blanks with the correct words.

❶ _____ forces make things move.

❷ _____ forces keep things in the same place.

❸ What is an example of an unbalanced force?

_____

■ Read each situation. Circle if the force being used is balanced or unbalanced.

❶ A child throws a ball to his brother.

Balanced   **Unbalanced**

❷ A girl stops a soccer ball with her foot.

Balanced   **Unbalanced**

❸ A cat pushes glass of water off a table.

Balanced   **Unbalanced**

❹ A boy places his backpack on the floor and it stays there.

Balanced   **Unbalanced**

Speed and Friction

Speed describes how quickly an object changes position. Force can change speed. The more force, the greater the change in speed. Force can also change direction.

When you first get on a scooter, you aren't moving. You use force to get going when you push off the ground with your foot. If you want to go faster, you push harder against the ground. This creates more force. You might also have the force of gravity helping you move if you are going downhill. This would increase your speed. If you want to stop, you also use force. You might use brakes, or you might stop with your foot. You use the force of your foot against the ground to stop.

Friction is the resistance of motion when one object rubs against another. Anytime two objects rub or move against each other, they cause friction. Some surfaces offer objects less friction and make objects easier to move like a tile floor or a dirt road. Other types of surfaces create more friction for moving objects like grass or mud.

The less friction on an object in motion, the faster its speed. The more friction, the slower it moves. If a child pedals a bike on pavement they will go faster than on grass because the pavement offers less friction or resistance against his tires.

■ Answer the questions.

❶ How does force affect the speed of a ball when you kick it? If you use more force, will it typically go faster or slower?

❷ What would happen to the speed of the ball in Question 1 if it was kicked on grass instead of pavement?

■ Write True or False for each statement.

1 A child will go faster on a water slide than on a regular slide due to friction.

2 A ball will roll slower on grass than on pavement.

3 Pulling a wagon across the sand is harder than pulling it across grass because there is more friction.

4 A child will go down a hill faster on grass than on snow.

5 Slippery surfaces create less friction.

Magnets and Forces

KEY POINTS

Magnets are certain kinds of metal or rock, like iron, steel, or nickel, that can attract some kinds of metals. Magnets are in things we use every day. People use magnets to hang things on the fridge or other metal surfaces. Magnets are used in some tablet cases to keep them shut, in recycling plants to sort metal, in computers, in compasses, and many other everyday objects.

Every magnet has two poles, which are called the north and south poles. If you try to put the south poles of two magnets together,

they will repel or push away from each other. The same thing will happen if you try to put the north ends of two magnets together. However, if you put the north end of one magnet near the south end of another, they will move towards each other and stick together! This force is called magnetism.

■ Answer the questions.

1 What are magnets made of?

_____

2 What do you call the force that makes magnets stick together?

_____

3 How are magnets used in everyday life?

_____

Date

Great Job Sticker

Circle the objects that are magnetic.

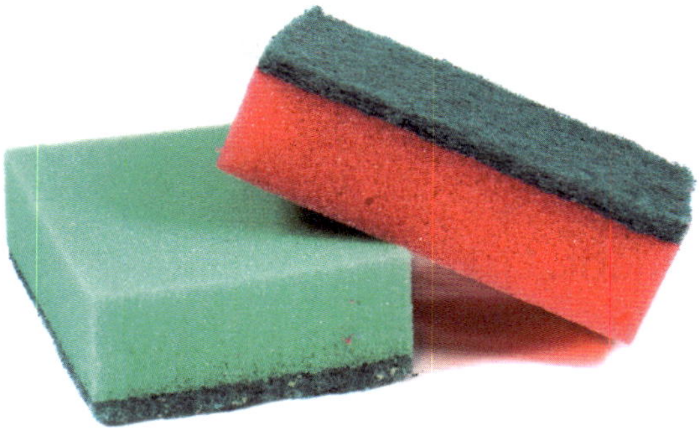

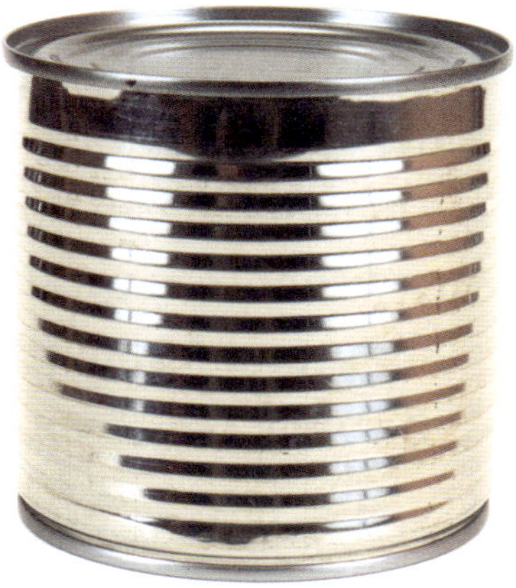

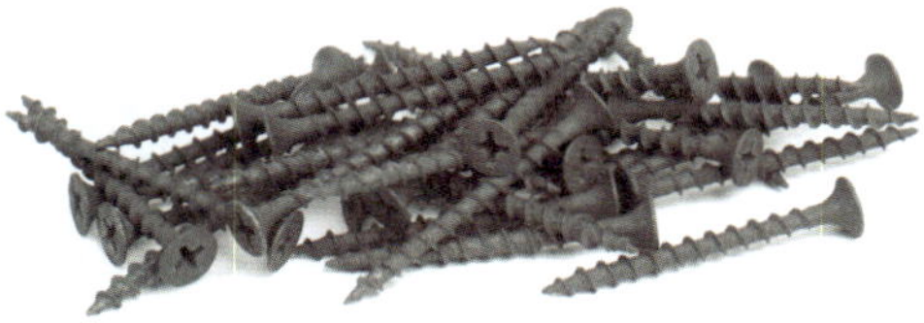

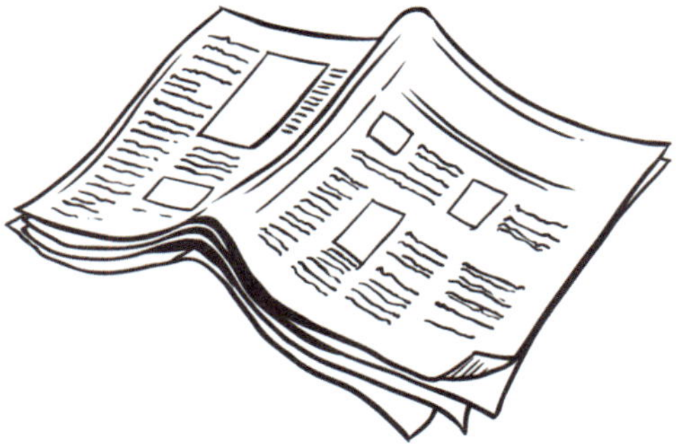

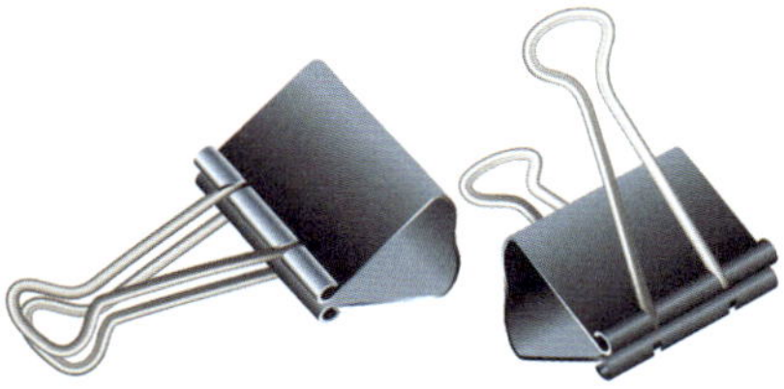

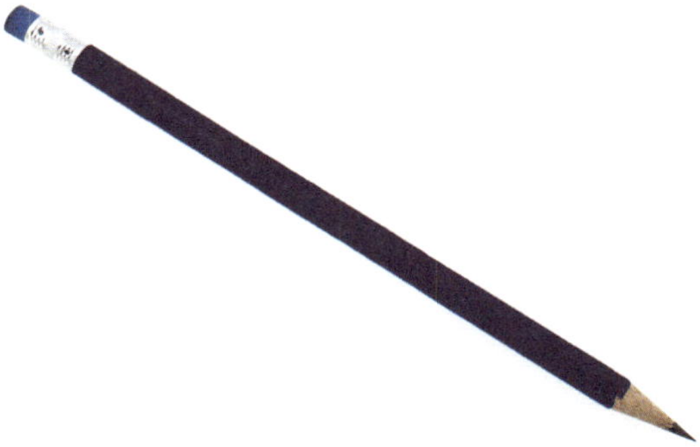

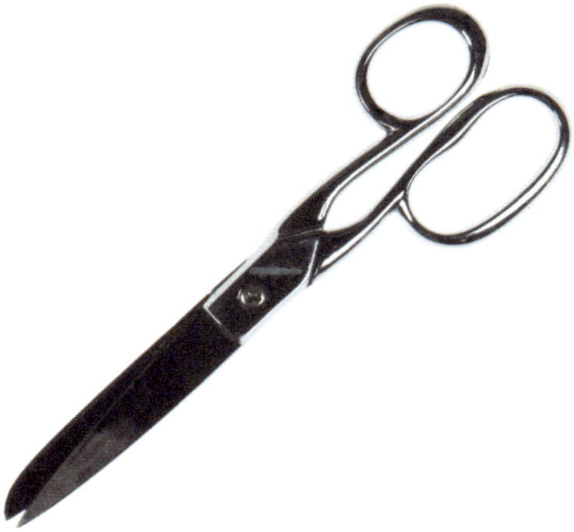

Brain Break
Science Journal 1

Magnets produce magnetic forces that attract the opposite forces in most metal objects. Find a magnet (it can be a refrigerator magnet!) and choose several objects from around your home and test to see if they are magnetic. List the objects and your answers in the chart below.

Magnetic	Non-magnetic

Art Break!

■ Color the flowers below. Use more force or color harder on one petal and use less force or color softer on another. Can you see a difference in the color? Try this technique with different colors. Create patterns with more and less force.

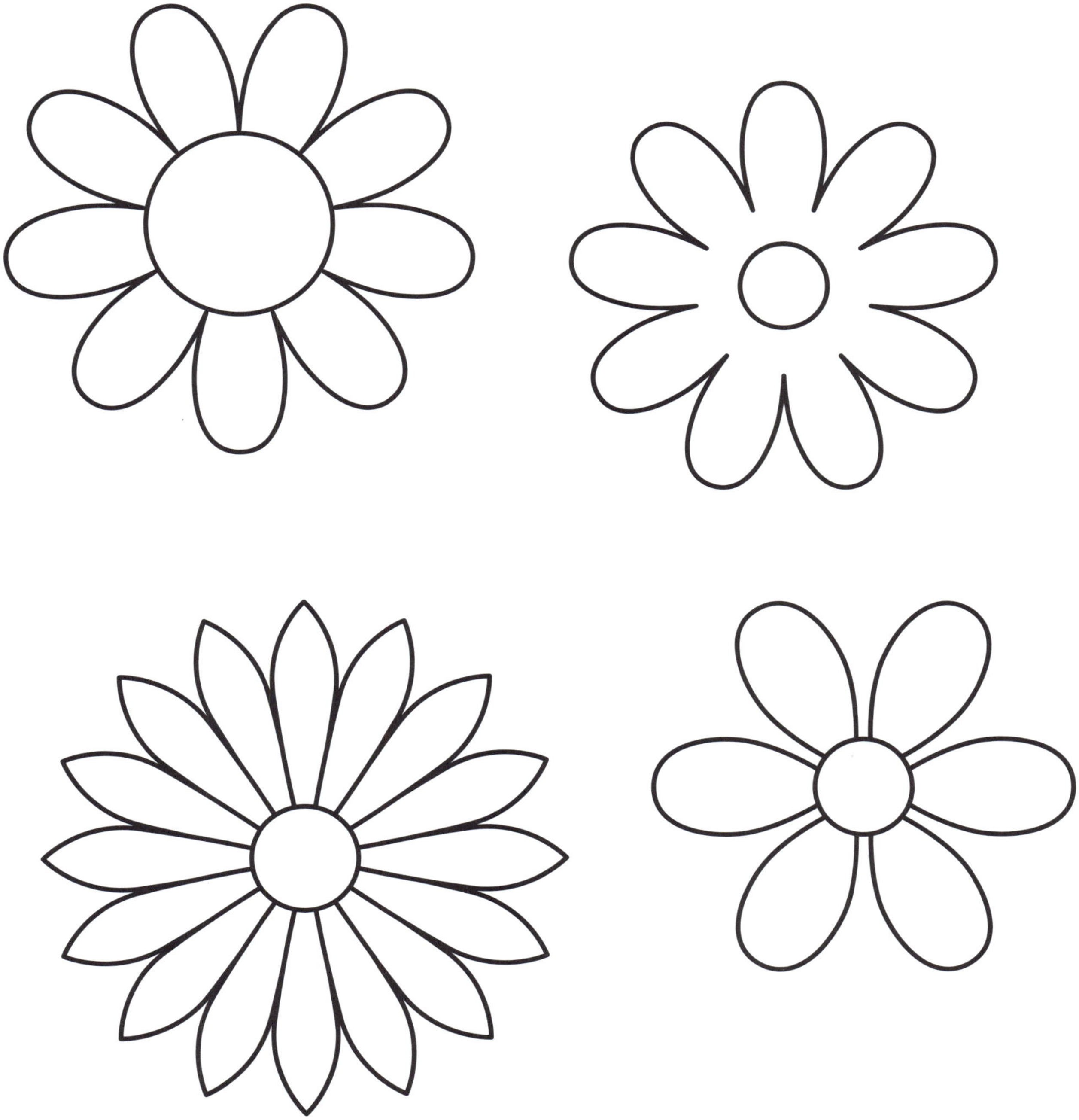

Exploration of America

KEY POINTS

The land now known as North America, made up of Mexico, the United States, and Canada, was first inhabited by humans around thirty thousand years ago. The first people to inhabit a land are called indigenous. The children of these original travelers became the people of the Americas, known in different places as Native Americans, American Indians, or First Nations. They went from Asia to North America across a land bridge that was exposed during the Ice Age. By the time Europeans arrived many thousands of years later, there were people living in almost all parts of the Americas.

In 1492, Christopher Columbus led the first Europeans to visit the Americas. The Spanish king and queen paid for his voyage. He was sailing west to try to find a faster way to get to Asia instead of going south around Africa. He never realized that he had come to a completely different continent. He called the indigenous people "Indians" because he thought he had landed in India. He actually landed in the Caribbean.

In the following years, many countries colonized the Americas. When a country colonizes a place, it means they build a settlement. People from their country move to live there. They claim the land as part of their original country. They try to control the indigenous people. They take resources from the land to trade and develop new towns.

Other European countries also wanted colonies in the Americas. The French established colonies in the Caribbean and in what are now eastern Canada and Louisiana. In Canada, they focused on collecting furs to sell in Europe. Because of this, they often worked with the indigenous people rather than fighting them to take their land.

■ **Answer the questions.**

❶ How did the first people get to the Americas?

❷ Which European countries mentioned in the Key Points colonized North America and the Caribbean?

❸ Who led the first Europeans to visit the Americas?

■ **Fill in the blanks to complete the statements.**

❶ The land known as _____ is made up of Mexico, The United States, and Canada.

❷ _____ crossed a land bridge from Asia to North America.

❸ _____ led the first Europeans to visit the Americas.

❹ Columbus called the indigenous people of the Americas _____ because he thought he had sailed to India.

❺ European countries like _____ set up colonies in North America, mainly in Canada and the Caribbean.

The Original Thirteen Colonies

KEY POINTS

Out of all of Britain's colonies in the Americas, there were a few mainland colonies that joined together to express their unhappiness with British rule. Thirteen colonies banded together to fight the American Revolutionary War against the British and became the first states in the United States. These colonies were made up of mostly English-speaking, Protestant, European settlers. They also had somewhat similar systems of government. These factors made it easier for them to decide to fight together.

The Thirteen Colonies are usually put into three main categories. The Southern Colonies were Georgia, South Carolina, North Carolina, Virginia, and Maryland. The Middle Colonies were Delaware, Pennsylvania, New Jersey, and New York. The New England Colonies, which were in the north, were Connecticut, Rhode Island, Massachusetts, and New Hampshire.

Most of the New England Colonies were started by people looking for a place where they could practice their Puritan religion without interference. Maryland, Pennsylvania, and Rhode Island were founded by Catholics and Quakers, who were often persecuted in England, as places where everyone could practice their religion. Most of the Southern Colonies were founded for the purpose of making money for the colonists and for Britain.

■ **Answer the questions.**

❶ Name at least two things the Thirteen Colonies had in common.

❷ What colonies made up the New England colonies?

❸ Which colonies were responsible for making money for the other colonies and Great Britain?

■ Write true or false for each statement.

1 The Thirteen colonies became the first U.S. states.

2 The Thirteen colonies were founded by European settlers.

3 New York was originally a Southern colony.

4 The Thirteen colonies were founded for religious freedom.

5 Most Southern colonies were founded to make money for Great Britain.

6 The Thirteen colonies wanted freedom from Spain.

> KEY POINTS

The colonists in the Thirteen colonies were used to a certain level of self-rule. When Great Britain started placing more taxes and tariffs on American goods in 1765 to help pay the debt they created during the French and Indian War, the colonists began to get angry. It was difficult to unite the Thirteen Colonies, but they eventually banded together. The Continental Congress was formed and included representatives from all thirteen colonies. They made big decisions about resisting the British and fighting against them.

The Revolutionary War officially started on April 19, 1775 with the Battles of Lexington and Concord in Massachusetts. The British army tried to take some of the revolutionaries' weapons. The revolutionaries were warned and beat the British in the battles.

On July 4, 1776, the Continental Congress adopted the Declaration of Independence. It declared that the Thirteen Colonies were no longer colonies of Great Britain but instead independent. It listed complaints against the British government and king. The war was difficult. The British had more weapons and better trained armies. But the colonists knew the land better and were more motivated to win. In 1778, the French decided to help the colonists.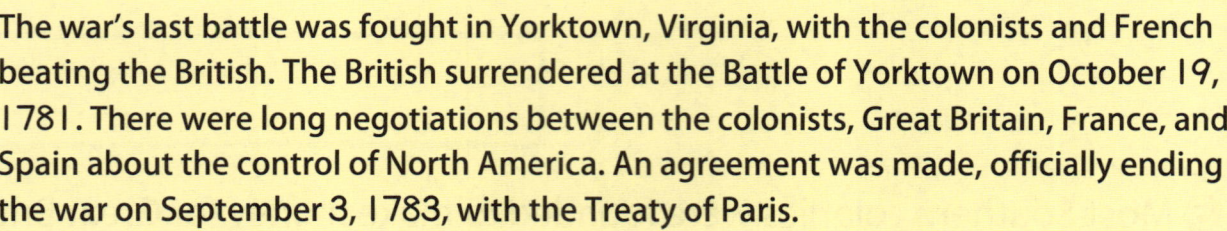

The war's last battle was fought in Yorktown, Virginia, with the colonists and French beating the British. The British surrendered at the Battle of Yorktown on October 19, 1781. There were long negotiations between the colonists, Great Britain, France, and Spain about the control of North America. An agreement was made, officially ending the war on September 3, 1783, with the Treaty of Paris.

■ **Answer the questions.**

❶ What did the Continental Congress do for the revolution?

❷ Which European country helped the colonists win the war?

■ Complete the timeline with the correct dates.

Colonies founded in America by Great Britain

1607

Britain started raising taxes and tariffs in the colonies in...

The official start of the Revolutionary War was in...

The French decide to support the colonies in the war in...

The date the Declaration of Independence was signed by Congress was in...

The last battle of the war was fought in Yorktown in...

The Treaty of Paris official ended the Revolutionary War in 1783.

1783

Key Figures of the American Revolution

KEY POINTS

Many people played a role in the Thirteen Colonies' fight to win the Revolutionary War.

George Washington fought as a commander for the British in the French and Indian War. He began to protest against unfair British policies in the late 1760s. He was part of the Continental Congresses. When fighting with the British started, he was chosen to lead the Continental Army. His leadership and strategy helped the colonists win the war. After the war, he was the president of the Continental Congress that created the Constitution, which designed the government for the United States. He was elected the first president of the United States and served for eight years.

Thomas Jefferson was also part of Virginia's colonial government and part of the Continental Congress. He was the main author of the Declaration of Independence, which declared that the Thirteen Colonies were no longer under British rule. He later became the third president of the United States.

Alexander Hamilton joined in the protests and wrote speeches and papers supporting the revolution. When the war started, he became George Washington's assistant. He helped Washington plan battles. He wrote letters to the Continental Congress to gather money, food, and other supplies for the soldiers. After the war ended, Hamilton worked to help the Thirteen Colonies become the United States. He helped write the U.S. Constitution and wrote many pamphlets to convince people to support it. When George Washington was president, Hamilton was the U.S.'s first Secretary of Treasury. He created the national banking system. He also advocated for the United States to abolish slavery.

Benjamin Franklin was a printer, writer, and inventor. He became a political leader in Philadelphia, Pennsylvania before the Revolutionary War. He created services to help people, like a hospital and a fire department. Franklin negotiated with the British to get rid of the Stamp Act, which imposed a lot of taxes on the colonists. When conflict with the British continued, Franklin joined the Continental Congress. He helped Jefferson write the Declaration of Independence. He went to France and convinced the French government to help the Thirteen Colonies fight against the British. After the war, he advocated for the abolishment of slavery and wrote his own autobiography.

■ Match the key figures.

Who was the main author of the Declaration of Independence? ●   ●

George Washington

Who was the leader of the Continental Army? ●   ●

Thomas Jefferson

Who created the United States' first national banking system? ●   ●

Alexander Hamilton

Who helped convince France to help the colonies fight against the British? ●   ●

Benjamin Franklin

Brain Break
Crossword Puzzle

■ Use the clues to complete the crossword puzzle.

Revolution
Washington
Jefferson
Hamilton
England
thirteen
colony
Franklin

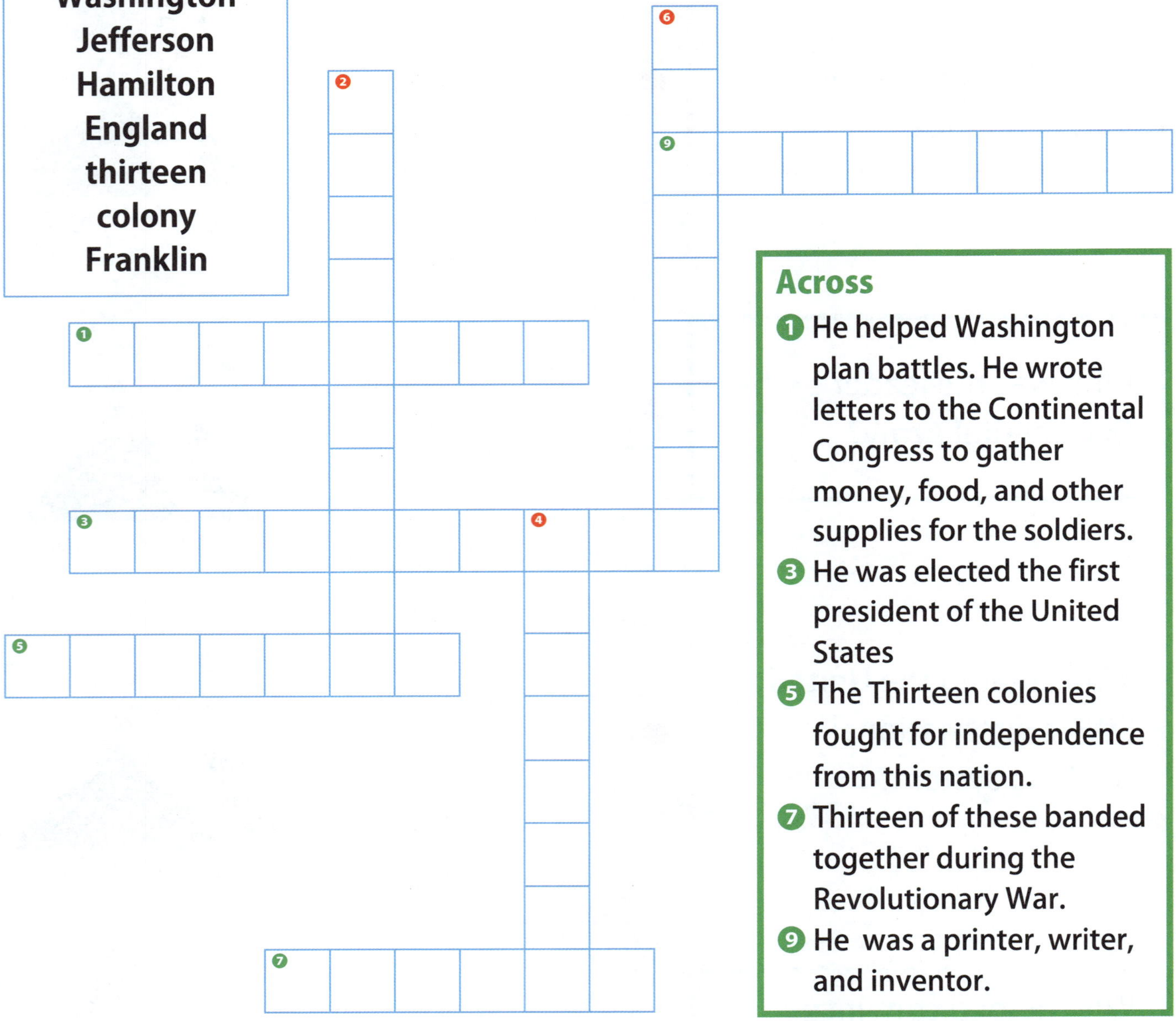

Across

1. He helped Washington plan battles. He wrote letters to the Continental Congress to gather money, food, and other supplies for the soldiers.
3. He was elected the first president of the United States
5. The Thirteen colonies fought for independence from this nation.
7. Thirteen of these banded together during the Revolutionary War.
9. He was a printer, writer, and inventor.

Down

2. This is fought to overthrow a government and gain freedom.
4. Number of original colonies under British control in America.
6. He is the main author of the Declaration of Independence.

Mindfulness Break!

KEY POINTS

A mantra is a phrase you can say out loud or in your head to make yourself feel happy and confident about yourself or in a situation.

Example: "Everything will be okay."

■ Complete the mantras below.

1 "Today I will be [   ] and will do my best!"

2 "I will be [   ] and [   ] to everyone I meet today."

3 "If something upsets me I will [   ]."

4 "When I face a challenge I will [   ]."

5 "If I am scared I will [   ]."

Computer Hardware

■ Look at the top picture. Then look at the bottom picture.
Circle five things that are different in the bottom picture.

■ Rearrange each word to find words related to the parts of a computer.

1 s c e e r n ➡

2 m u o s e ➡

3 w e c a b m ➡

4 p r e t i n r ➡

5 s p a k e e r ➡

6 k e y b a r o d ➡

■ Find and circle five keyboards from below that help you when writing a email.

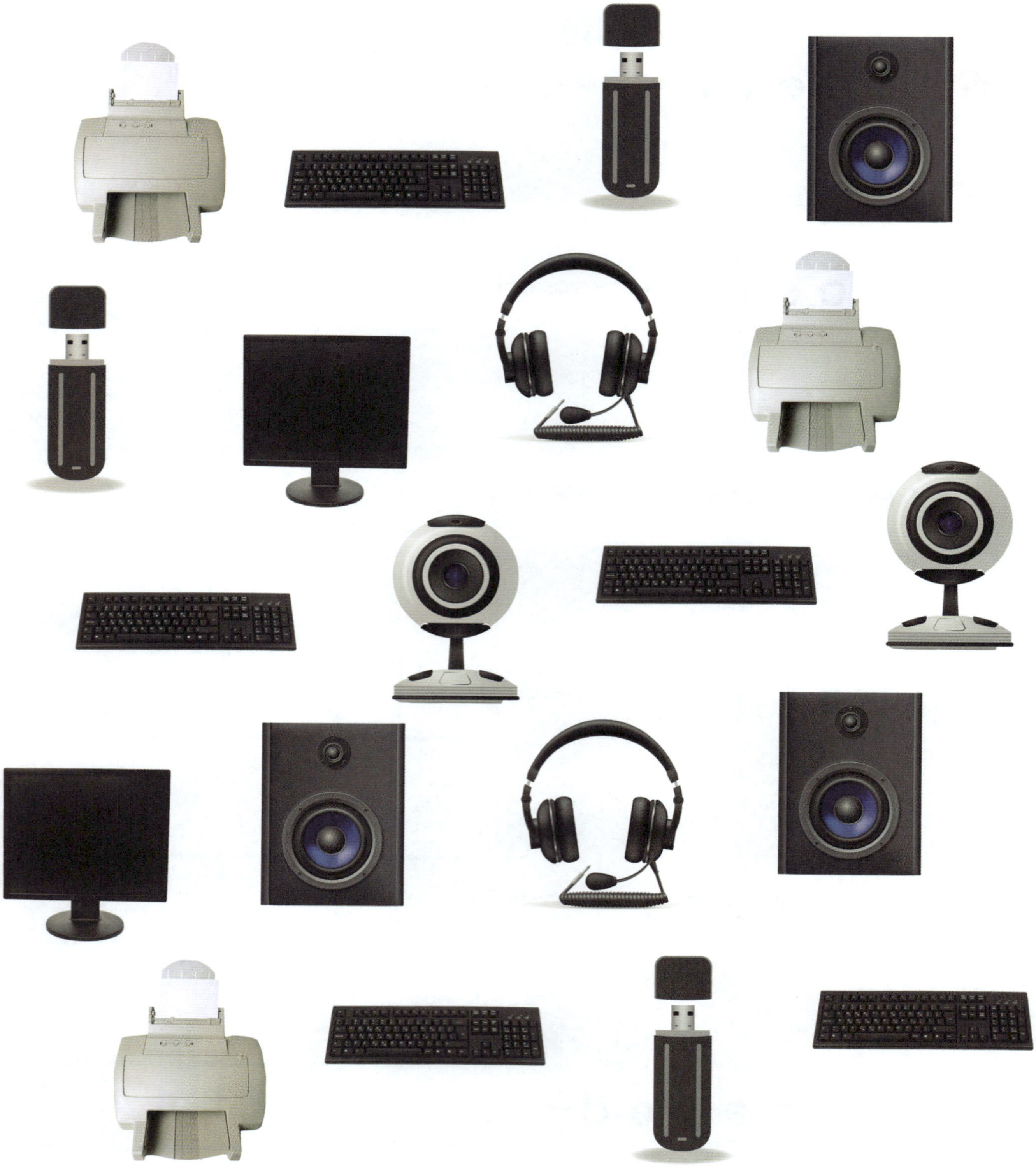

■ Write a check mark (✔) below the picture for the correct answer to the question.

❶ Which object can take a picture?

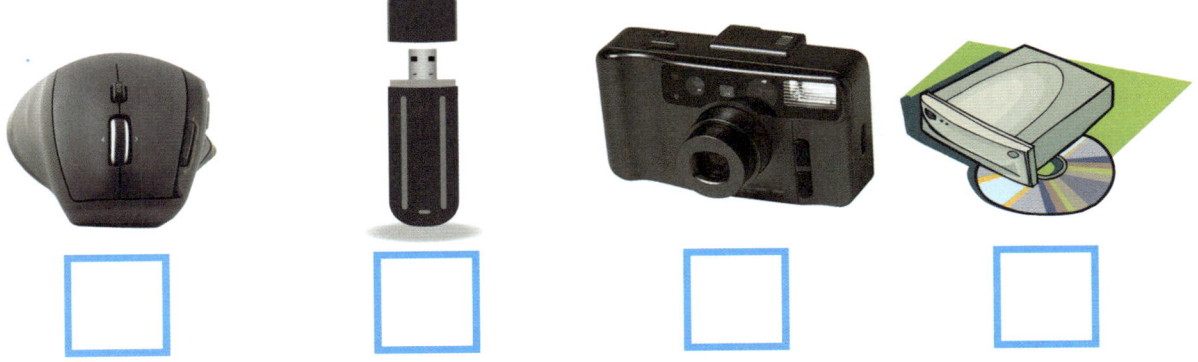

❷ Which object can send a photo?

❸ Which object can play music?

Keyboard Skills

■ Fill in the missing keys highlighted in blue on the keyboard.

■ Color the keyboard using the guide below.

Backspace key →	**Green**
Enter key →	**Red**
Shift keys →	**Yellow**
Spacebar key →	**Blue**
Number Keys →	**Orange**

Secret Code

KEY POINTS

You can use a secret code to convert a message into other letters, numbers, or symbols. Using such codes to protect privacy is considered very important in today's technologically advanced world.

■ Use the table below to read the secret codes.
Write the answer in each box.

	0	1	2	3	4	5	6	7	8	9
Secret code	2	5	9	1	6	3	8	0	4	7

❶ 3 5 7 ⟶ | 5 | 1 | |

❷ 2 4 6 1 ⟶ | | | | |

❸ 4 6 8 3 5 ⟶ | | | | | |

❹ 9 0 1 0 2 7 ⟶ | | | | | | |

■ Use the table below to read the secret codes.
  Then circle the largest number.

0	1	2	3	4	5	6	7	8	9
Secret code 7	E	9	b	R	l	r	B	4	e

① 4 1   1 9   9 7

② E b   r R   E e

③ l R 4   l 4 R   R 4 l

④ R 9 r 7   9 e l R   B 4 E 7

Physical Education Break!

It's important to move your body and exercise!
Try this fun activity below to break up your studying!

- Get a die or borrow a die from a board game.
  Roll the die and complete the exercise it lands on.
  Repeat at least 2 times or as many times as you want.

20 Arm Circles

10 Jumping Jacks

1-minute Run In Place

20 Toe Touches

10 Squats

1-minute March In Place

Unit **2** Table of Contents

Use this page to keep track of your progress throughout the book. Place a check mark in the box when you have completed a section.

Language Arts

Reading

Math

Science

Social Studies

Technology

Possessive Nouns

KEY POINTS

Possessive nouns are nouns that show ownership. They are usually formed by adding an apostrophe and an *s* (*'s*) to the end of the word. For example, if you are referring to a book that belongs to Oona, you would say *Oona's* book.

Here are a few more examples:

chalk belonging to the teacher ⟶ the teacher's chalk

hairbrush belonging to Linda ⟶ Linda's hairbrush

If the noun ends with an s, you can just add an apostrophe to the end.

a steering wheel belonging to the bus ⟶ the bus' steering wheel.

■ Circle the correct possessive for each noun.

❶   **Laura**   **Lauras**   **Laura's**

❷   **class**   **classes**   **class'**

❸   **cat**   **cats'**   **cat's**

❹   **houses**   **houses'**   **house's**

■ Write the correct possessive for each noun.

1 dinosaur

2 door

3 Molly

4 Douglas

5 cars

6 goose

7 Jess

8 principal

Spelling: Word Families and Suffixes

KEY POINTS

Many words have parts added onto the end called suffixes. For example, we often add -*ing* or -*ness* to the end of a word. But some words change when you add a suffix to the end. We can look for word families to help find these patterns.

_____t	+ ting	_____y	_____y + ness
sit	sitting	happy	happiness
knit	knitting	lazy	laziness
wet	wetting	easy	easiness
jot	jotting	messy	messiness

■ Add the suffix below to each word.

① **trot** **(ing)**

② **sleepy** **(ness)**

③ **strut** **(ing)**

④ **creamy** **(ness)**

KEY POINTS

Here is another word family that changes when a suffix is added.

_____y	+ies
cry	cries
fly	flies
try	tries
fry	fries

■ Add the suffix, making sure to follow the word family pattern.

❶ dry

❷ pry

❸ shy

❹ deny

Titles

> **KEY POINTS**
>
> We use capital letters to write the titles of books, movies, plays, TV shows, and more. Using capital letters at the beginning of each word helps set the title apart from the rest of the sentence so that the reader knows it is a title.
>
> But not every word gets capitalized. Articles (*the, an, a*) are lowercase unless they are the first word of the title. So are prepositions, which include *over, through, between, in, among.* And conjunctions (*but, or, and*) are also lowercase.

■ **Write the titles below with correct capitalization.**

❶ goodnight moon

_____

❷ the hungry caterpillar

_____

❸ romeo and juliet

_____

❹ charlie and the chocolate factory

_____

■ If the title is written correctly, put a check. If it is incorrect, put an x.
Then rewrite it correctly.

❶ War and Peace

❷ the Great Gatsby

❸ Alice's Adventures In Wonderland

❹ The Lion, the Witch, and The Wardrobe

❺ Pride And Prejudice

❻ of Mice And Men

Punctuating Dialogue

KEY POINTS

When a person speaks in a text, it is called dialogue. These words are surrounded by quotation marks. For example: She said "Hi!"

If the dialogue comes at the end of the sentence, add the end punctuation inside the quotes. If it is in the middle of the sentence, use a comma inside of the quotes.

She said, "I'd like to go to the beach."

"I'd like to go to the beach," she said.

■ Add the correct punctation inside the quotation marks.

❶ "Hi there [ ] " she said.

❷ I said, "I'm going home [ ] "

❸ "Wait for me [ ] " he said.

❹ Sasha said, "Let's go to the library [ ] "

Date

Great Job Sticker

Add the correct punctuation in each piece of dialogue.

This morning, I woke up and heard my mom say,

"Get out of bed ☐ "

"One more minute ☐ " I answered.

"You're running late ☐ " she insisted.

I got dressed quickly and brushed my teeth.

I asked her, "Can I have cereal for breakfast ☐ "

She said, "Yes, but hurry ☐ "

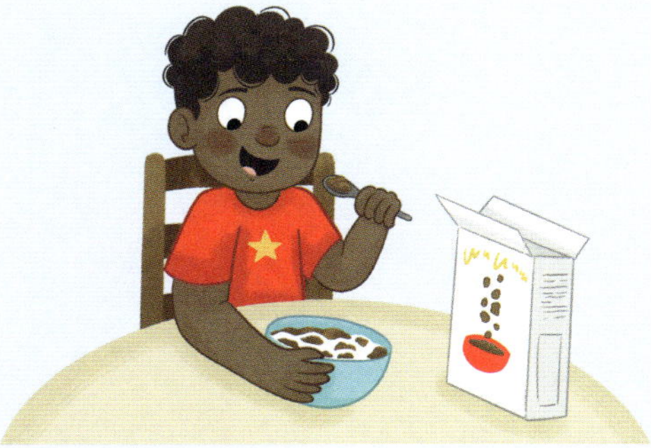

I ate quickly and put my shoes on.

"Come on ☐ " I yelled.

But now my mom wasn't ready. She called back,

"I'll be right there ☐ "

Brain Break
Let's Make Up a New Word!

■ You've learned a lot of rules about language in these activities Now it's time to make up a word of your own. Imagine you could add one word to the English language. Write the word below, and provide a definition. Then use it in a sentence!

Word:

Meaning:

Definition:

Mindfulness Break!

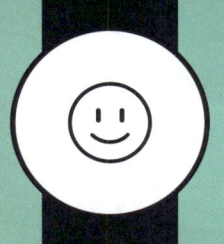

Write a letter to someone to make them feel better.

KEY POINTS

When you read a story or book the text can give you important details about the characters, plot, and setting.

■ Use the text to answer the questions. Quote a line or two from the passage to support your answer.

> Jared was excited to learn how to swim. He put on his bright green goggles and climbed into the shallow end of the pool. At first, he was scared, but his teacher, Coach Megan, helped him float on his back. Then she gave Jared a kickboard and told him to swim across the pool. Jared kicked his legs and moved his arms, just like Coach Megan showed him. Slowly, he started to swim across the pool. When he reached the
>
>  other side, Jared felt very happy and proud. It made him want to keep practicing and get even better at swimming.

1 How did Jared feel about learning to swim?

_____

_____

2 What helped Jared be more confident in his ability to swim?

_____

_____

■ Answer the questions based on the reading passage. Quote a line or two to support your answer.

Samantha was excited for her first day at a new school. She wore her favorite purple shoes which matched her new purple backpack. When she walked into the classroom, she had butterflies in her stomach. But she took a deep breath and smiled at the other kids around her. She sat in a desk next to a girl named Lily was wearing purple glasses! Lily smiled happily at Samantha. She said, "Hi, my name is Lily!" Samantha said "hi" and asked if Lily wanted to play at recess. Lily agreed! By the end of the day, Samantha had made a new friend. She climbed onto the bus to go home looking forward to the next day and making more friends.

❶ How did Samantha feel about her first day at a new school?

_____

_____

❷ What made Samantha less worried about making friends?

_____

_____

❸ How did she feel at the end of the school day?

_____

_____

Learning from Fables

KEY POINTS

Fables are stories that offer a clear message or moral to teach a lesson. They have been told orally from generation to generation to help children learn.

■ **Use the text to answer the questions.**

The Lion and the Mouse - Aesop Fables

A Lion was asleep in the forest, his great head resting on his paws. A shy little Mouse came upon him unexpectedly. She rushed to get away and accidentally ran across the Lion's nose. The Lion woke from his nap with a start and grabbed the Mouse in his huge paw. "Don't eat me!" begged the poor Mouse. "Please let me go and some day I will repay you. "The Lion laughed at the thought that a Mouse could ever help him. But he was generous and decided let the Mouse go.

A few days later, while hunting in the forest, the Lion was caught in the ropes of a hunter's net. He struggled and struggled, but was unable to escape. He let out an angry roar that filled the forest. Luckily, the Mouse heard and quickly found the Lion struggling in the net. She climbed up one of the big ropes holding the Lion down and began to chew through it. After the Mouse chewed through a few ropes the Lion was able to break free. "You laughed at me when I said I would repay you for not eating me," said the Mouse. "But as you can see, sometimes even a Mouse can help a Lion." The Lion gave the Mouse a grateful nod before bounding away.

① **What is the moral of this fable?**

_____

_____

② **What sentences from the fable support your moral?**

_____

_____

■ Answer the questions based on the reading passage.

The Mice and the Cat - Aesop's Fables

A group of Mice lived peacefully on a farm. Their only problem was the farmer's Cat who would catch and eat them. One day, the Mice got together to try and come up with a plan to help them stay safe when the Cat was around.

They talked and talked all day and night, but no mouse could come up with a good idea for how to come up with a way to warn the other mice that the Cat was coming. Finally, the littlest Mouse had a thought and said, "I have an idea that should work very well. All we have to do is to hang a bell about the Cat's neck. When we hear the bell ringing we will know she is coming and have time to run away!"

All the Mice were surprised that they had not thought of this plan before. They were so excited they began to shout with joy and celebrate. But while they were celebrating, an old Mouse stood up and said: "I will admit the little Mouse's plan is a very good one. But I have one question: Who will put the bell on the Cat?"

❶ What is the moral of this fable?

_____

_____

❷ What is a sentence from the fable that supports your moral?

_____

_____

❸ Have you faced a situation like this in your daily life?

_____

_____

Describing Characters

KEY POINTS

Part of what makes story fun to read is having well-written characters. A good writer describes their characters' looks, personality, motivations, and feelings. How a character behaves can affect the outcome of a story or situation in a book.

Examples of Character Traits

Physical Traits

Hair color: brown, blonde, black, red
Eye color: brown, blue, green, hazel, grey
Height: tall, short, average
Body Shape: large, small, round, squat

Personality Traits

Happy, moody, charismatic, solemn, angry, motivated

Motivation Traits

Wanting to win, supportive, out for revenge, trying to save someone or something, being a hero

Descriptive Traits

Type of clothes, hobbies, age

■ Try and describe yourself as a character using examples of character traits from above.

_____

_____

_____

■ **Answer the questions based on the reading passage.**

> Molly woke up excited and jumped out of bed. The day was finally here! Today she would go to the amusement park with her family. This year she was nervous to see if she was finally tall enough to ride the Looping Rollercoaster. Molly had always been shorter than her classmates. Molly braided her long brown hair and put on her favorite pair of sunglasses that were shaped like yellow stars.
>
> Once in the car, Molly and her sister talked non-stop about what rides they wanted to do first.
>
> "I want to do the Merry-Go-Round," her sister said.
>
> "And I want to try the Looping Rollercoaster!" said Molly. Her father smiled at her in the review mirror and said, "We can try that first, and see if you're tall enough."
>
> At the park, Molly grabbed her father's hand and pulled him along to the rollercoaster. She ran right up to the height chart and spun around.
>
> "Looks like you can ride this year!" her father said happily. Molly jumped up and down with joy before racing onto the ride line.

❶ List Molly's physical traits.

_____

_____

❷ Write an example of a personality trait of Molly's.

_____

_____

❸ How do the character traits make Molly more interesting?

_____

_____

Illustrations in Stories

KEY POINTS

When a book or story has an illustration, it helps contribute to what is conveyed by the words in a story. An illustration can add information and help the reader feel more connected with the story.

■ Use the illustration to answer questions about the story that might not be in the text.

Gillian's parents gave her a new bike for her 12th birthday. She was so excited to ride it. The bike had streamers coming from the handlebars, a basket, and a bell. After having cake with her family she went out to ride her new bike.

Gillian put on her helmet and mounted her new bike. She rode up and down the sidewalk from her house to the local park.

At the park, Gillian saw her best friend, Phillip.

"Wow, what a cool bike!" said Phillip. "Now we can ride around the lake together!" Gillian nodded in agreement and the two friends took off around the lake. Gillian's new bike pedaled smoothly and she was even able to beat Phillip in a race!

❶ What color is Gillian's new bike?

❷ What is Gillian feeling from the look on her face and the description in the story?

■ Use the illustration to answer questions about the story that might not be in the text.

It was Halloween! Max was getting ready to go Trick-or-Treating with his friends. Max put on his hat and cape to complete his costume. Max was going as a wizard! He grabbed his pumpkin pail and headed out the front door with his parents.

Max waited on the sidewalk for his friends. He could see them coming. "I love your costume," said Max's friend Jenna when she reached him. "I love your costume too!" said Max. Jenna did a twirl in her costume. "Look, here comes Henry." "Wow, what a scary costume, Henry!" Jenna said. "Yeah it's great!" added Max. "Thanks! I like your costumes too. Did you see Anna's costume? Her mom made it and it's awesome." Max and Jenna turned around to see Anna and her mom coming toward them. They both had huge smiles on their faces when they saw her costume. "That's an awesome costume!" Max said. "Your mom is really talented." Anna smiled and said, "Thank you! Now let's go get some candy!"

❶ What is Jenna's costume?

_____

❷ Why is Henry's costume scary?

_____

❸ What kind of costume did Anna's mom make her?

_____

Brain Break
Let's Write a Story with Your Own Character!

■ Use the writing skills learned in this section to write a story with your own character.

1 What would their traits be? Physical, personality, motivation?

2 Add an illustration of your character and setting.

Mindfulness Break!

■ Fill in the boxes with your plan.

Situation: You did not make the team or club you tried out for...

❶ What happened?

❷ Why did it happen?

❸ Can I change the outcome?

❹ If yes: how?

❺ If no: then what's next?

❻ How does it make me feel?

Multiplication 1

■ Complete the multiplication table. Then, solve the problems below.

1 × Table

$1 \times 1 = 1$ $1 \times 6 =$

$1 \times 2 = 2$ $1 \times 7 =$

$1 \times 3 =$ $1 \times 8 =$

$1 \times 4 =$ $1 \times 9 =$

$1 \times 5 =$ $1 \times 10 =$

When multiplying by 1 the answer is always the number being multiplied, $1 \times 7 = 7$.

① $1 \times 4 =$ ② $1 \times 7 =$ ③ $1 \times 5 =$ ④ $1 \times 10 =$

⑤
$$\begin{array}{r} 1 \\ \times 2 \\ \hline 2 \end{array}$$

⑥
$$\begin{array}{r} 1 \\ \times 6 \\ \hline \end{array}$$

⑦
$$\begin{array}{r} 1 \\ \times 9 \\ \hline \end{array}$$

⑧
$$\begin{array}{r} 1 \\ \times 8 \\ \hline \end{array}$$

■ Complete the multiplication table. Then, solve the problems below.

2 × Table

$2 \times 1 = 2$

$2 \times 2 = 4$

$2 \times 3 =$

$2 \times 4 =$

$2 \times 5 =$

$2 \times 6 =$

$2 \times 7 =$

$2 \times 8 =$

$2 \times 9 =$

$2 \times 10 =$

Did you find that the answers are increasing by 2?

❶ $2 \times 1 =$

❷ $2 \times 4 =$

❸ $2 \times 8 =$

❹ $2 \times 5 =$

❺
$$\begin{array}{r} 2 \\ \times 10 \\ \hline 20 \end{array}$$

❻
$$\begin{array}{r} 2 \\ \times 3 \\ \hline \end{array}$$

❼
$$\begin{array}{r} 2 \\ \times 6 \\ \hline \end{array}$$

❽
$$\begin{array}{r} 2 \\ \times 2 \\ \hline \end{array}$$

Multiplication 2

■ Complete the multiplication table. Then, solve the problems below.

3 × Table

$3 \times 1 = 3$ $3 \times 6 =$

$3 \times 2 = 6$ $3 \times 7 =$

$3 \times 3 =$ $3 \times 8 =$

$3 \times 4 =$ $3 \times 9 =$

$3 \times 5 =$ $3 \times 10 =$

The answer to a multiplication problem is called the **product**.

❶ $3 \times 3 =$ ❷ $3 \times 5 =$ ❸ $3 \times 7 =$ ❹ $3 \times 9 =$

❺ $\begin{array}{r} 3 \\ \times 4 \\ \hline \end{array}$ ❻ $\begin{array}{r} 3 \\ \times 8 \\ \hline \end{array}$ ❼ $\begin{array}{r} 3 \\ \times 6 \\ \hline \end{array}$ ❽ $\begin{array}{r} 3 \\ \times 2 \\ \hline \end{array}$

■ Complete the multiplication table. Then, solve the problems below.

4 × Table

$4 \times 1 = 4$ $4 \times 6 =$

$4 \times 2 = 8$ $4 \times 7 =$

$4 \times 3 =$ $4 \times 8 =$

$4 \times 4 =$ $4 \times 9 =$

$4 \times 5 =$ $4 \times 10 =$

You can read
a multiplication problem like
4×2 as "four times two."

❶ $4 \times 3 =$ ❷ $4 \times 10 =$ ❸ $4 \times 9 =$ ❹ $4 \times 1 =$

❺ $\begin{array}{r} 4 \\ \times 5 \\ \hline \end{array}$ ❻ $\begin{array}{r} 4 \\ \times 8 \\ \hline \end{array}$ ❼ $\begin{array}{r} 4 \\ \times 4 \\ \hline \end{array}$ ❽ $\begin{array}{r} 4 \\ \times 2 \\ \hline \end{array}$

Multiplication 3

■ Complete the multiplication table. Then, solve the problems below.

5 × Table

$5 \times 1 = 5$ $5 \times 6 =$

$5 \times 2 = 10$ $5 \times 7 =$

$5 \times 3 =$ $5 \times 8 =$

$5 \times 4 =$ $5 \times 9 =$

$5 \times 5 =$ $5 \times 10 =$

You can also say
"five groups of two"
for 5×2.

❶ $5 \times 4 =$ ❷ $5 \times 6 =$ ❸ $5 \times 7 =$ ❹ $5 \times 2 =$

❺ $\begin{array}{r} 5 \\ \times 8 \\ \hline \end{array}$ ❻ $\begin{array}{r} 5 \\ \times 3 \\ \hline \end{array}$ ❼ $\begin{array}{r} 5 \\ \times 9 \\ \hline \end{array}$ ❽ $\begin{array}{r} 5 \\ \times 1 \\ \hline \end{array}$

■ Complete the multiplication table. Then, solve the problems below.

6 × Table

$6 \times 1 = 6$ $6 \times 6 =$

$6 \times 2 = 12$ $6 \times 7 =$

$6 \times 3 =$ $6 \times 8 =$

$6 \times 4 =$ $6 \times 9 =$

$6 \times 5 =$ $6 \times 10 =$

Did you find that the answers
are increasing by 6?

❶ $6 \times 2 =$ ❷ $6 \times 7 =$ ❸ $6 \times 6 =$ ❹ $6 \times 4 =$

❺ $\begin{array}{r} 6 \\ \times 10 \\ \hline \end{array}$ ❻ $\begin{array}{r} 6 \\ \times 8 \\ \hline \end{array}$ ❼ $\begin{array}{r} 6 \\ \times 3 \\ \hline \end{array}$ ❽ $\begin{array}{r} 6 \\ \times 5 \\ \hline \end{array}$

Multiplication 4

■ Complete the multiplication table. Then, solve the problems below.

7 × Table

$7 × 1 = 7$ $7 × 6 =$

$7 × 2 = 14$ $7 × 7 =$

$7 × 3 =$ $7 × 8 =$

$7 × 4 =$ $7 × 9 =$

$7 × 5 =$ $7 × 10 =$

You can read
a multiplication problem like
7 × 2 as "seven times two."

❶ $7 × 5 =$ ❷ $7 × 2 =$ ❸ $7 × 6 =$ ❹ $7 × 9 =$

❺ $\begin{array}{r} 7 \\ × 3 \\ \hline \end{array}$ ❻ $\begin{array}{r} 7 \\ × 7 \\ \hline \end{array}$ ❼ $\begin{array}{r} 7 \\ × 1 \\ \hline \end{array}$ ❽ $\begin{array}{r} 7 \\ × 10 \\ \hline \end{array}$

■ Complete the multiplication table. Then, solve the problems below.

8 × Table

$8 \times 1 = 8$ $8 \times 6 =$

$8 \times 2 = 16$ $8 \times 7 =$

$8 \times 3 =$ $8 \times 8 =$

$8 \times 4 =$ $8 \times 9 =$

$8 \times 5 =$ $8 \times 10 =$

You can also say
"eight groups of two"
for 8×2.

❶ $8 \times 4 =$ ❷ $8 \times 3 =$ ❸ $8 \times 5 =$ ❹ $8 \times 8 =$

❺ $\begin{array}{r} 8 \\ \times 7 \\ \hline \end{array}$ ❻ $\begin{array}{r} 8 \\ \times 2 \\ \hline \end{array}$ ❼ $\begin{array}{r} 8 \\ \times 10 \\ \hline \end{array}$ ❽ $\begin{array}{r} 8 \\ \times 6 \\ \hline \end{array}$

Multiplication 5

■ Complete the multiplication table. Then, solve the problems below.

9 × Table

$9 \times 1 = 9$ $9 \times 6 =$

$9 \times 2 = 18$ $9 \times 7 =$

$9 \times 3 =$ $9 \times 8 =$

$9 \times 4 =$ $9 \times 9 =$

$9 \times 5 =$ $9 \times 10 =$

Did you find that the answers are increasing by 9?

❶ $9 \times 3 =$ ❷ $9 \times 7 =$ ❸ $9 \times 5 =$ ❹ $9 \times 6 =$

❺ $\begin{array}{r} 9 \\ \times 4 \\ \hline \end{array}$ ❻ $\begin{array}{r} 9 \\ \times 9 \\ \hline \end{array}$ ❼ $\begin{array}{r} 9 \\ \times 1 \\ \hline \end{array}$ ❽ $\begin{array}{r} 9 \\ \times 2 \\ \hline \end{array}$

■ Complete the multiplication table. Then, solve the problems below.

10 × Table

$10 \times 1 = 10$ $10 \times 6 =$

$10 \times 2 = 20$ $10 \times 7 =$

$10 \times 3 =$ $10 \times 8 =$

$10 \times 4 =$ $10 \times 9 =$

$10 \times 5 =$ $10 \times 10 =$

Did you find a pattern when
you multiply by 10?

❶ $10 \times 9 =$ ❷ $10 \times 3 =$ ❸ $10 \times 1 =$ ❹ $10 \times 7 =$

❺
$$\begin{array}{r} 10 \\ \times 10 \\ \hline \end{array}$$

❻
$$\begin{array}{r} 10 \\ \times\ 2 \\ \hline \end{array}$$

❼
$$\begin{array}{r} 10 \\ \times\ 6 \\ \hline \end{array}$$

❽
$$\begin{array}{r} 10 \\ \times\ 5 \\ \hline \end{array}$$

Brain Break
Multiplication Facts "True" or "False"

■ Write a check mark (✔) if the multiplication facts are true or false.

Multiplication Table

×	1	2	3	4	5
1	1	2	3	4	5
2	2	4	6	8	10
3	3	6	9	12	15
4	4	8	12	16	20
5	5	10	15	20	25
6	6	12	18	24	30
7	7	14	21	28	35
8	8	16	24	32	40
9	9	18	27	36	45
10	10	20	30	40	50

You can switch the order of numbers, and the answer is always the same. This is called the **commutative property of multiplication**.

Ex: $5 \times 6 = 30$ and $6 \times 5 = 30$

 True ☐ False

1, 25, 49, 64, 81, and 100 show only once in this table. They are products obtained by multiplying the same numbers.

 True  False

	6	7	8	9	10
	6	7	8	9	10
	12	14	16	18	20
	18	21	24	27	30
	24	28	32	36	40
	30	35	40	45	50
	36	42	48	54	60
	42	49	56	63	70
	48	56	64	72	80
	54	63	72	81	90
	60	70	80	90	100

You can see a mirror image of the other in this table.

☐ True ☐ False

×	1	2	3	4	⋯
1	1	2	3	4	⋯
2	2	4	6	8	⋯
3	3	6	9	12	⋯
4	4	8	12	16	⋯
⋮	⋮	⋮	⋮	⋮	⋱

Whether you look vertically or horizontally at a multiplying number in this table, the answer is always the same.

☐ True ☐ False

×	6
1	6
2	12
3	18
⋮	⋮

×	1	2	3	⋯
6	6	12	18	⋯

Animals are Living Things

KEY POINTS

Living things, also called organisms, are things that can move, feel, grow, and create new life. Animals, plants, and fungi (like mushrooms, yeast, and mold) are all living things.

Animals can move, using their own energy (not just drifting in the wind or floating in a river). Some animals move by walking, running, climbing, swimming, flying, jumping, or slithering. Non-living things move when they are moved by the wind, the water, or by living things.

Animals can feel. Some animals, like humans, can feel with a lot of detail. For example, if you touch something with your eyes closed, you might be able to guess what it is just by noticing what shape and texture it is. Some animals can only feel if something is hot or cold. Non-living things, like rocks or water, can't feel anything.

Animals can grow. When animals like kittens are born, they are very small and can't take care of themselves. They can't open their eyes until they are one or two weeks old! They get energy through drinking their mother's milk. They use this energy to grow and develop. Eventually they grow up to be adult cats.

Animals can create new life. They have babies that can grow up to be adults and have their own babies. This continues the life cycle of the animal.

■ **Answer the questions.**

1 What are the three types of living things?

_____

2 What are some traits that make living things different from non-living things?

_____

3 What are some ways non-living things can be moved?

_____

■ **Fill in the blanks with the correct words.**

① _____ can move, feel, grow, and create new life.

② Rocks, water, and soil are examples of

_____ .

③ Animals can move using their own

_____ .

④ Humans can _____ different textures and temperatures.

⑤ _____ can create new life by producing seeds.

Animal Life Cycles

KEY POINTS

All living things go through a life cycle. A life cycle is a series of changes that a living thing goes through. All members of the same species will go through similar stages. All frogs will start as eggs, which hatch into tadpoles. The tadpoles grow legs and become froglets. They lose their tails and grow bigger and become adult frogs. The adult frogs lay eggs that then hatch into tadpoles, starting the process over again.

Some animals, like frogs and butterflies, change a lot in each life stage. Tadpoles breathe underwater and have tails instead of arms or legs–very different from frogs!

Caterpillars turn into butterflies–they go from having lots of legs and no wings to having six legs and wings! Other animals, like baby turtles and horses, just look like smaller versions of their parents.

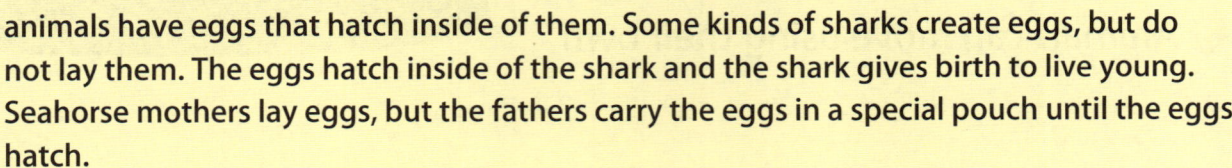

Some animals lay eggs in order to reproduce, or create new life. Most fish, reptiles, amphibians, insects, and birds lay eggs. Some animals have eggs that hatch inside of them. Some kinds of sharks create eggs, but do not lay them. The eggs hatch inside of the shark and the shark gives birth to live young. Seahorse mothers lay eggs, but the fathers carry the eggs in a special pouch until the eggs hatch.

Almost all mammals give birth to live young instead of laying eggs. Dogs give birth to live puppies which they care for until the are old enough to take care of themselves. Other animals like marsupials give birth to their young when they are very small and not very developed. These babies live in their mothers' pouches until they are developed enough to survive outside of it. Kangaroos, opossums, and koalas are all examples of marsupials.

■ **Answer the questions.**

❶ What is a life cycle?

❷ What type of animals lay eggs?

❸ What makes marsupials different from other animals?

■ Complete the life cycle of a frog.

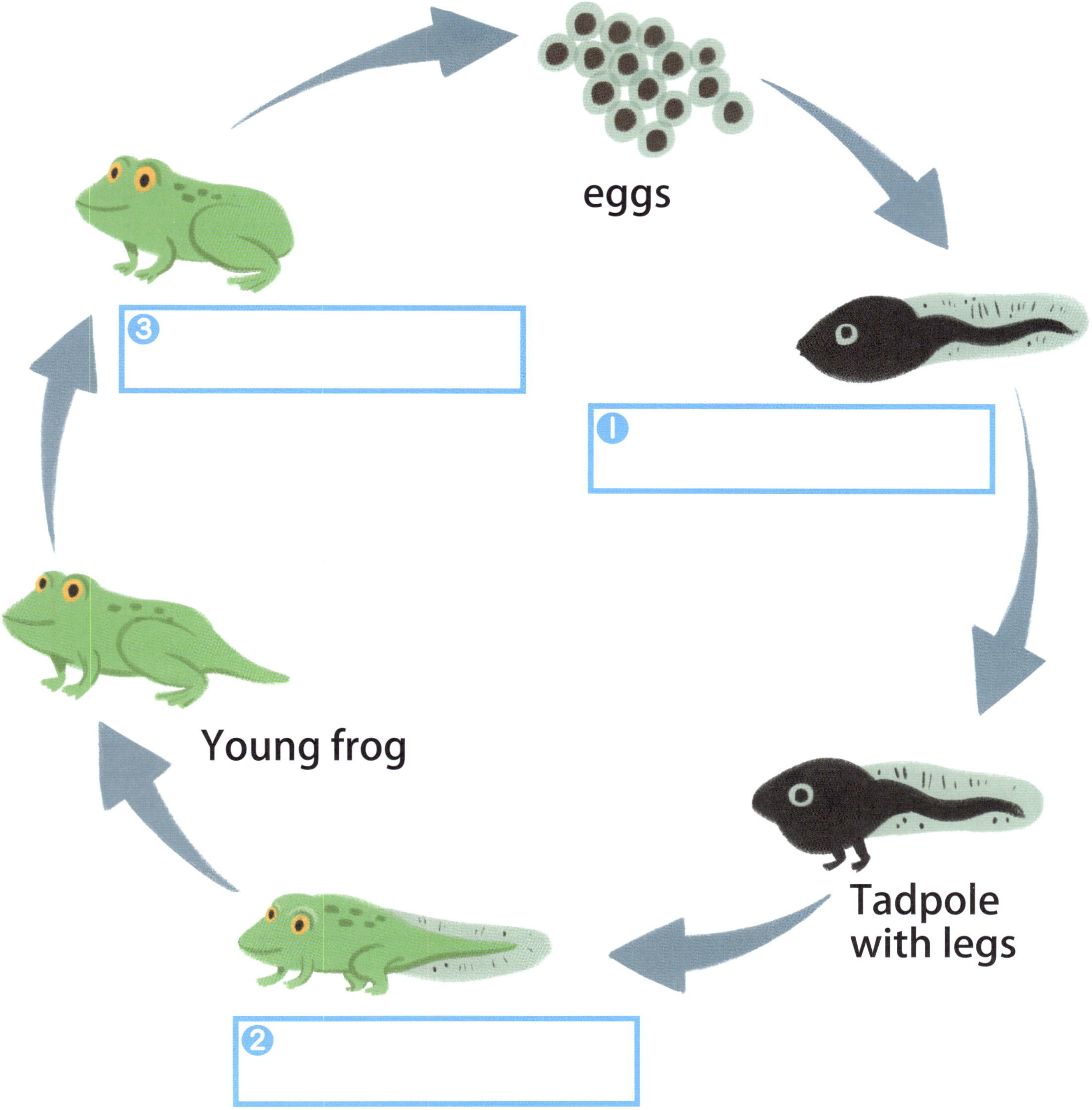

eggs

③

①

②

Young frog

Tadpole
with legs

Animals and Offspring

KEY POINTS

Some animals care for their young for years after they are born. Others lay their eggs and leave. Some animals have one or two babies at a time. Others lay one thousand eggs at one time! There are many different kinds of parents in the animal world.

Mammals usually care for their young until they are able to take care of themselves. Baby mammals drink milk created by their mothers when they are young. This milk gives them energy to grow and develop. For most kinds of mammals, the mothers take care of the young without help from the fathers.

Most birds are born helpless, with no feathers and with their eyes closed. Bird parents must care for their eggs and young. They keep them warm, protect them from predators, and feed them once they are born. For most kinds of birds, both the mother and father take care of their young. Birds can lay between one and twenty eggs at a time, depending on the kind of bird.

Many reptiles can already find their own food and care for themselves when they are born. Most reptiles do not take care of their young. They lay their eggs in a protected area, like a hole, and leave them. However, some reptiles guard their nests. Some even take care of their young. Some kinds of reptiles lay just one egg at a time, while others lay more than one hundred!

Amphibians, like frogs, often lay their eggs and leave them to take care of themselves, but some amphibians guard their eggs or young. Some even feed their young. Sometimes the mother does this and sometimes the father does this, depending on the kind of amphibian. It is very rare for both of them to stay with their young.

Fish usually lay many eggs at once–up to one thousand! Many fish lay their eggs and leave, but others stay with the eggs. They protect the eggs and then protect the young fish after they hatch. It is more common that fish fathers stay with the eggs. Fish mothers usually don't.

Date

Great Job Sticker

Match the animals to their young.

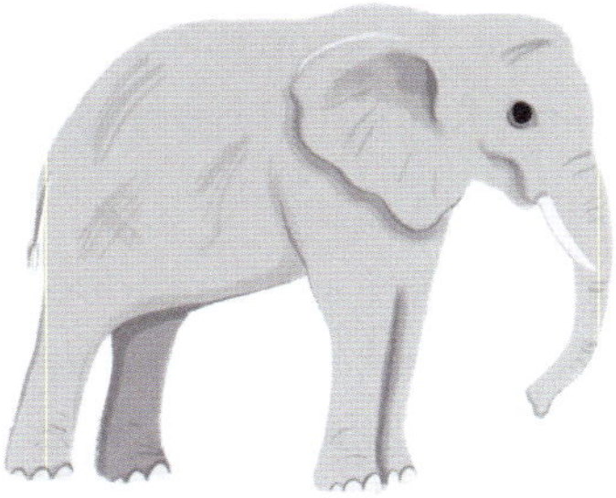
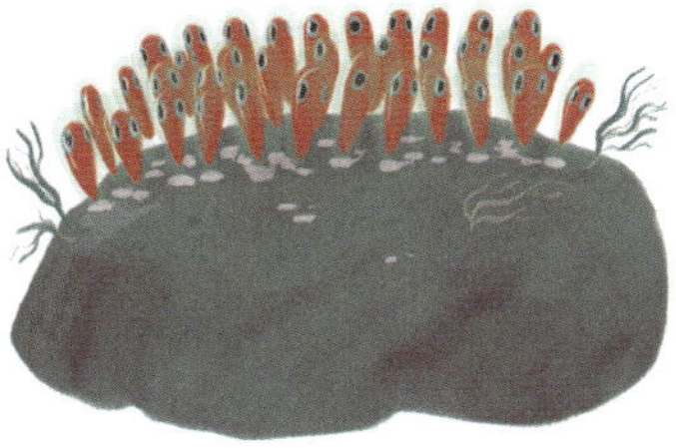
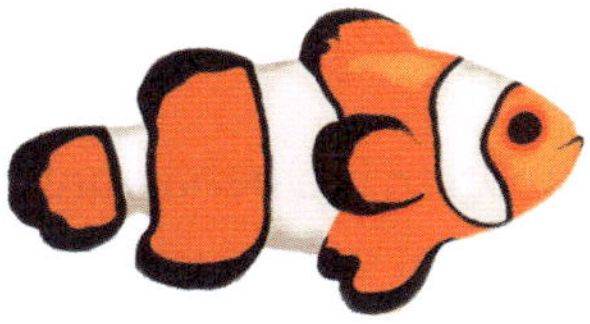
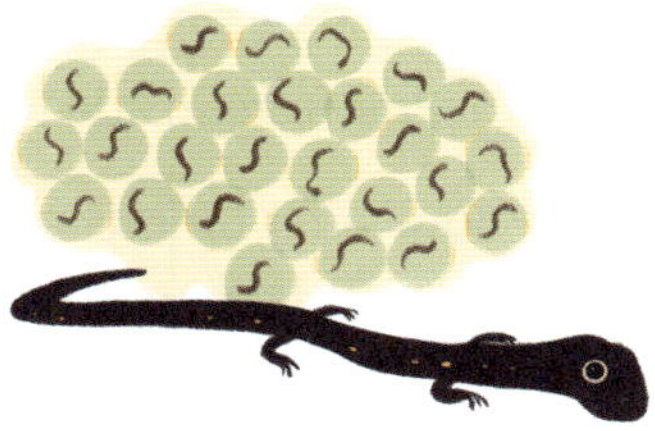
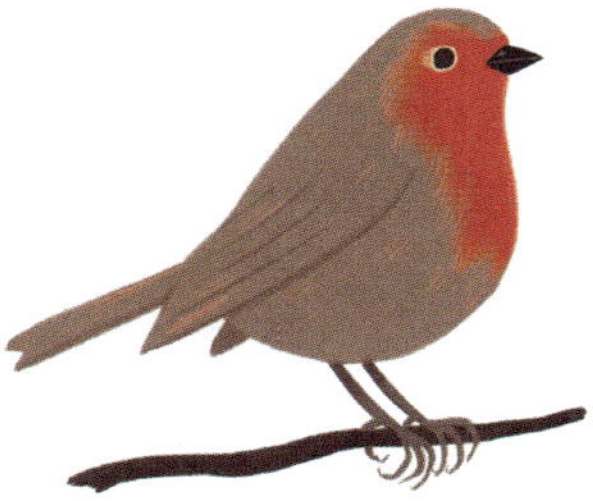
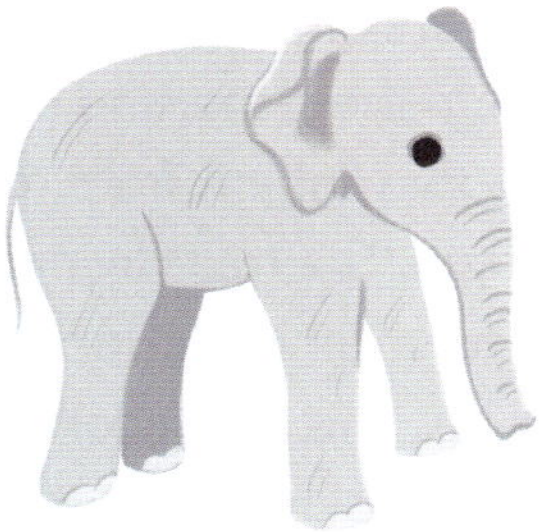
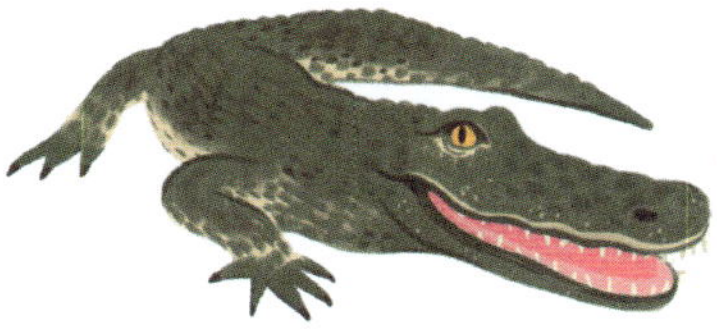
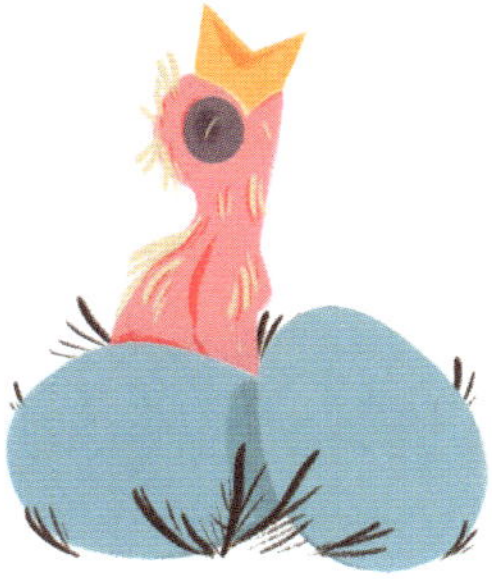
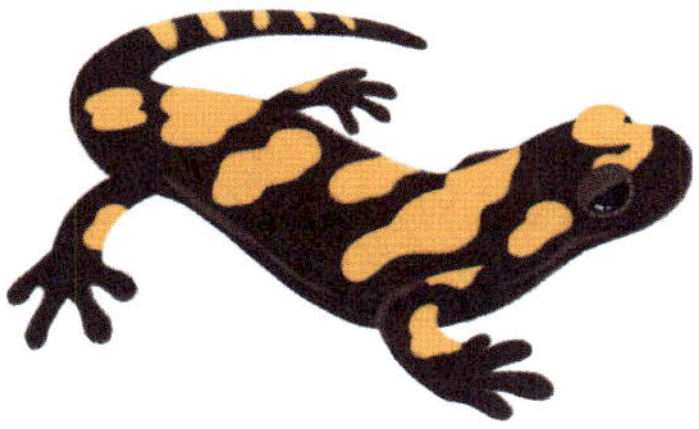
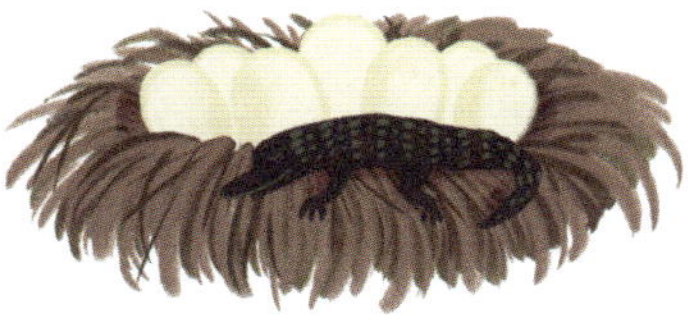

Inherited Traits and Adaptations

KEY POINTS

There are millions of species, or kinds of animals, on Earth! Different species of animals are adapted to different environments and to different roles in that environment. If all animals ate the same thing, not very many animals would be able to survive. They would all compete for the same food. That is a reason why different animals have adapted to eat different things.

Adaptations are traits that living things inherit from their parents that help them survive and reproduce. Adaptations can be physical, meaning they are a part of an animal's body, or behavioral, meaning they are something the animal does. Physical adaptations are traits in animals' bodies. For example, fur that helps an animal camouflage so that it can hide from predators or sneak up on prey. Giraffes' long necks are a physical adaptation that allow them to reach leaves that other animals can't, so they don't have to compete for them. Hummingbirds' long, narrow beaks are a physical adaptation that allow them to drink nectar from inside flowers.

Behavioral adaptations are things that animals do that help them survive. Hibernation is a behavioral adaptation that many animals have. It helps them survive cold winters. Schools of fish swim together in large groups as a behavioral adaptation to protect themselves from predators and to have a better chance of finding food.

There are differences in how animals of the same species look and act. Not all cats are the same, and neither are all seagulls. These differences come from traits they inherit from their parents and from the environments in which they grew up. The traits living things inherit from their parents are complicated, but, for example, puppies will usually look like a combination of their two parents. This is true for other animals as well as plants and other living things. If an animal has traits that help it survive in the environment where it lives, it is more likely to have more babies that have similar traits. This is how certain traits can become more common in a species.

■ **Answer the questions.**

❶ **What are adaptations?**

❷ **Why are adaptations important?**

❸ **Write some examples of physical adaptations.**

■ Write whether the adaptation is physical or behavioral.

❶ A bear hibernating.

❷ A giraffe's long neck.

❸ Fish swimming together in schools.

❹ A tiger's fur being striped for camouflage.

Brain Break
Science Journal 2

Animals inherit different traits from their parents. If the two dogs below had puppies, what combination of traits could be inherited?

Traits:

Traits:

Puppy **1**

_____

Puppy **2**

_____

Puppy **3**

_____

■ Pick one of the puppies from your Science Journal. Draw it below. Make sure to include all the inherited traits!

Rules and Laws

KEY POINTS

Good rules and laws are both designed to keep people safe, help individuals or groups resolve conflicts, and protect people's rights. Laws are decided on and enforced by governments. Rules can be made by anyone for many reasons. Adults can also make rules for their families.

Parents might have a rule that a child always has to hold their hand in parking lots or near roads. This is a rule for keeping the child safe from cars. Not all families have the same rules. Some families might have a rule that kids can only have thirty minutes of screen time a day, or that they can only eat dessert on Mondays and Fridays. Other families might have different rules about screen time and desserts or not have any rules about these topics.

Laws are created by governments. They can be different from state to state or town to town. Others are federal laws that apply to everyone in the country. There are even international laws that apply to all countries that have agreed to them. Laws apply to all people equally. If anyone breaks a law, no matter if they are rich or poor, they will face the same consequences.

In the United States and most other democratic countries, laws are created by elected representatives and sometimes by judges. Laws are supposed to stop people from stealing from or hurting other people, either on purpose or by accident. They also create order and safety. For example, laws about how fast cars can drive reduce car accidents. Laws about how restaurants operate keep people from getting food poisoning.

■ **Answer the questions.**

❶ Who creates laws?

_____

❷ Who can create rules?

_____

❸ What is a rule at your school that you think is important to follow?

_____

■ Use the Key Points to fill in the blanks.

❶ Rules and laws are created to keep people

in society.

❷ Laws are made by

and rules can be made

by anyone.

❸ Many families have their own

created to

keep kids and other family members safe.

❹

laws apply to everyone in a country and

are created by that country's government.

❺ In the United States, laws are created by

.

Laws and Punishment

KEY POINTS

If you break a rule at school, you might have to apologize, miss out on a fun activity, or even talk to the principal. If you break a rule at home, you might get a stern talk, time out, or grounding. Breaking any rule can led to punishment. A punishment is a consequence given to the person who broke the rule by the person who made it. Punishments are meant to teach people not to break rules in the future.

Laws are different because they are enforced by the government, not teachers or adults in your family. Police officers can arrest or fine people who break laws. For more minor crimes, like driving faster than the speed limit, people usually just have to pay a fine. For more serious crimes, like hurting another person or stealing something valuable, people are often arrested and taken to jail.

The government can then prosecute people. To prosecute someone for a crime is to take them to court to see if they are guilty or not-guilty of a crime. Judges and sometimes juries decide whether or not a person is guilty and what their

punishment should be. Juries are groups of regular people who listen to the facts presented about the crime and decide the outcome.

If someone is found to be guilty in a court of law, they are then sentenced to, or given, a punishment. That punishment could be paying a fine, doing community service, or spending time in jail or prison.

■ **Answer the questions.**

❶ What is one difference between a rule and a law?

_____

❷ What is an example of a serious crime?

_____

■ Write true or false for each statement.

❶ A punishment is a consequence for breaking a rule or law.

❷ Breaking a rule at home might lead to grounding or a time out.

❸ Laws are different because they are enforced by the government.

❹ Police officers are the ones who make the laws.

❺ For breaking the law and committing serious crimes, a person can go to jail.

❻ One role of a judge is to decide what punishment to give a person who broke the law.

Unit 2 Social Studies

State Laws

KEY POINTS

Federal laws apply to everyone in the United States. A federal government is a government that unites, or brings together, a number of states. In the case of the US, it unites 50 states and 16 territories.

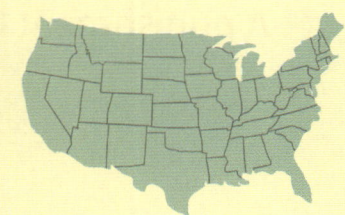

There are also state laws that apply only to people in that state. State and local laws cannot contradict, or say the opposite of, federal laws. Federal laws are the most important laws in the United States. If a state law contradicts a federal law, it is invalid, meaning it can't be enforced.

There are some laws that are frequently different between states. Laws about marriage and divorce, required punishments for certain crimes, gun control laws, and laws for businesses can vary from state to state. For example, in some states, it is very easy for an adult to buy a gun. In other states, people have to go through a long process to show that they know how to safely use and store a gun before they are allowed to buy one.

State laws are different because states are different. People's state representatives make laws that should represent what the people want and think is important.

Some states have strange laws that were created many years ago, but people still follow today.

It is illegal to hunt camels in Arizona.	It is illegal to change the clothes of a store front mannequin unless the shades are down in Georgia.	In West Virginia, hats are banned in movie theaters.
In North Dakota, you can't light fireworks after 11 p.m.	It is against the law in Pennsylvania to sleep in your refrigerator.	In Indiana it is illegal to ride a horse faster than 10 miles per hour.

Unit 2

■ Fill in the state where the strange law must be followed.

① In this state, hats are banned in movie theaters.

② You can't hunt camels in this state.

③ You can't light fireworks after 11 p.m. here.

④ If you're in this state, don't ride your horse faster than 10 mph.

⑤ Make sure the shades are down when changing the clothes on a mannequin in this state.

⑥ Never sleep in your refrigerator in this state.

Rights and Responsibilities

KEY POINTS

Being a United States citizen gives you both rights and responsibilities.

RIGHTS

- US citizen adults are able to vote in elections at the local, state, and federal levels.
- They have freedom of speech and assembly. That means that people can say, act, and gather however they want, as long as they do not hurt, endanger, or stop others from expressing themselves.
- US citizens have freedom of religion. As long as they do not hurt or endanger others, they can believe or not believe in anything they want.
- US citizens have the right to keep and bear arms, within reasonable restrictions. This means that US citizens can have guns or other weapons, as long as they have followed all of the rules of their state or district.
- US citizens have the right to be considered innocent until found guilty. They have the right to a speedy and fair trial by a jury of peers. This means that the government does not have the right to keep someone in jail for a long time while they wait to have a trial where the judge or jury decides if the person is guilty or not. The government needs to make the trial happen as quickly as possible.
- US citizens are allowed to serve on juries, run for elected office, and apply for jobs with the federal government.
- US citizens have freedom to pursue "life, liberty, and the pursuit of happiness." This means that they can make their own choices about their lives.

RESPONSIBILITIES

- Voting is both a right and a responsibility. US citizens should vote in all elections in their areas.
- US citizens should stay informed, learning about issues and candidates before voting in elections.
- Serving on a jury is also both a right and a responsibility. US citizens must serve on a jury if called to.
- US citizens must pay federal, state, and local taxes honestly and on time.
- US citizens must obey federal, state, and local laws.
- In times of war, US citizens must support their country. Some may have to serve in the military.
- US citizens should participate in their communities through volunteering, helping neighbors, getting involved in schools, local politics, and local organizations.
- US citizens must respect the rights and beliefs of others. Being tolerant and respectful of others is essential if we want to live in a country where everyone can be free to be themselves.

■ Circle Right or Responsibility for each statement. If it is both, then circle both.

❶ Voting   **Right**   **Responsibility**

❷ Freedom of Speech   **Right**   **Responsibility**

❸ Serving on a jury   **Right**   **Responsibility**

❹ Obeying federal laws   **Right**   **Responsibility**

❺ Innocent until found guilty   **Right**   **Responsibility**

❻ To run for office   **Right**   **Responsibility**

❼ The pursuit of life, liberty, and happiness   **Right**   **Responsibility**

Brain Break
Word Search

■ Find the word below in the Word Search puzzle.

rule	law	government	state
right	crime	punishment	jail

G	O	V	E	R	N	M	E	N	T
W	F	C	G	T	E	O	P	M	Q
E	G	Z	D	F	R	H	B	O	A
R	J	A	I	L	B	W	T	I	S
G	T	S	A	C	V	E	Q	U	E
J	Y	G	H	O	M	R	C	T	U
K	U	R	U	L	E	G	R	H	I
L	I	A	K	P	N	C	I	S	O
O	M	W	R	L	K	X	M	B	P
P	U	N	I	S	H	M	E	N	T
B	W	S	B	T	Z	D	D	K	M
Y	C	F	C	A	X	Q	P	O	L
R	I	G	H	T	Z	Y	U	I	A
C	V	A	S	E	D	H	J	L	W

Mindfulness Break!

KEY POINTS

Gratitude is feeling thankful for the people and things in your life.

■ Draw or write something you are grateful for in each box.

Coding 1

■ The turtle robot follows the block's commands. ⬆ and ➡ represent the robot's direction.

Command of the block

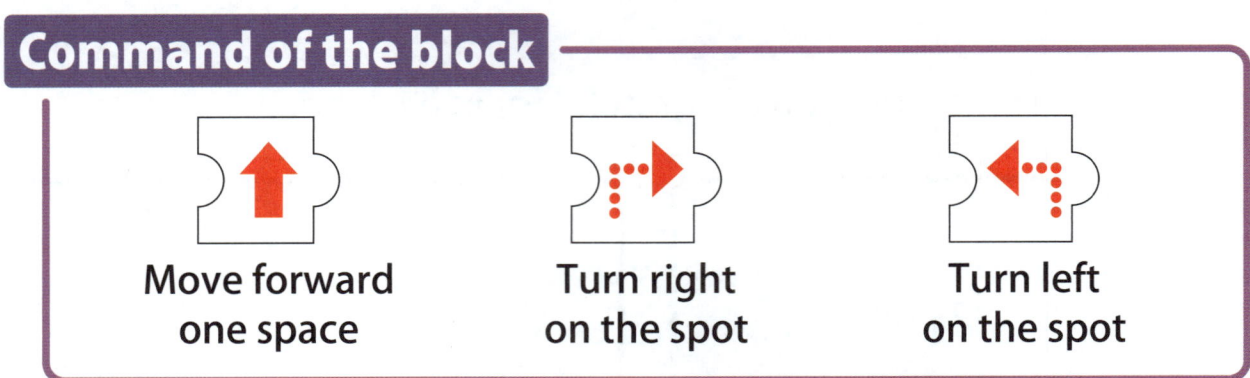

| Move forward one space | Turn right on the spot | Turn left on the spot |

What space does the robot end up in if you follow the code direction arrows in red? Write a check mark (✓) in the box.

❶ START ⬆ ⬆ ↦ ⬆ ⬆ GOAL

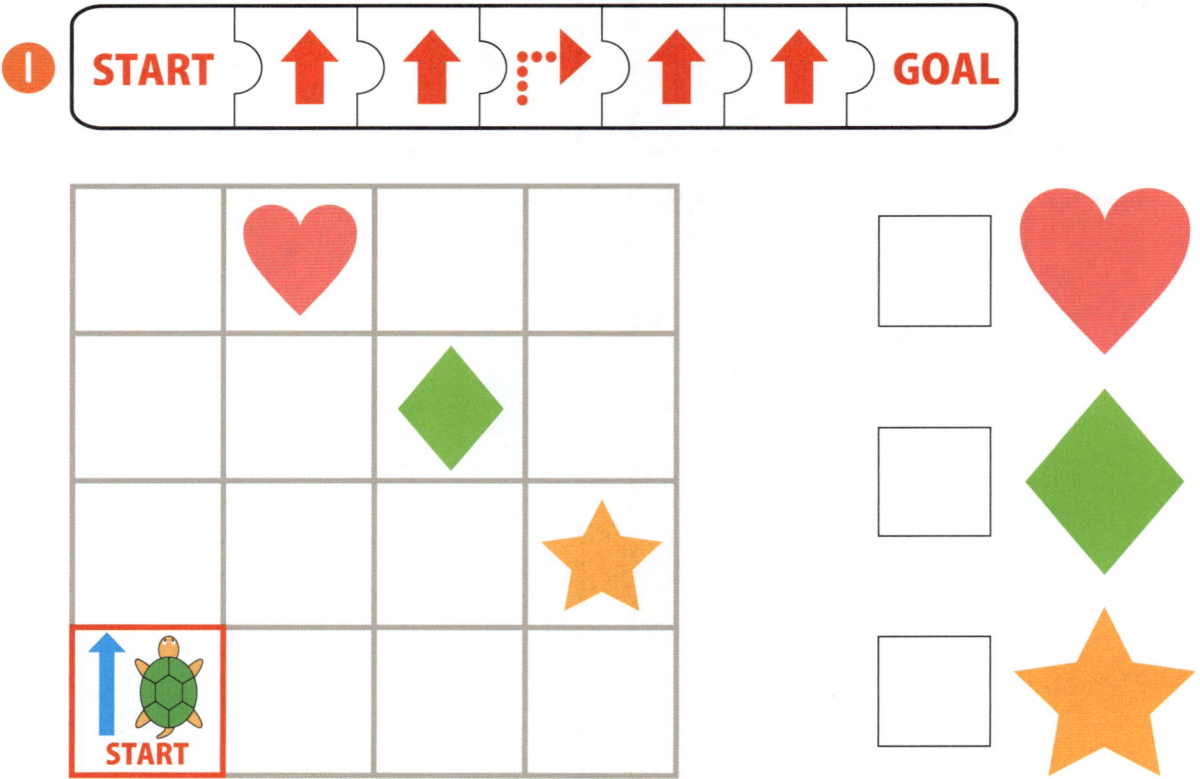

2
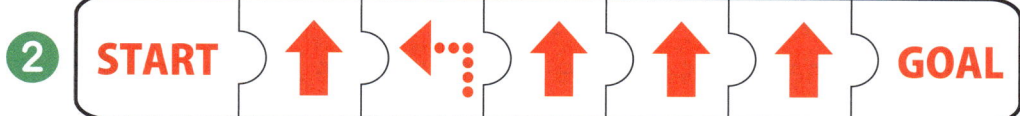

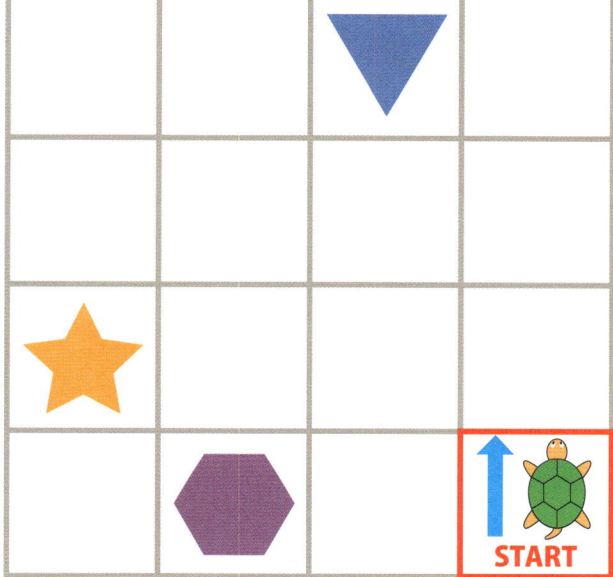

3
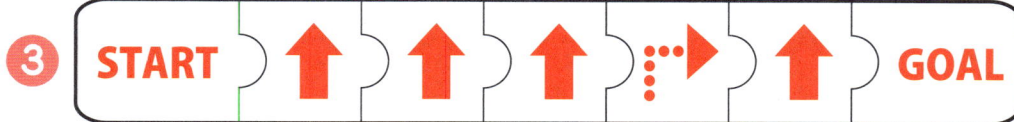

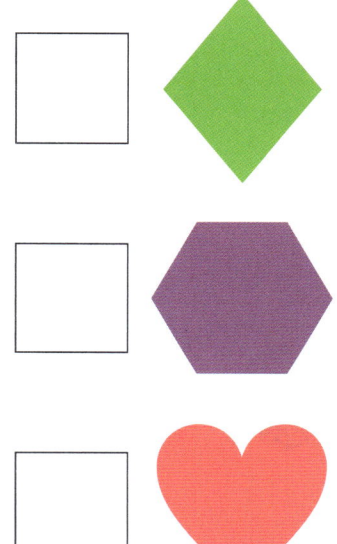

Coding 2

■ See the flowchart on the right-hand page. Which animals can the turtle robot meet if it follows the steps? Write the numbers in the order in which the robot meets them. ⬆ represents the robot's direction.

Date

Great Job Sticker

Start

↓

Move 2 steps

↓

Turn right

↓

Move 1 step

↓

Turn left

↓

Move 3 steps

↓

Turn right

↓

Move 2 steps

↓

Turn right

↓

Move 4 steps

↓

Turn left

↓

Move 2 steps

↓

Turn left

↓

Move 3 steps

↓

End

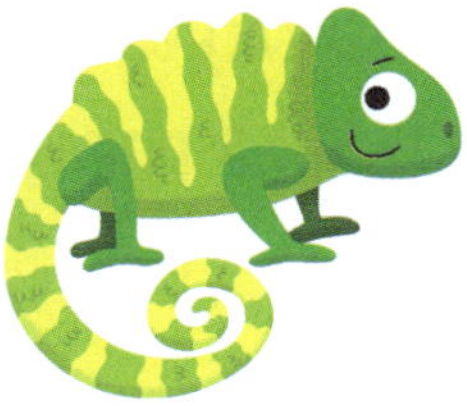

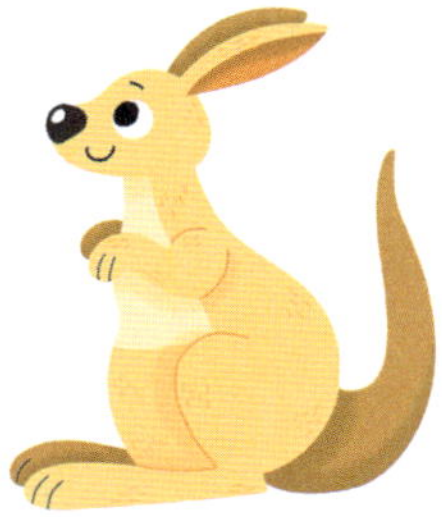

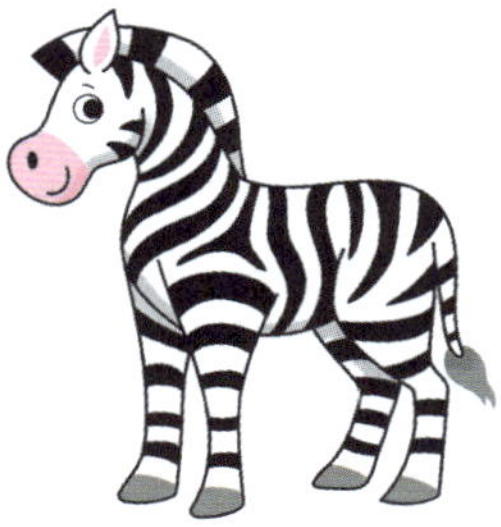

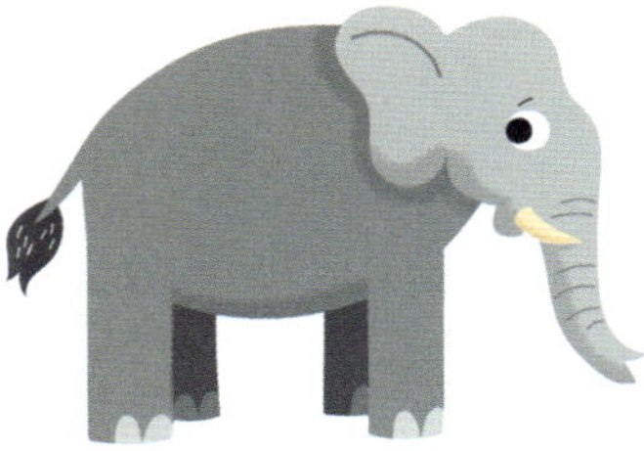

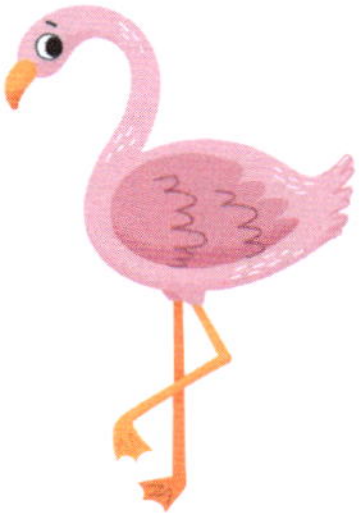

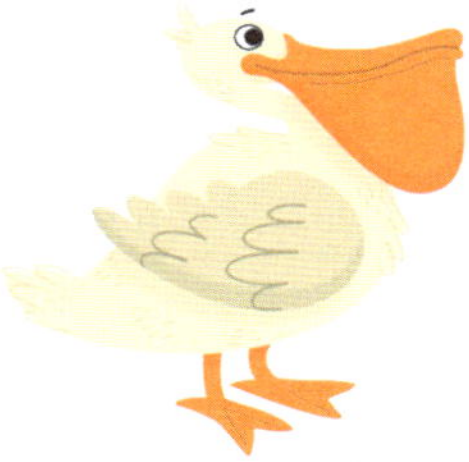

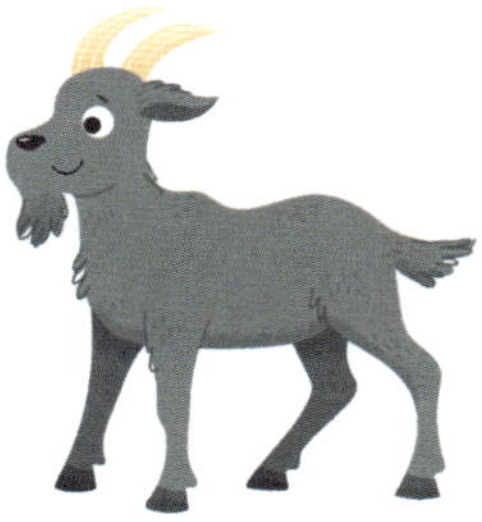

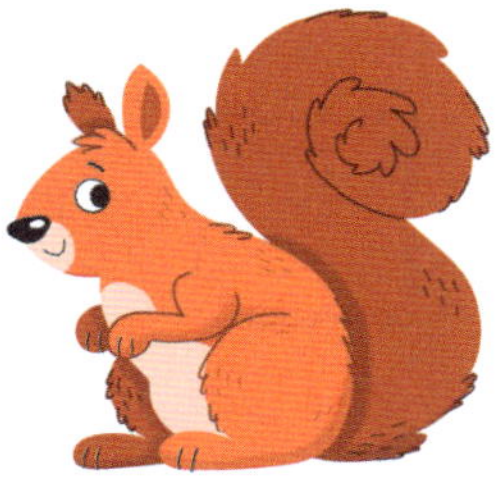

■ The car robot follows the arrow command blocks below. Which commands are needed to get the robot to the following locations on the grid? Write a check mark (✔) in the box. ⬆ represents the robot's direction.

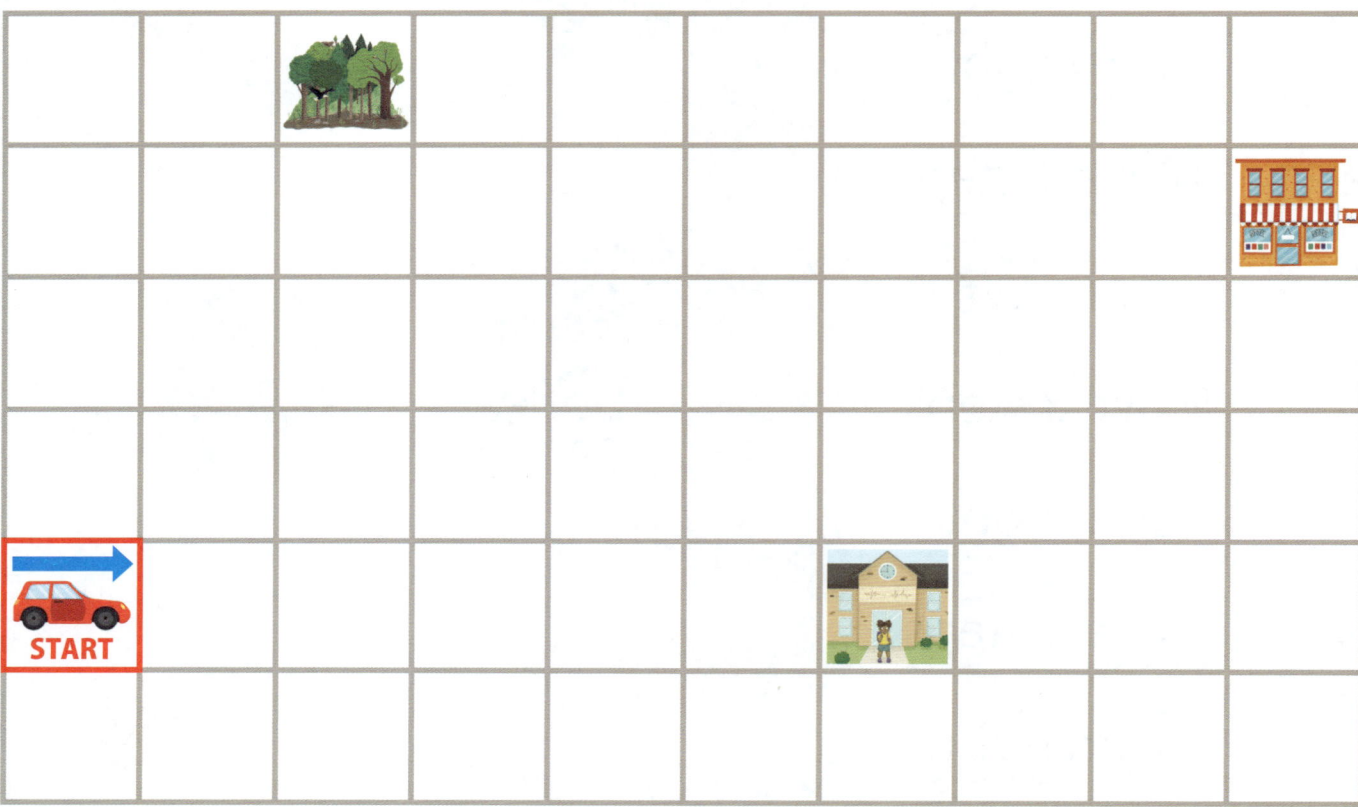

❶ Go to the school

☐  repeat 6 times

☐  repeat 4 times

☐ 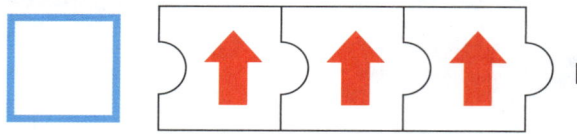 repeat 3 times

2 Go to the park

repeat 2 times

repeat 2 times

repeat 2 times

3 Go to the book store

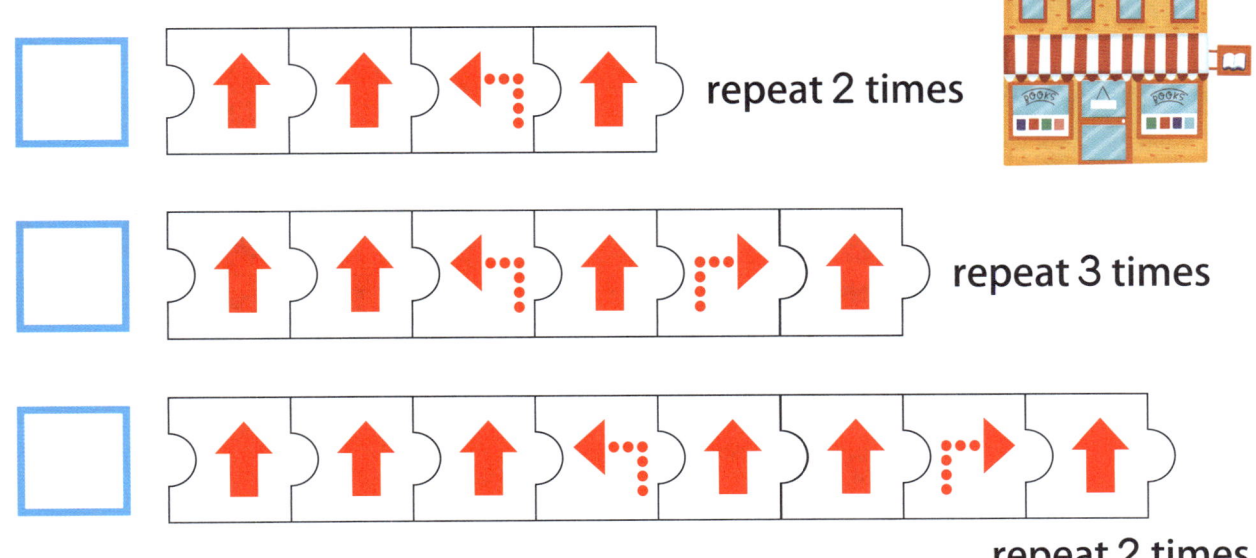

repeat 2 times

repeat 3 times

repeat 2 times

■ The robot will travel the forked road with the following rules. Choose the correct place for the robot to arrive and write a check mark (✓) in the box.

Rules

When the robot sees a yellow triangle ▲ , it will go straight ahead.
If the robot sees a red circle ● , it will go right.
If neither of the above two applies, it will go left.

1 ☐   ☐   ☐

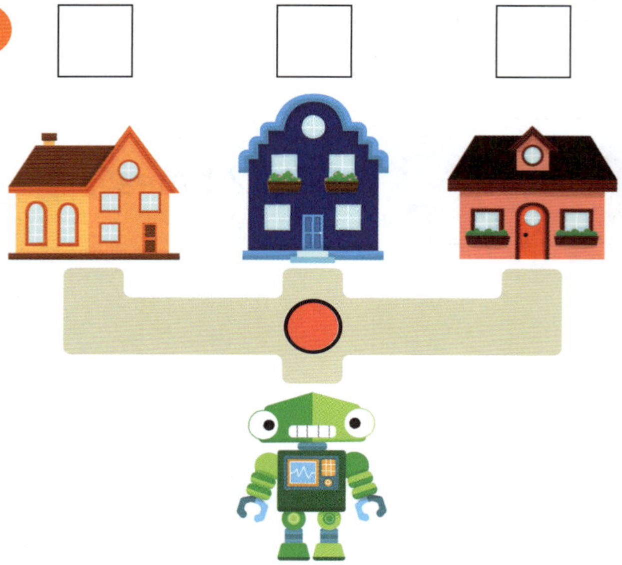

2 ☐   ☐   ☐

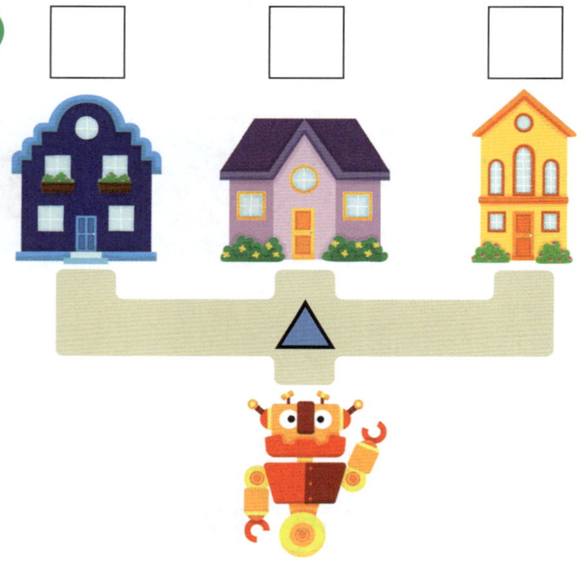

3 ☐   ☐   ☐

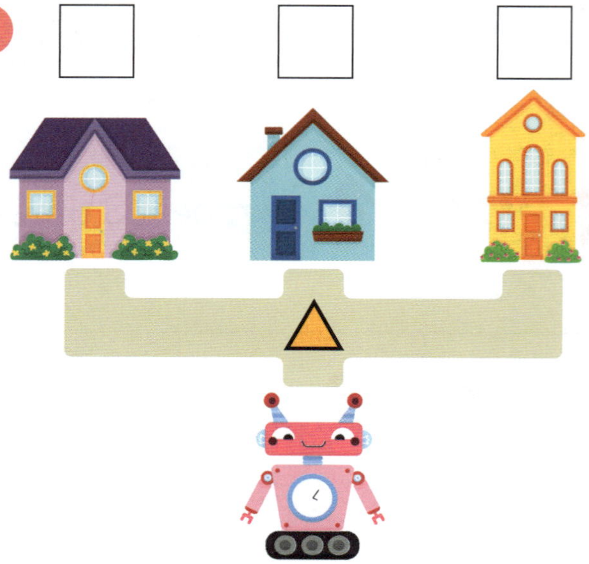

4 ☐   ☐   ☐

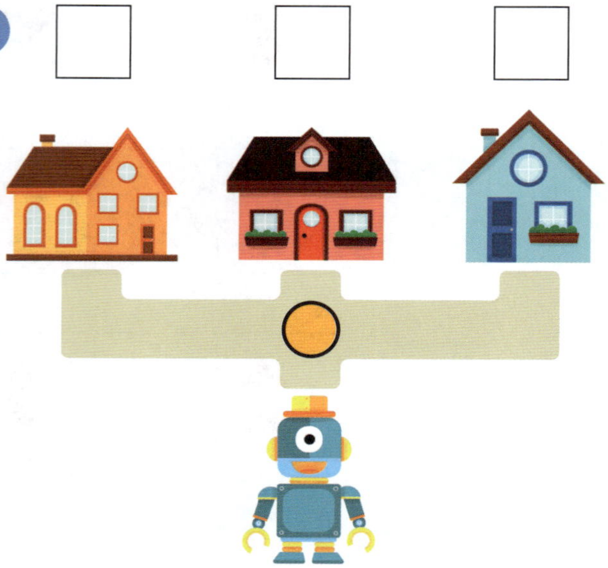

5 □ □ □ □ □ □

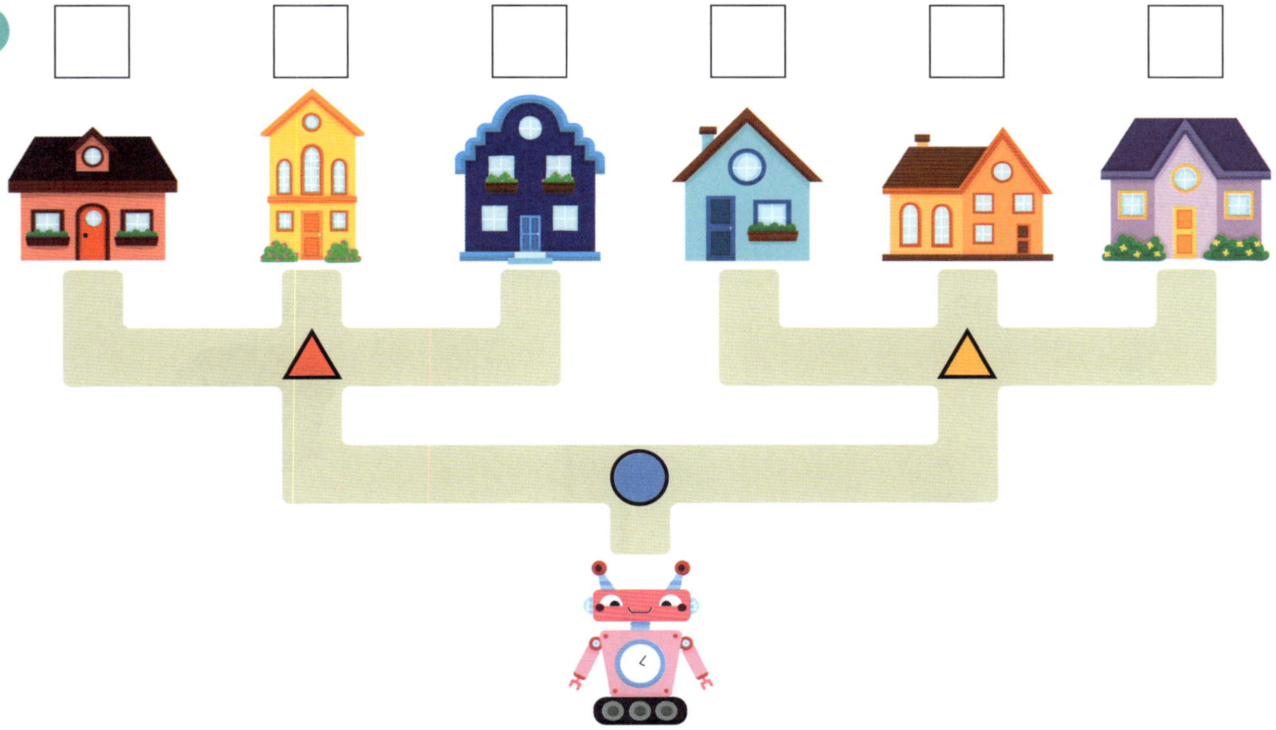

6 □ □ □ □ □ □

It's important to move your body and exercise!
Try this fun activity below to break up your studying!

■ Try the yoga poses! Use the images and directions to help you do each one correctly.

Tree Pose

Stand on one leg. Bend the knee of the leg you are not standing on, place the bottom of your foot on the inside of your leg, and then balance.

Butterfly Pose

Sit on your behind with your back straight. Bend your legs and place the bottom of your feet together.

Mountain Pose

Stand up straight with your feet apart and your arms out to the side with palms facing foward. Imagine being strong and unmovable like a mountain.

Frog Pose

Squat down with your knees apart and your arms resting between your knees. Touch your hands to the ground. Hold.

Unit **3** Table of Contents

Use this page to keep track of your progress throughout the book. Place a check mark in the box when you have completed a section.

Reading Comprehension: Story Elements

KEY POINTS

Stories have key points like characters, names, settings, and details that tell you what the story is about.

■ Use the text to answer the questions.

> Liam was excited for his family camping trip. He packed his backpack by himself. He packed his flashlight, water bottle, teddy bear, and some snacks. Then he got in the car with his mom, dad, and little brother to drive to the campsite.
>
> When they arrived at the campsite, Liam saw tall trees and a sparkling lake. He helped his dad set up the tent. His brother helped his mom build a fire. They roasted hotdogs for dinner and then his mom surprised them with marshmallows to make s'mores!
>
> Liam got nervous when it got dark and made sure his flashlight and teddy bear were close to him in his sleeping bag. Suddenly, he heard a weird hooting noise outside the tent. Liam turned his flashlight on and carefully unzipped the tent window. He shone his flashlight outside and saw a big owl in the tree. Liam woke his brother to show him the owl. Both boys were so excited that Liam forgot to be afraid.
>
> The next day, Liam told his mom and dad about the owl. It was the highlight of his camping trip. He couldn't wait to go to school on Monday and tell his friends.

❶ Describe the setting of Liam's family trip.

_____

_____

❷ What helped Liam be less afraid of the dark while camping?

_____

_____

■ **Answer the questions based on the reading passage.**

Sophie was nervous as she stood by her science project at the school fair. She had worked hard to make a volcano that erupted with colorful baking soda and vinegar. She had even made the baking soda pink, so the lava would be her favorite color.

When the judges came by, she took a deep breath and explained how her volcano worked. They watched in amazement as the lava bubbled up and flowed down the sides. Sophie felt proud that her experiment worked!

Later that day, the principal announced the winner. "The Third Grade blue ribbon goes to...Sophie!" Everyone clapped and cheered around her.

Sophie smiled as she accepted her ribbon. That night, she proudly showed her blue ribbon to her parents and siblings. They surprised her with pizza, her favorite, for dinner! Sophie was happy and excited to do more science projects in the future.

❶ What did Sophie make for the science fair?

_____

❷ Did Sophie win the science fair?

_____

❸ What did the outcome of the science fair do for Sophie?

_____

_____

Reading Comprehension: Main Topic

All texts have a main idea or topic. You can determine the main topic of a piece by reading it and putting together the information and details. Details, major and minor, support the main idea by telling how, what, when, where, why, how much, or how many. Finding the topic, main idea, and supporting details helps you understand the points the writer is trying to express.

■ **Use the text to answer the questions.**

The platypus is a unique animal that lives in Australia. They are mammals with fur, but they have soft bill-like mouths and paddle-shaped feet. They love to swim in freshwater rivers and streams. Platypuses eat small insects, worms, and fish. They can even dive underwater and hold their breath for a long time! They use their sensitive bills to search for food in the mud at the bottom of the river.

Platypuses are nocturnal, which means they mainly come out and hunt and play at night. Platypuses build their homes near the water. They dig burrows along river banks. These keep them safe from predators. Platypuses are also unique because they are one of the few mammals that lays eggs!

❶ What is the main topic of this passage? Add one quote to support your answer.

_____

_____

❷ What traits make the platypus a unique animal?

_____

_____

■ Answer the questions based on the reading passage.
  Quote a line or two to support your answer.

Cricket is a popular sport played in many countries, like England, Australia, and India. In cricket, two teams take turns to bat and bowl. The batting team tries to score runs by hitting a ball and running between two sets of wickets or wooden posts. The bowling team tries to get the batters out by hitting the wickets or catching the ball once it is hit. The game is played on a big, grass field and can last a long time.

One famous cricket player is Sachin Tendulkar from India. He played for many years and scored more runs than anyone else in cricket history! He started playing cricket when he was a young child and worked very hard to become a great

player. Cricket fans all around the world admire him for his skills and his kind sportsmanship. He was the captain of India's National Cricket team and holds the record for receiving the most "Player of the Match" awards.

❶ What is the main point of this passage?

_____

_____

❷ What are the key details that support the topic?

_____

_____

❸ Why is Sachin Tendulkar relevant to this passage?

_____

_____

Reading Comprehension: Context Words

KEY POINTS

When reading and answering questions about different types of reading passages, sometimes there are specific words or procedures for responding to the questions.

For example, in historical text words like "past" and "present" are used to indicate time. In a scientific text, words like "cause" and "effect" are used to demonstrate what happens in a experiment.

■ **Use the text to answer the questions.**

Clara Barton was a brave woman who lived in the 1800s. She cared deeply about helping people, especially during times of war. During the Civil War, she worked as a nurse, tending to soldiers who were hurt. Barton would even go to the battlefields to bring food, medicine, and comfort to injured soldiers. Her dedication earned her the nickname, "The Angel of the Battlefield."

In 1881, Barton founded the American Red Cross. This organization was formed to help people in emergencies like wartimes, natural disasters, and during times of illness. Barton wanted to make sure that all people received help, no matter where they lived or the challenges they faced.

Thanks to Barton's efforts, the American Red Cross continues to help people around the US today. Clara Barton's kindness and leadership made a big difference in many lives.

❶ What words in this passage show you that this is about a historical person?

_____

❷ What is the main topic of the text?

_____

_____

■ **Answer the questions based on the reading passage.**

Starting a vegetable garden is a fun and exciting project! Below are some steps to making a successful garden.

First, find a sunny spot in your yard or on your balcony where plants can grow. You want to clear the area of weeds and rocks, and use a shovel to turn the soil. This will help the plants grow better.

Next, decide what vegetables you want to plant and that will do well in your area, like tomatoes, carrots, or cucumbers. You can buy seeds or small seedlings from a local garden center. Make sure to follow the instructions when planting the seeds or seedlings so they have enough space to grow.

After planting, make sure to water your plants consistently. Keep the soil wet, but be careful not to overwater. You should check your garden every day to see if the plants need more water or if there are any weeds.

The biggest thing to know about growing vegetables is to be patient! It will take some time for them to grow big and ripe enough to eat. Look for signs that your vegetables are ready by watching for size and color changes. Finally, when they are ready, pick them carefully from the ground or cut them from the plant.

❶ What is the main topic of this passage?

_____

_____

❷ List some of the procedural words from the passage.

_____

❸ Why is it important to following the procedure presented in this passage?

_____

_____

KEY POINTS

Another important skill to develop when reading is the ability to compare and contrast the most important points and key details presented in two different text about the same topic.

For example, reading an informational text will teach you something different about a topic than an opinion text about the same topic. Both types of texts have main points they try to make, but they go about it in different ways.

Informational Text

Red pandas are small mammals that live in the mountains of Asia. They have reddish-brown fur, white faces, and bushy tails. Red pandas are known for their playful behavior. They love climbing trees and rolling around on the ground with each other. Red pandas mostly eat bamboo, but will also eat fruits and berries when they can find them. They are nocturnal which means they are most active at night.

Red pandas are endangered animals, which means there are not many left in the wild. Their habitat is being lost to human development as people cut down trees to build farms and homes. There are many organizations trying to protect their habitats today and save red pandas from becoming extinct. Zoos around the world are also working to help red pandas by teaching people about them and helping keep them safe.

Opinion Text

My favorite animal is the red panda! They are a super cute and special animal. Red pandas are reddish colored with white faces that look like masks. They also have fluffy striped tails. Their habitat is in the mountains of Asia. They love to climb trees and are very playful. Red pandas mostly eat bamboo but also like to eat fruit. I think it is amazing that they are super active at night and sleep during the day.

Unfortunately, red pandas are in danger because their homes are being cut down. That is why I think it is important to tell people about red pandas. I want to help protect them by teaching people about how special they are. They are not just super adorable animals, but are also important to our world.

■ Answer the questions using the two text.

❶ What is the main topic of both texts?

_____

❷ What is the writers' main objective for each text?

_____

❸ Which text provides the best understanding of the topic?

_____

❹ Explain why you chose your answer in question ❸.

_____

_____

■ List of the facts that are the same between both texts.

Brain Break
Let's Make a Recipe!

KEY POINTS

Order is important when it comes to a recipe. Use the words below and complete the recipe.

■ Complete the recipe.

Word Box

| Next | First | Finally | Then | After |

To Bake a Cake!

[_____] , pre-heat the oven to 350 degrees and gather your ingredients. Next, put the wet ingredients into a bowl: milk, eggs, melted butter or oil.

[_____] , put the dry ingredients into a second bowl: flour, sugar, and spices.

[_____] that, mix the dry ingredients into the wet ingredient bowl.

[_____] pour the batter evenly into to cake pans. Bake the cake for 30 minutes. Take it out and let it cool.

[_____] , ice your cake with frosting and enjoy!

Mindfulness Break!

■ Draw a place that you feel peaceful and calm.

Think of a place that makes you feel happy and calm. You can imagine you are there whenever you feel sad or stressed.

Narrative Writing: Elements of a Story

KEY POINTS

Narrative writing tells a story, and there are certain things that all stories have. Stories have characters, and events that happen to those characters. Those events are what make up the plot of the story.

■ Read the story below. Circle the characters and write three events below.

Once upon a time, three pigs decided to build themselves houses. The first pig used straw. The second pig used sticks. The third pig used bricks. One day a wolf came. He blew down the first house. Then he blew down the second house! But he couldn't blow down the third house.

Events: ❶ _____

_____

❷ _____

_____

❸ _____

_____

■ In a few activities, you will write a story of your own. There is an optional prompt below. You can choose to use this prompt, or you can make up any story you wish. Use this page to choose your characters and events. Make sure to list the events in the order in which they happen.

Prompt (optional): Write about an interesting dream you had recently. Who was in it? What happened?

Characters:

Events: ❶

②

❸

④

Narrative Writing: Details

KEY POINTS

Stories contain details, like descriptions of actions, thoughts, and feelings. They also contain dialogue, which is when characters speak.

■ Read the story below.

> "Lucy?" I called. "Are you there?" I was standing in the doorway to my room. I thought I had heard my sister coming up the stairs. But no one answered.
> I started to worry. If it wasn't Lucy, then who was making that noise? I ran into the hall .
> Then I heard a little meow. It was just our cat!

❶ Underline the dialogue in the story above.

❷ What is one action that the narrator takes?

_____

❸ What sentence describes the narrator's thoughts?

_____

❹ What sentence shows how the narrator feels?

_____

Date

Great Job Sticker

List five details to include in your story.

1

2

3

4

5

Narrative Writing: Temporal Words

KEY POINTS

Temporal words are words that help show time. These include words like, *before, after, first, later, yesterday, today, tomorrow.*

■ Use the temporal word to create a sentence.

❶ before

_____

❷ after

_____

❸ first

_____

❹ later

_____

❺ yesterday

_____

❻ tomorrow

_____

KEY POINTS

Temporal phrases also help show time. However, temporal phrases have more than one word. Some examples include, *after that, later on, not long after, after a few minutes, the next day, before that.*

■ Use the temporal phrase to write a sentence.

❶ **after that**

_____

❷ **not long after**

_____

❸ **after a few minutes**

_____

❹ **the next day**

_____

❺ **later on**

_____

❻ **before that**

_____

Writing a Story

■ Write your story, using the story elements and details that you wrote already, and try to include a few temporal words or phrases.

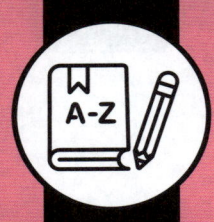

Brain Break
Write a Summary of Your Favorite Story

■ Write a summary of your favorite story below. You can write about a book, movie, or any other type of story.
Make sure to include the characters and the events that happen.

Mindfulness Break!

KEY POINTS

An important part of being mindful is having self-awareness. Self-awareness is a person's ability to recognize and understand facts and feelings about themselves.

■ Fill in each bubble with a comment about yourself to practice self-awareness.

I am a good person because...

What I like most about myself is...

I am thoughtful when I...

I am unique because...

My special talent is...

I am helpful when I...

Division 1

■ Find a missing number, and complete each problem.
You can pick the number from the hint below.

❶ $2 \times \boxed{} = 6$ ❷ $3 \times \boxed{} = 12$ ❸ $4 \times \boxed{} = 24$

> **Hint for ❶ ❷ ❸** $\underline{3}$ $\underline{6}$ $\underline{4}$

❹ $1 \times \boxed{} = 9$ ❺ $5 \times \boxed{} = 40$ ❻ $\boxed{} \times 7 = 14$

> **Hint for ❹ ❺ ❻** $\underline{2}$ $\underline{9}$ $\underline{8}$

❼ $\boxed{} \times 7 = 28$ ❽ $3 \times \boxed{} = 30$ ❾ $5 \times \boxed{} = 25$

> **Hint for ❼ ❽ ❾** $\underline{10}$ $\underline{5}$ $\underline{4}$

❿ $\boxed{} \times 9 = 27$ ⓫ $5 \times \boxed{} = 35$ ⓬ $\boxed{} \times 8 = 32$

> **Hint for ❿ ⓫ ⓬** $\underline{4}$ $\underline{3}$ $\underline{7}$

KEY POINTS

You can use multiplication facts to help solve division problems. Division and multiplication are inverse or opposite operations.

6 divided by 2 is 3.   **2 times 3 is 6.**

$$6 \div 2 = \boxed{3} \longrightarrow 2 \times \boxed{3} = 6$$

14 divided by 7 is 2.   **2 times 7 is 14.**

$$14 \div 7 = \boxed{2} \longrightarrow 2 \times \boxed{7} = 14$$

■ Solve.

❶ $12 \div 3 = 4$ ❷ $9 \div 9 =$ ❸ $24 \div 8 =$

❹ $20 \div 4 =$ ❺ $16 \div 8 =$ ❻ $40 \div 10 =$

❼ $3 \overline{)6}$ $\,^2$ ❽ $7 \overline{)35}$ ❾ $6 \overline{)18}$ ❿ $5 \overline{)20}$

Division 2

■ Find a missing number, and complete each problem.
You can pick the number from the hint below.

① $6 \times \boxed{} = 12$　② $7 \times \boxed{} = 21$　③ $8 \times \boxed{} = 40$

Hint for ① ② ③　2　5　3

④ $10 \times \boxed{} = 70$　⑤ $9 \times \boxed{} = 54$　⑥ $\boxed{} \times 2 = 16$

Hint for ④ ⑤ ⑥　6　7　8

⑦ $\boxed{} \times 6 = 36$　⑧ $7 \times \boxed{} = 63$　⑨ $9 \times \boxed{} = 27$

Hint for ⑦ ⑧ ⑨　9　3　6

⑩ $\boxed{} \times 2 = 20$　⑪ $8 \times \boxed{} = 56$　⑫ $\boxed{} \times 4 = 36$

Hint for ⑩ ⑪ ⑫　7　9　10

KEY POINTS

• The number being divided is called the **dividend**.
• The number to divide is called the **divisor**.
• The answer to a division problem is called the **quotient**.

dividend   divisor   quotient
↓   ↓   ↓
$12 \div 6 = 2$

$$\begin{array}{r} 6 \leftarrow \textbf{quotient} \\ \textbf{divisor} \rightarrow 9\overline{)54} \leftarrow \textbf{dividend} \end{array}$$

■ Solve

❶ $21 \div 7 =$ 　　　**❷** $40 \div 8 =$ 　　　**❸** $24 \div 4 =$

❹ $64 \div 8 =$ 　　　**❺** $49 \div 7 =$ 　　　**❻** $30 \div 3 =$

❼ $8\overline{)16}$ 　　**❽** $9\overline{)72}$ 　　**❾** $7\overline{)35}$ 　　**❿** $8\overline{)56}$

Multiplication and Division

■ Find a missing symbol (× or ÷), and complete each problem.

1 4 ☐ 2 = 2

2 16 ☐ 2 = 8

3 3 ☐ 5 = 15

4 6 ☐ 5 = 30

5 9 ☐ 9 = 1

6 21 ☐ 7 = 3

7 24 ☐ 6 = 4

8 6 ☐ 7 = 42

9 50 ☐ 10 = 5

10 40 ☐ 8 = 5

11 6 ☐ 9 = 54

12 9 ☐ 3 = 3

13 1 ☐ 9 = 9

14 81 ☐ 9 = 9

15 8 ☐ 2 = 4

KEY POINTS

0× and ×0

0 means "nothing." Multiplying 0 and any other number always gives you 0.

$$0 \times 3 = 0 \qquad 6 \times 0 = 0$$

0÷

0 divided by any number always gives you 0.

$$0 \div 4 = 0 \qquad 0 \div 9 = 0$$

■ Solve.

❶ $0 \times 7 =$

❷ $0 \times 2 =$

❸ $0 \times 5 =$

❹ $3 \times 0 =$

❺ $9 \times 0 =$

❻ $1 \times 0 =$

❼ $0 \div 8 =$

❽ $0 \div 4 =$

❾ $0 \div 10 =$

Multiplication with Regrouping

KEY POINTS

How to multiply 2-digit numbers without regrouping

Example: 13×2

```
    1 3
  ×   2
    6
```

```
    1 3
  ×   2
  2 6
```

Step 1: Multiply digits in the ones place.
Step 2: Multiply the tens digit by the ones digit.

■ Solve.

1
```
    12
  ×  4
```

2
```
    14
  ×  2
```

3
```
    23
  ×  3
```

4
```
    22
  ×  4
```

5
```
    11
  ×  1
```

6
```
    31
  ×  2
```

7
```
    11
  ×  3
```

8
```
    22
  ×  2
```

9
```
    32
  ×  3
```

KEY POINTS

How to multiply 2-digit numbers with regrouping

Example: 16×2

$$
\begin{array}{r}
{}^{1}16 \\
\times 2 \\
\hline
2 \\
\end{array}
\qquad
\begin{array}{r}
{}^{1}16 \\
\times 2 \\
\hline
32 \\
\end{array}
$$

Step 1: Multiply digits in the ones place.

Step 2: Regroup to tens place.

Step 3: Multiply the tens digit by the ones digit. Don't forget to add the digit that was regrouped.

■ Solve.

1
$$
\begin{array}{r}
17 \\
\times 2 \\
\hline
\end{array}
$$

2
$$
\begin{array}{r}
15 \\
\times 3 \\
\hline
\end{array}
$$

3
$$
\begin{array}{r}
13 \\
\times 4 \\
\hline
\end{array}
$$

4
$$
\begin{array}{r}
24 \\
\times 3 \\
\hline
\end{array}
$$

5
$$
\begin{array}{r}
19 \\
\times 4 \\
\hline
\end{array}
$$

6
$$
\begin{array}{r}
14 \\
\times 5 \\
\hline
\end{array}
$$

7
$$
\begin{array}{r}
16 \\
\times 6 \\
\hline
\end{array}
$$

8
$$
\begin{array}{r}
12 \\
\times 7 \\
\hline
\end{array}
$$

9
$$
\begin{array}{r}
12 \\
\times 8 \\
\hline
\end{array}
$$

Word Problems

■ Answer the following word problems.

❶ There are 4 cars on the street. Each car is carrying 2 people. How many people are in the cars in all?

$$4 \times 2 = \boxed{} \text{ people}$$

❷ A house has 7 rooms. Each room contains 5 chairs. How many chairs are in the house?

$$7 \times \boxed{} = \boxed{} \text{ chairs}$$

❸ Sheila has 3 jars. Each jar contains 9 marbles. How many marbles does she have in all?

$$\boxed{} \times \boxed{} = \boxed{} \text{ marbles}$$

❹ Theo has 8 shirts. Each shirt has 6 buttons. How many buttons are there in all?

$$\boxed{} \times \boxed{} = \boxed{} \text{ buttons}$$

■ Answer the following word problems.

❶ Eliot finds 9 shells on the beach. He puts them into groups of 3.
How many groups does he have?

$$9 \div 3 = \boxed{} \text{ groups}$$

❷ A vet divided 24 treats evenly among 6 cats.
How many treats did each cat get?

$$24 \div \boxed{} = \boxed{} \text{ treats}$$

❸ A theater has 56 seats. There are 8 seats in each row.
How many rows are there?

$$\boxed{} \div \boxed{} = \boxed{} \text{ rows}$$

❹ Mila has 40 bricks. She divides them evenly into 5 stacks.
How many bricks are in each stack?

$$\boxed{} \div \boxed{} = \boxed{} \text{ bricks}$$

Brain Break
Multiplication and Division Match!

■ Match the multiplication problems that have the same answer.
(You may not need to do some calculations.)

2 × 4 ●	● 8 × 7
3 × 6 ●	● 16 × 6
8 × 7 ●	● 4 × 2
25 × 3 ●	● 4 × 21
6 × 16 ●	● 6 × 3
21 × 4 ●	● 3 × 25

■ Complete each equation with the missing symbol (× or ÷).

$8 \boxed{} 9 = 36 \boxed{} 2 = 24 \boxed{} 3$

$4 \boxed{} 7 = 7 \boxed{} 4 = 14 \boxed{} 2$

$81 \boxed{} 9 = 45 \boxed{} 5 = 3 \boxed{} 3$

$54 \boxed{} 9 = 48 \boxed{} 8 = 42 \boxed{} 7$

$8 \boxed{} 7 = 14 \boxed{} 4 = 28 \boxed{} 2$

$5 \boxed{} 2 = 80 \boxed{} 8 = 20 \boxed{} 2$

Ecosystems

KEY POINTS

An ecosystem is made up of the living and non-living things in an area. Plants, animals, and other living things are parts of an ecosystem. Non-living things like rocks, water, wind, and temperature are also parts of an ecosystem.

All parts of an ecosystem affect each other. If one part changes, that will make other parts change, too. For example, if all of the wolves in an ecosystem die or move away, there will not be as many predators. More prey animals like deer will survive. Those animals will eat more plants. They might eat too many plants for the plants to be able to reproduce. Eventually, there might not be enough plants for the animals to eat.

All parts of an ecosystem are important. Plants are important for the animals that eat them. The animals that eat the plants are often important for the plants, too. Squirrels, birds, and other animals often help spread the plants' seeds so that the plants can reproduce.

Ecosystems can be big or small. A huge coral reef is an ecosystem, with corals, fish, seagrasses, algae, and other living things. Tide pools are also ecosystems. These are tiny ponds left on rocks when the ocean's waves don't reach as far during low tide. They have algae that use the sun's energy to make their own food, sea snails that eat the algae, and sea stars that eat the snails.

■ **Answer the questions.**

❶ What is an ecosystem made up of?

❷ How do parts of an ecosystem affect each other?

❸ What might happen if an ecosystem changes in a major way? For example, if all the squirrels were taken away?

■ Use the picture below to answer the questions.

1 Write what could happen to the mouse population if the eagles all suddenly left the ecosystem.

_____

_____

_____

2 Write what could happen to the wild berry bushes if the eagles all suddenly left the ecosystem.

_____

_____

_____

3 How could humans help rebalance the ecosystem after the eagles all left?

_____

_____

_____

Diversity in an Ecosystems

KEY POINTS

Ecosystems are complex. In order for an ecosystem to thrive, all of the plants and animals that live there have to survive and perform their roles. To survive, all living things need energy. Plants rely on soil, water, and the sun for energy. Animals rely on plants as well as other animals for energy. The exchange of energy from plants to animals is called a food chain. A food web is made up of the many food chains of animals in an ecosystem.

A food chain is made up of producers like plants, and consumers like animals. Some animals eat plants and some animals eat other animals. The animals that get eaten are called prey and the animals that eat them are called predators.

Each predator usually eats many different kinds of prey. Their prey eat many different kinds of other prey and plants. Each plant is usually eaten by many different kinds of animals. Each living thing has its role and is important to the ecosystem as a whole. Diverse ecosystems, which have many different kinds of living things, are usually healthier and more stable than less diverse ecosystems. They are better able to adapt to and survive changes.

■ Answer the questions.

❶ What do all living things need to survive?

_____

❷ What is a food chain?

_____

❸ What type of animal would be a predator?

Ⓐ **fox**　　　Ⓑ **mouse**　　　Ⓒ **skunk**　　　Ⓓ **rabbit**

Date

Great Job Sticker

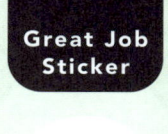

Write the correct letter in the blank to complete each food chain.

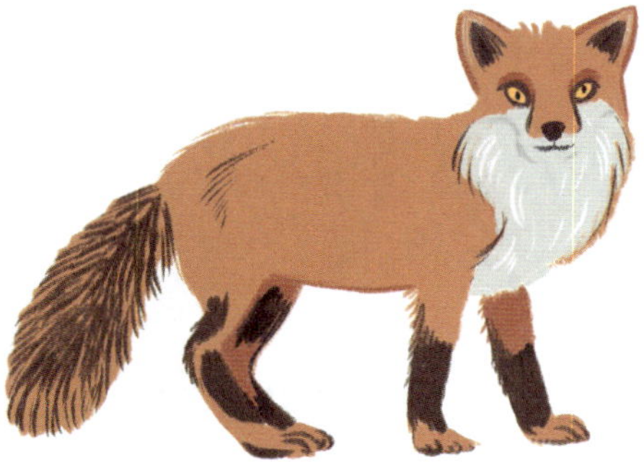

Ⓐ Fox

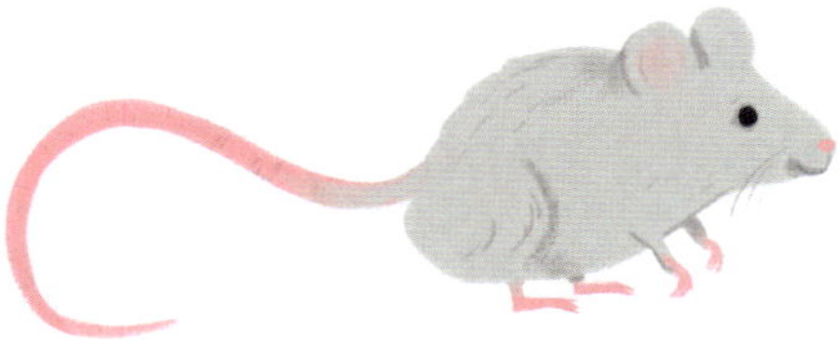

Ⓑ Mouse

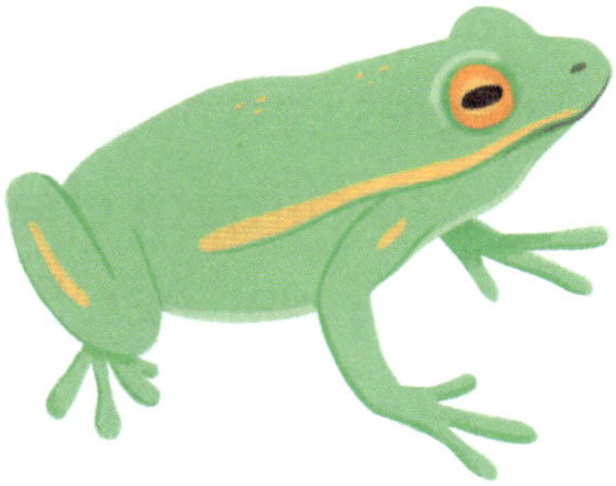

Ⓒ Frog

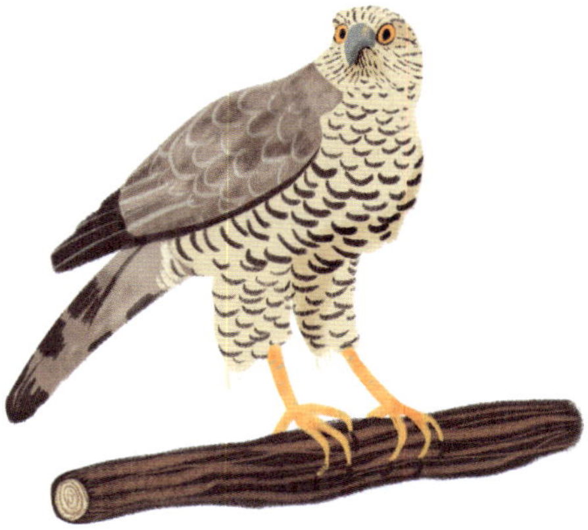

Ⓓ Hawk

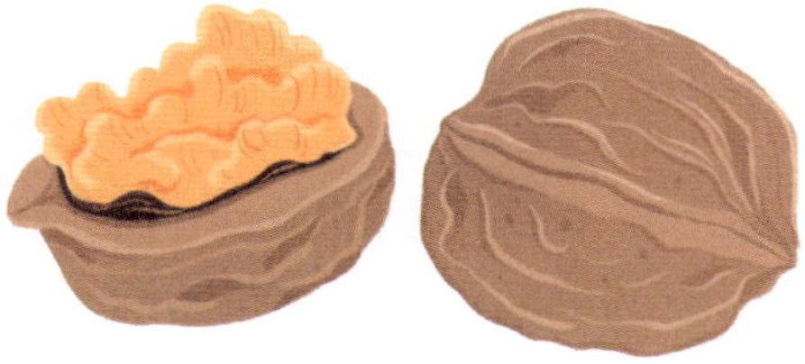

Ⓔ Walnuts

1. grass ← mouse ← ☐
2. walnut ← ☐ ← hawk
3. fly ← ☐ ← hawk

Effects of a Changing Ecosystem

KEY POINTS

Changes to ecosystems can affect all the organisms, that live there. Temperature changes, natural disasters, and invasive species can all majorly disrupt ecosystems. Due to climate change, most ecosystems are getting warmer. Some plants, animals, and other organisms cannot survive at these temperatures. For example, ocean water is getting warmer and more acidic. This is killing coral, which is the base for coral reef ecosystems.

Natural disasters like hurricanes, wildfires, earthquakes, tornadoes, and tsunamis can quickly change an ecosystem. Hurricanes and tsunamis often cause flooding. If an ecosystem is flooded, plants may be uprooted and die. Seeds that would have sprouted may be washed away or destroyed.

Wildfires are another unpredictable natural disaster that can have a big impact on an ecosystem. Bigger wildfires kill more plants and animals and make it harder for the ecosystem to recover. When organisms are already endangered and only live in a small area, wildfires can cause them to go extinct.

Invasive species are organisms that are brought (accidentally or on purpose) from their native ecosystem to another ecosystem. They often cause damage to the ecosystem they are introduced, because they have too many offspring which take resources from native species. Wild pigs are an example of an invasive species in the United States. They are originally from Europe and Asia.

They can eat most foods, they are strong and smart, and they have a lot of babies. They dig up plants with their tusks, destroying native plants and farmers' crops. These actions disrupt the food webs of native plants and animals which rely on those resources to survive.

■ Write true or false for each statement.

❶ Changes to an ecosystem can affect the plants and animals that live there.

❷ Climate change does not affect ecosystems.

❸ Natural disasters are normal and do not change the ecosystem.

❹ Wildfires can quickly change an ecosystem and harm the living things in them.

❺ Invasive species are living things that change the ecosystems they are brought to.

❻ Native animals in an ecosystem benefit from the introduction of invasive animals.

Humans and Ecosystems

KEY POINTS

Natural disasters and invasive species are not the only things that can cause damage to ecosystems. Humans have damaged ecosystems by cutting down forests (deforestation), draining wetlands, spreading invasive species, and by polluting. We have also caused climate change by using fossil fuels like gas and coal. Climate change is making the Earth warmer and increasing natural disasters like hurricanes. However, there are ways that humans can help ecosystems recover!

To fight climate change, governments need to make big companies use renewable energy instead of fossil fuels. Fossil fuels are burned to make energy. Burning them releases carbon into the air, which causes the Earth to get warmer. Renewable energy sources, like solar and wind energy, never run out and do not have to be burned. Solar energy comes from the sun and is collected by solar panels. Wind energy is collected by wind turbines that spin when there is wind.

Regular people can also choose to use renewable energy. Some people have solar panels on their houses or buy renewable energy from their power companies. People can also use fewer fossil fuels and limit pollution by walking, riding a bike, taking public transportation like the bus or subway, or carpooling.

Reforestation is a method of regrowing a forest that was cut down or burned down for human needs. Reforestation can create new, healthy ecosystems. This can also help with climate change because more trees can filter more carbon from the air. People can help remove invasive species from ecosystems. Many parks have programs where people gather to remove invasive plants. Some groups work to hunt invasive animals so that native animals can thrive. People can also plant native plants in their gardens. These help native insects and other animals survive, which benefits the native ecosystem.

■ **Answer the questions.**

❶ What type of damage can humans cause to an ecosystem?

_____

_____

❷ What can people do to help stop climate change to an ecosystem?

_____

_____

■ Match the solution to the ecosystem problem.

Deforestation	●	●	Ride a bike
Climate change	●	●	Plant new trees
Invasive plants	●	●	Allow groups to hunt invasive animals
Burning fossil fuels by driving	●	●	Use renewable energy, like solar power
Invasive animals	●	●	Remove invasive plants

Brain Break
Science Journal 3

What kind of ecosystem do you live near? Describe the key features below.

Art Break!

■ Choose an ecosystem different from the one you live near. Draw it below. Make sure to include habitat, animals, plants and food sources for all.

Landforms

KEY POINTS

Landforms are naturally-formed geographic features on the surface of the earth. There are many kinds of landforms. Below are some examples.

Valleys are long depressions in the land, where the land is lower than the area around it. Valleys are often between hills or mountains. Many valleys have rivers flowing through them. Rivers can form valleys over thousands of years by eroding soil. Glaciers and the movement of the earth's plates can also form valleys.

Hills are landforms that are taller than the area around them but shorter than mountains. They are usually shorter than 1,000 feet (300 meters) and have rounded tops.

Plateaus are large regions that are higher than the areas around them and mostly flat. They have cliffs or steep drops on at least one side.

Mountains are landforms that are much taller than the area around them. They normally have steep sides. Their tops can be rounded or pointed. Mountains are usually parts of mountain ranges, or groups of mountains. Mountains are formed by volcanic activity or by the earth's plates slowly moving towards each other.

Plains are flat regions at low elevations. That means they are not high above sea level.

Islands are pieces of land that are surrounded by water on all sides. Islands can be in oceans, lakes, rivers, ponds, or other bodies of water.

■ Fill in the blank to complete each statement.

❶ [_____] are landforms that are much taller than the

land around them. They have steep sides and are usually part of ranges.

❷ Flat regions at low elevations are called

[_____] .

❸ Pieces of land that are surrounded by water on all sides are called

[_____] .

❹ [_____] are large regions of land that are higher

than the land around them. They usually have flat tops and steep sides.

❺ [_____] are long depressions in the land, where the

land is lower than the area around it.

❻ Landforms that are taller than the area around them but are shorter

than mountains are called [_____] .

KEY POINTS

A body of water is any area of land covered by water. Oceans, bays, lakes, ponds, rivers, estuaries, streams, and creeks are kinds of bodies of water. Some have saltwater, some have freshwater, and some have brackish water, which is a mix of saltwater and freshwater.

Oceans are giant, salty bodies of water. Winds, currents, and tides keep the ocean's water in motion. There are five oceans on Earth: the Atlantic, the Pacific, the Indian, the Arctic, and the Southern, or Antarctic. However, all of the oceans are connected to each other and there are no borders between them. Water moves between all of the oceans, so scientists often describe Earth as having just one ocean. Earth's oceans cover almost 71% of its surface.

Ponds are small, shallow, freshwater bodies that are surrounded by land.

Lakes are large, freshwater bodies that are surrounded by land. Freshwater is not salty.

Rivers are long, flowing, freshwater bodies that are surrounded by land. Rivers can be wide, narrow, deep, or shallow. Rivers usually start as creeks or streams that flow together to make rivers.

■ Write true or false for each statement.

❶ A body of water is any area of land covered by water.

❷ Giant salty bodies of water with currents and tides are called oceans.

❸ Lakes are usually freshwater.

❹ Freshwater is not salty.

❺ All oceans are connected and water moves between them.

❻ Rivers are long flowing bodies of freshwater.

❼ Ponds are bigger than lakes.

KEY POINTS

A map is a drawing of all or part of a planet's surface (usually Earth's). A map is always smaller than the place it represents. Most maps are flat. Some maps are on globes. Since Earth is round, globes give the most accurate representation of Earth.

Topographic maps show the shape, size, and location of land and water. They often show natural features like landforms and bodies of water.

Political maps show borders between countries, even though there are not really lines separating one country from another. They can also show cities, states, and provinces.

Maps sometimes show roads, train routes, bus routes, or hiking paths. Some maps show the entire world. Others show just one building or one neighborhood. They can be detailed enough that you can use it to figure out directions to get somewhere.

Before people had smartphones that would tell them how to get places, they relied on special maps called roadmaps with highways and streets on them. They used roadmaps to find routes to get from one place to another. Some people still use them for this purpose.

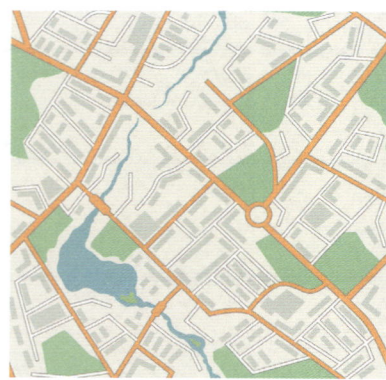

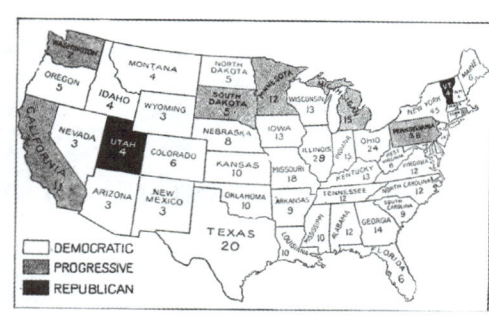

■ Circle what type of map would you use for each situation.

1 You are camping and need to find the way to the lake to go canoeing.

political map   topographical map   town map

2 The bus route from your house to the library.

political map   topographical map   town map

3 The border between the U.S. and Canada.

political map   topographical map   town map

4 A map to help your parents drive from your home to Disney World.

political map   topographical map   town map

5 You are doing a report on how many lakes are in your state.

political map   topographical map   town map

Map Scale

KEY POINTS

When using a map, you should look at the scale. The map scale tells you how much smaller the map is than the place it represents. For example, on the map scale below, 1 inch is equal to 1.576 miles.

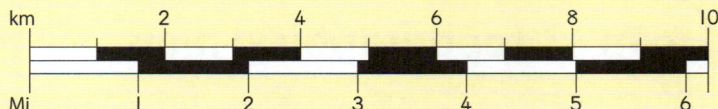

You should also look at the map key. Map keys tell you what each symbol on the map means. Dots may represent cities while stars represent capitals. Red lines might represent highways, while blue lines represent other roads.

Maps have compass roses. They show which directions north, east, south, and west are on the map. Many maps have north at the top, but this is not always the case. You should always check to see which direction is which on the map you are looking at.

To use a map to get from one place to another, you should first figure out where you are on the map and where your destination is on the map. You can then look at the available routes between you and your destination. Notice when you will be turning left or right. Make sure you are planning to walk on streets or paths, not the highway.

■ **Answer the questions.**

1 What is a map scale?

2 What is a compass rose?

■ Determine how far each place is from the starting point.

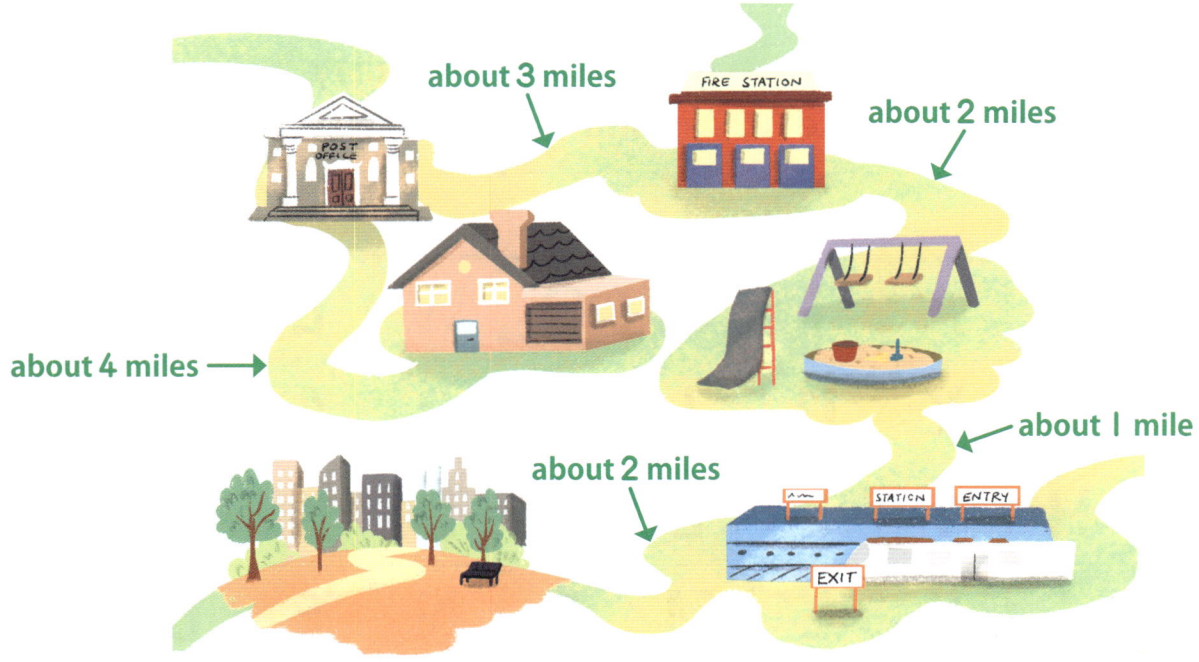

❶ Fire station to home.

about _____ miles

❷ Home to the park.

about _____ miles

❸ Home to the train station.

about _____ miles

❹ City square to the post office.

about _____ miles

❺ Post office to the train station.

about _____ miles

Brain Break
Word Search

■ Find the words below in the word search.

hill	plateau	mountain	valley	plain
island	lake	pond	ocean	river

P	L	A	I	N	Q	W	L	E	V
R	T	Y	U	I	O	P	A	A	A
G	H	I	L	L	F	D	K	S	L
H	J	K	L	M	P	N	E	B	L
D	P	S	A	Z	L	X	C	V	E
M	O	U	N	T	A	I	N	O	Y
F	N	G	H	J	T	K	L	P	O
T	D	Y	O	C	E	A	N	U	I
R	E	W	Q	Z	A	X	C	V	B
J	H	G	F	D	U	S	A	M	N
I	S	L	A	N	D	C	O	I	E
K	L	W	T	Y	R	I	V	E	R

KEY POINTS

Setting goals is an important step to achieving the things you want. You can use mindfulness to help you figure out your goals , how to set them, and how to achieve them.

■ Use the chart below to set some goals for your current school year.
List the steps needed to achieve them.
Record if you meet your goals in the future.

My goal:	My goal:	My goal:
The steps:	The steps:	The steps:
Did I achieve my goal:	Did I achieve my goal:	Did I achieve my goal:

Counting Money 1

■ Count the money in each wallet. Then write the amount in the box below.

1

$ 1.30

2

$

3

$

4

$

■ Draw a line from each amount to the item it can buy.

$ 3.45

$ 2.07

$ 2.30

$ 3.22

Counting Money 2

■ Count the money in each wallet. Then write a check mark (✓) in the box under the wallet with the largest amount.

1

2

3

Date

Great Job Sticker

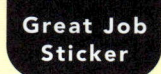

There are many different types of money. Circle the combination of bills and coins that add up to $1.50 in red. Then circle the combination of bills and coins that add up to $2.49 in blue.

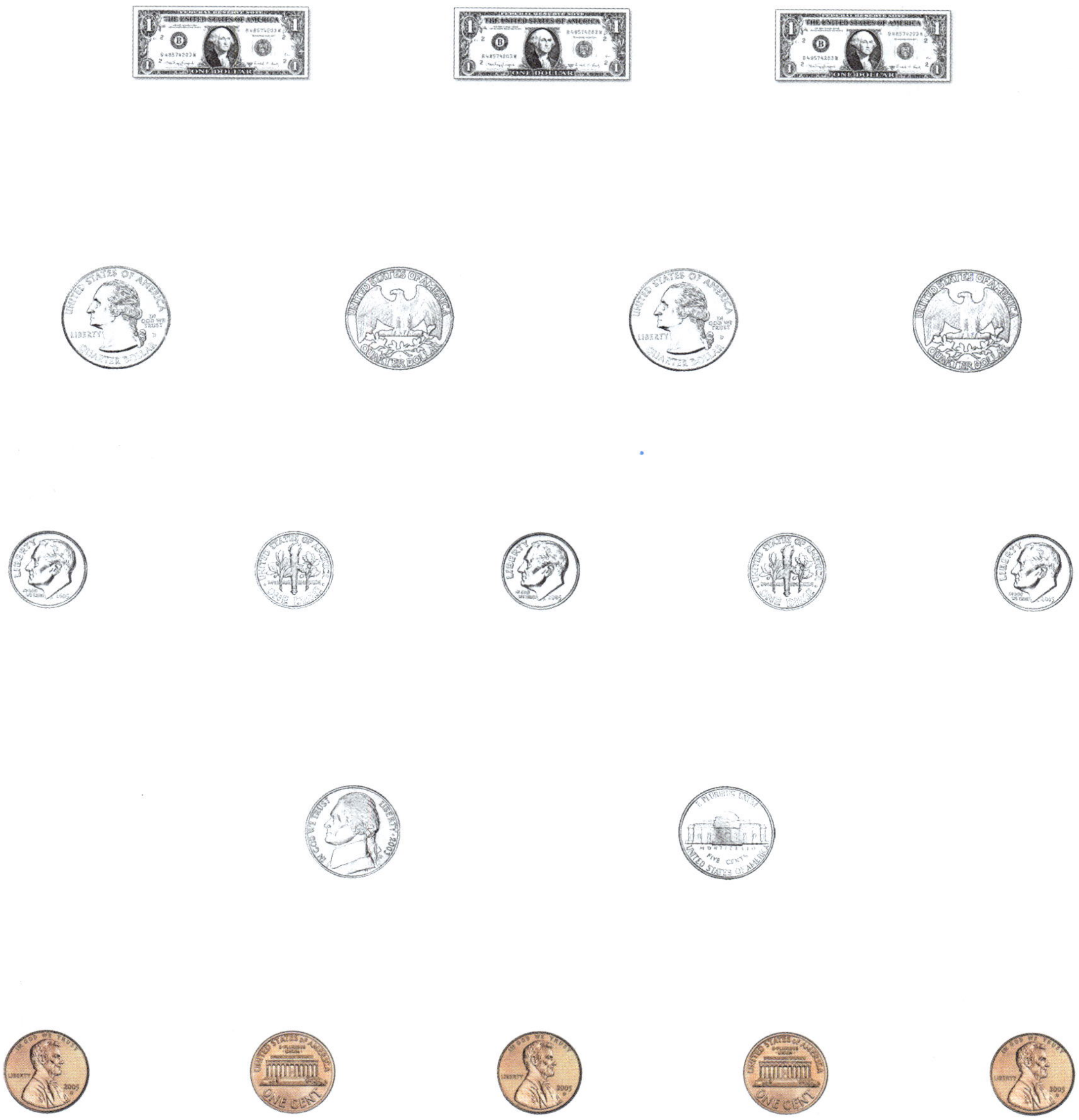

Making Change

■ You are in a store and are about to buy some stationery. How much change will you get back after paying? Write the number in the screen of each cash register.

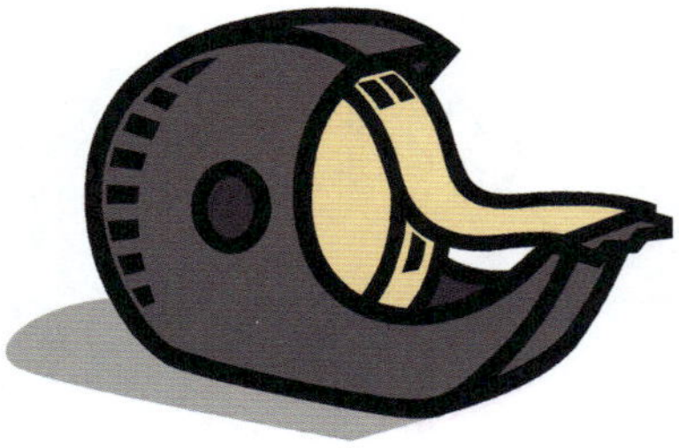

$ 1.40

$ 2

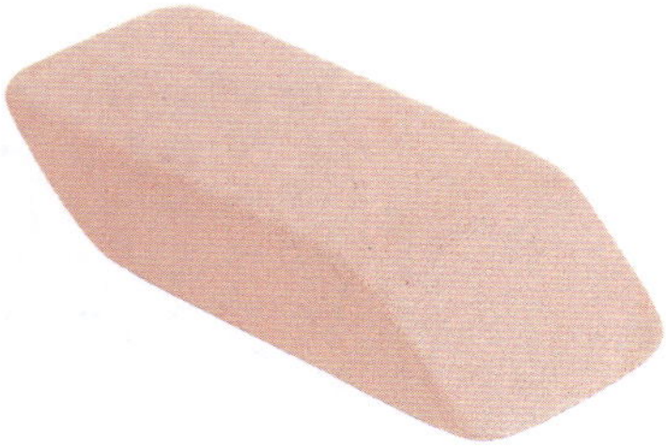

$ 0.50

$ 3

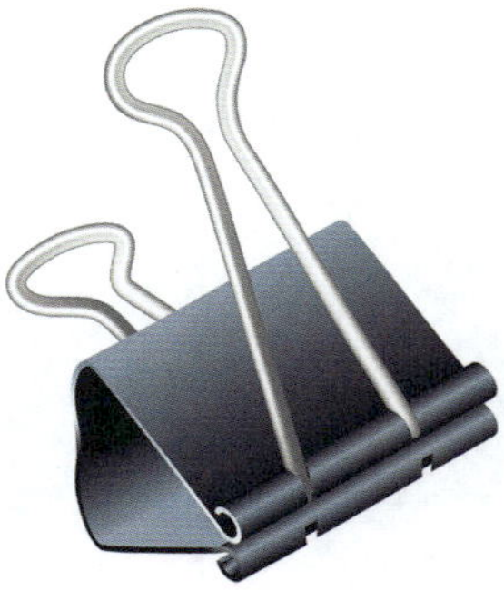

$ 0.10

$ 1.65

$ 4.15

$ 1.20

$ 5

1

Change
$ 0.30

2

Change
$

3

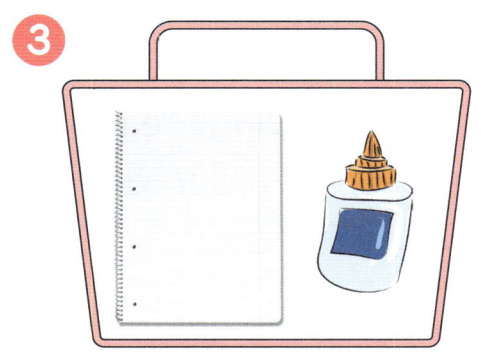 

Change
$

4

Change
$

Unit 3 Personal Finance

Finance Words

■ Draw a line to match each finance word with its definition.

| Income | | Things we need in order to live like food and water. |

| Budget | | Jobs that we do for other people for money. |

| Needs | | It is a plan you make to help spend or save money wisely. |

| Wants | | Things we would like to have. But we don't really need them in order to live. |

| Goods | | The money you get for working a job or performing a task. |

| Services | | Things people buy or sell. |

Date

Great Job Sticker

Look at each picture and circle if the picture shows a good or a person performing a service.

1 Doctor

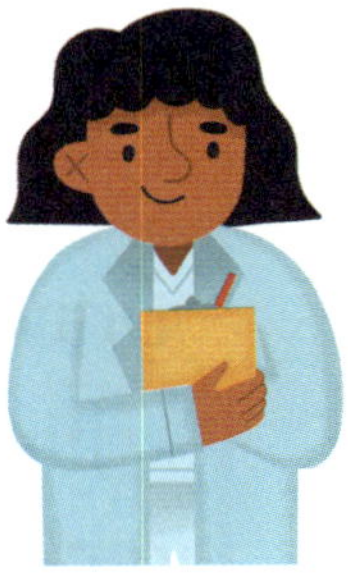

Good Service

2 Clothes

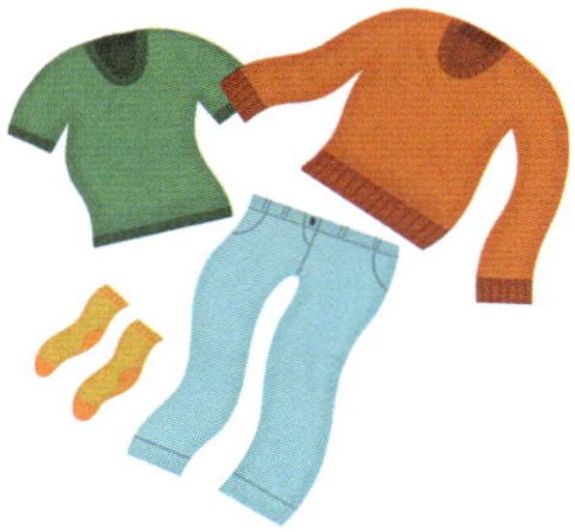

Good Service

3 Food

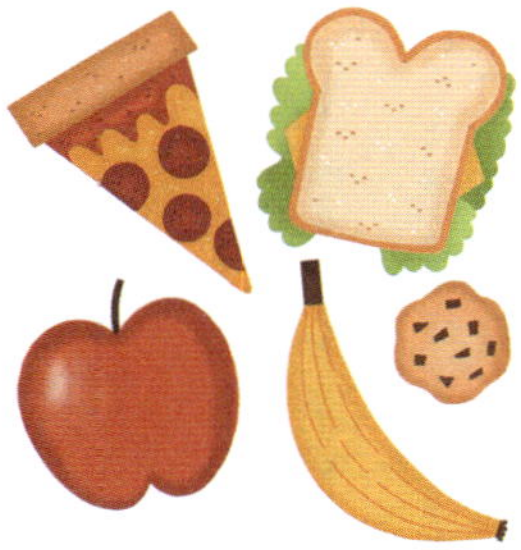

Good Service

4 Toys

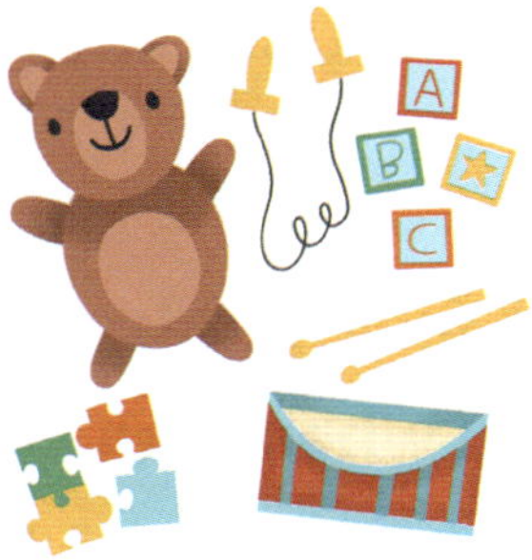

Good Service

5 Chef

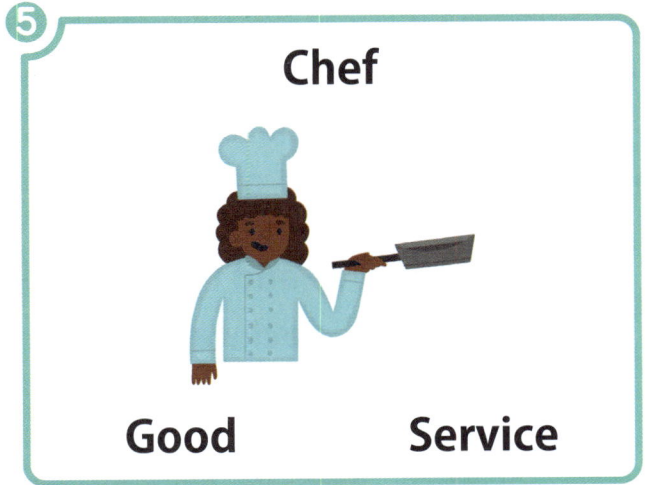

Good Service

6 Hair Stylist

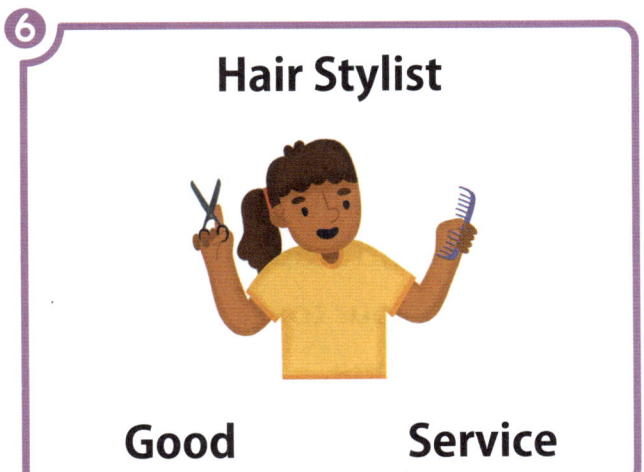

Good Service

Physical Education Break!

It's important to move your body and exercise!
Try this fun activity below to break up your studying!

■ Pick a few of the options below to draw with sidewalk chalk and make your own "Activity Line."

Draw a bunch of bubbles and jump from one to the other to "pop" them.	Draw a flower vine and walk along the length. Make it as long or short as you want.	Draw a "lava" pit and jump over it. Add rocks you can hop on to be safe if you want to make it bigger.
Draw a few spirals and spin when you get to them.	Draw a few large circles along the path and stop for a "dance party" when you reach them.	Draw lily pads along the path and "frog hop" from one to the next.
Draw triangles along the path and stop and touch your toes in each one.	Draw a straight line as long as you want and run as fast as you can along it.	Draw a zigzag line and try and walk backwards along it.

Unit **4** Table of Contents

Use this page to keep track of your progress throughout the book. Place a check mark in the box when you have completed a section.

Opinion Piece 1

KEY POINTS

Opinion texts are a form of writing that shares the writer's thoughts and feelings about a topic with the reader. The writer of an opinion text offers reasons why they feel a certain way about a topic and presents examples to support their reasons. The reader might not always agree with the writer's opinion.

For example, a writer might write that: summer is the best season. They would give reasons like: the temperature is warm and you can be outside all day doing activities. Then they would give examples like: you can go swimming or play baseball, and you get to have ice cream!

■ Read the text below. Draw a box around the main opinion. Underline the reasons. Circle the examples.

I believe that cats are better than dogs. First, cats are usually more independent and can take care of themselves when you are busy. They don't need to be walked outside often like dogs do. This makes cats easier to care for. Cats are also calmer and quieter than dogs, which can be nice when you want to relax. Dogs have a lot more energy and bark a lot. Cats are playful too. You can play with them more easily than a dog because you can play with them inside with string or small toys. Cats

are good companions because they will sleep with you and not take up as much space as a big dog. Overall, cats make great pets that would be happy in most homes!

■ Answer the questions based on the reading passage.

> I think doing chores is a great way for kids to learn responsibility. When kids help with tasks at home like cleaning their room or washing dishes, they start to understand that everyone has a role to play in their family. This teaches them that their actions matter and that they can help out and make a big difference in their homes. Completing chores also gives kids a sense of accomplishment. When they finish a task, they can feel proud of what they have done.
>
> In addition, doing chores helps kids develop important skills for the future. They can learn how to manage their time and take care of their things. They can learn that these skills are not just useful at home, but can help them in school and in the future. A kid will be more likely to clean up after themselves in school if they learned to clean up after themselves at home.
>
>
>
> By making chores a regular part of a kid's day, they can also become more organized and responsible. Overall, chores are not just work, they are valuable lessons that help kids grow up to be responsible adults.

❶ What is the writer's main opinion in this text?

_____

❷ What reasons do they give? Include examples to support their reasons.

_____

_____

❸ Do you agree or disagree with their opinion? Why or why not?

_____

Opinion Piece 2

Opinion texts can help the reader learn more about different topics as well as help them decide which opinion they agree with based on the reasons and examples provided in the text.

■ Read the texts below that offer two different opinions on the same topic. Answer the questions on the following page.

Passage 1

Video games are a good hobby for kids. Video games can help children build certain skills. Kids learn creativity as they work through games. Each video game is set up differently, but most video games have some sort of problem to solve. Kids who play video games can grow their problem solving skills. These types of skills can be used in other parts of their lives like in school or after school. Parents often think of sports like soccer or basketball as being a team activity. However, video games can build teamwork skills too. Kids who play games with others learn team skills by working together during the game. They protect, help, and guide teammates. Also, when people play video games, they need to have a strategy, or a plan, in order to win. These skills can be learned in sports, but they can also be gained from playing video games.

Passage 2

Video games are not a good hobby for kids. Many parents believe that gaming is a bad thing. Some video gamers become addicted, and that is a major problem. Kids who are addicted choose to only spend their time playing games. They do not take care of chores, school work, or any other important things in life.

Video games can be bad for a child's health. Video game players skip meals or lose sleep because they stay up too late playing games. Sitting in front of a game for more than two hours a day is also bad for a child's health. Kids need to be active through exercise. Without exercise, kids can become overweight and have other health problems. In addition, video games can cause backaches, headaches, and strained eyes.

Lastly, some video games are violent. This can lead to kids bullying each other while playing. Instead of being good teammates, video game players can be mean to each other. This type of environment does not create positive relationships with with other kids or people in the real world.

Date

Great Job Sticker

1 What main topic is being discussed in both texts?

2 Does Passage 1 have a positive or negative opinion of the topic?

3 Include examples to support your claim in Question 2.

4 Does Passage 2 have a positive or negative opinion of the topic?

5 Include examples to support your claim in Question 4.

6 Do you agree with the opinion in Passage 1 or Passage 2? Explain why?

7 What reason would you add to one of the passages to support your opinion?

Argumentative Text

KEY POINTS

Argumentative texts are pieces that argue to support a point. The author takes a stand on a particular issue and tries to support it with reasons and facts. The author is trying to convince the audience to agree with them. The author often starts by researching the topic to make sure they have the facts they need to make a strong argument. The goal of an argumentative text is to get the reader to agree with the writer's stand on an issue.

■ Read the text and answer the questions.

Homework is important because it helps students practice what they've learned in school. When kids do their homework, they can improve their understanding of what they learned in class. Studies show that students who complete homework score better on tests. They have more chances to practice  the material and solve problems or answer questions correctly. Homework also teaches responsibility and time management skills, which are essential skills for success in the future. By doing homework, students get a chance to explore topics more deeply. It can also help them prepare for the next day's lessons by making sure they understand the material taught before. Overall, homework is a valuable part of learning that can help children succeed in school.

❶ What is the main argument of this text?

_____

❷ List two facts that support the writer's argument.

_____

■ Read the text and answer the questions.

Eating breakfast is very important because it helps your body and brain start the day strong. When you eat a healthy breakfast, you get energy from the foods you eat. Fruits like bananas or oranges, whole grains like toast or oatmeal, and proteins like eggs or sausage, give your body the energy it  needs to work throughout the day. This energy can help you stay focused in school and be more active. Studies show that kids who eat breakfast do better in classes and have more energy to play and learn. Kids who don't eat breakfast before school can have trouble focusing and be more sleepy due to hunger.

Additionally, breakfast can help you stay healthy. When you skip breakfast, you might feel hungry later and choose unhealthy snacks to fill you up until lunch. When you are hungry your body will tell you it wants fatty or sugary food to satisfy it and make you feel full quickly. But this is not good fuel for your body. Eating a good breakfast can keep you full until lunchtime and help your make better food choices throughout the day. So, by starting your day off with a nutritious meal, you can support your body and mind. This will make it easier to succeed at school and do the activities you enjoy.

❶ What is the main argument of this text?

_____

❷ List three facts the writer gives to support it.

_____

_____

❸ Do you agree with the writer's argument? Give a reason from the text to support your answer.

_____

Persuasive Text

KEY POINTS

In a persuasive text, the writer presents one side of a debatable topic. They use facts, reasons, and personal feelings on a subject to persuade the reader to agree with them. They typically do not mention the opposing viewpoint by not providing evidence or examples.

■ Read the passage and answer the questions.

Recess is the best part of the school day! It's the time when kids gets to play, run around, and have fun with their friends. But the day would be even better if recess were longer. Longer recess would give kids more time to enjoy  playing outside, get fresh air, and even have time to relax. The school day can be tiring and stressful for kids, they need more unstructured time to play and let out their energy. Longer recess will lead to happier kids, which will help make them better able to focus in class. Schools should consider making recess longer to give kids the time they need to recharge. Overall this will lead to more fun and better learning.

❶ What is the writer trying to persuade the reader of in this text?

_____

❷ List two reasons the writer gives to support this position.

_____

_____

■ Answer the questions based on the reading passage.

Books are better than movies! When you read a book, you can imagine what the characters and settings look like in your own way. Each reader gets to create their own picture in their mind which makes the story unique and special to them. Books also give more details about the plot and the characters' feelings. A lot can be learned about what they think and feel, and that can change the way they act throughout the story. Another reason books are better than movies, is that books help you improve your reading skills while also being entertained. They teach you how to use your imagination. Books can also be enjoyed anywhere and at anytime. You can read at home, one the bus, or in a park. If you get interrupted you can

stop and save your place with a bookmark for later. While movies are fun, they can't match the adventure of diving into a good book. So more people should choose books over movies and discover amazing new worlds through reading!

❶ What is the writer trying to persuade the reader of in this text?

_____

❷ List two reasons the writer gives to support their position.

_____

❸ What information might be missing from this text about the writer's opinion?

_____

❹ Did the writer's text persuade you to agree with their thoughts?

_____

Brain Break
Let's Try Writing a Persuasive Text!

Persuasive texts might sometimes seem like they are trying to convince the reader to believe something unusual or not commonly agreed with. So let's have some fun with that idea!

Try writing a persuasive piece about a made-up animal. Use the skills you practiced in this section to convince your reader that it is real!

■ Write a persuasive text about a made-up animal to convince your reader it is real. Include reasons and facts to support it.

_____

_____

_____

_____

_____

_____

_____

_____

_____

Mindfulness Break!

KEY POINTS

Mindfulness is about listening to your body and your feelings. It can help you know when you are happy, stressed, excited or worried.

Worrying is when you think a lot about something that makes you scared, nervous, or anxious. It is important to be aware of when you feel worried so you can try and stay calm or overcome that feeling.

Worrying is normal, and everyone worries! You might worry about a spelling test or going to a new place for the first time or going to the doctor's office.

One way to be mindful of your worries and to keep them controlled is to practice writing them down.

■ Use the box below to write down some of your current worries.

Informational Writing: Gathering Facts

KEY POINTS

The purpose of an informational text is to share information about a topic. That means that informational texts contain facts that tell about a specific subject. For example, an informational text about frogs would contain facts that tell the reader about frogs.

■ Read the text below. Then write three facts you learned.

> The next time you hear a funny noise coming from a pond or lake, look to see if it's a frog! Many frogs live in and around bodies of water. They mainly eat bugs, but they may also eat small fish. While we think of them as saying "ribbit ribbit," they actually make a range of different sounds. Some frogs  make a sound that sounds like whistle or a trilling sound. And of course, frogs are great at jumping. If you don't look quickly enough, they may leap away before you spot them!

❶

❷

❸

■ In a few activities, you will write your own informational text about an ecosystem of your choice. Choose the ecosystem you would like to write about. Then write four facts about the ecosystem. For example, what is the weather like? What plants and animals live there? What places have this ecosystem? Ask an adult to help you search for information online if you don't know enough about your ecosystem.

Ecosystem:

_____

_____

_____

_____

Informational Writing: Linking Words and Phrases

KEY POINTS

Linking words are words that join two or more ideas and show how they relate to each other. They are an important tool that writers use to make their ideas connect together smoothly. Some linking words include: *also, another, and, more, but.*

Examples:

Deer are active early in the morning. They are *also* active around sunset.

I have two books about owls at home, *and* one more at school.

Dolphins are very intelligent. *Another* example of a smart animal is a pig.

■ Use each linking word to write one to two sentences.

❶ before

_____

❷ after

_____

❸ first

_____

❹ later

_____

❺ yesterday

_____

■ Practice using linking words to join the facts that you wrote in the previous activity. Use at least four linking words.

1

_____

2

_____

3

_____

4

_____

Informational Writing: Structure

KEY POINTS

Informational texts usually have an introduction that gets the reader's interest and tells them what the text will be about. They also typically have a conclusion that ties the text together.

■ Read the text below. Circle the introduction and underline the conclusion.

You might think hermit crabs wouldn't be very social. Hermits usually keep to themselves, right? But actually hermit crabs work together in a fascinating way. Hermit crabs live in shells that they find, and as they grow bigger they often need to get new, bigger shells. When a new shell washes up on the shore, the hermit crabs line up by size. The biggest one will take the new shell, and the next largest will take the first crab's old shell. Then they will keep trading down the line, so that each crab gets a slightly bigger shell. It's just like getting your older sibling's hand-me-downs!

■ Draft an introduction and a conclusion for your informational text.

Introduction

Conclusion

Writing an Informational Piece

■ Write an informational text about an ecosystem of your choice. Make sure to use facts, linking words, an introduction, and a conclusion.

Brain Break
Draw a Picture!

■ Use the space below to draw a picture of an animal that lives in the ecosystem you wrote about.

Mindfulness Break!

KEY POINTS

Recognizing and acknowledging your emotions is an important part of practicing mindfulness. As you complete the wheel below, remember that everyone experiences these emotions, emotions are always changing, and there are no "good" or "bad" emotions.

■ Use the wheel below to draw a moment and time when you may have felt the listed emotion.

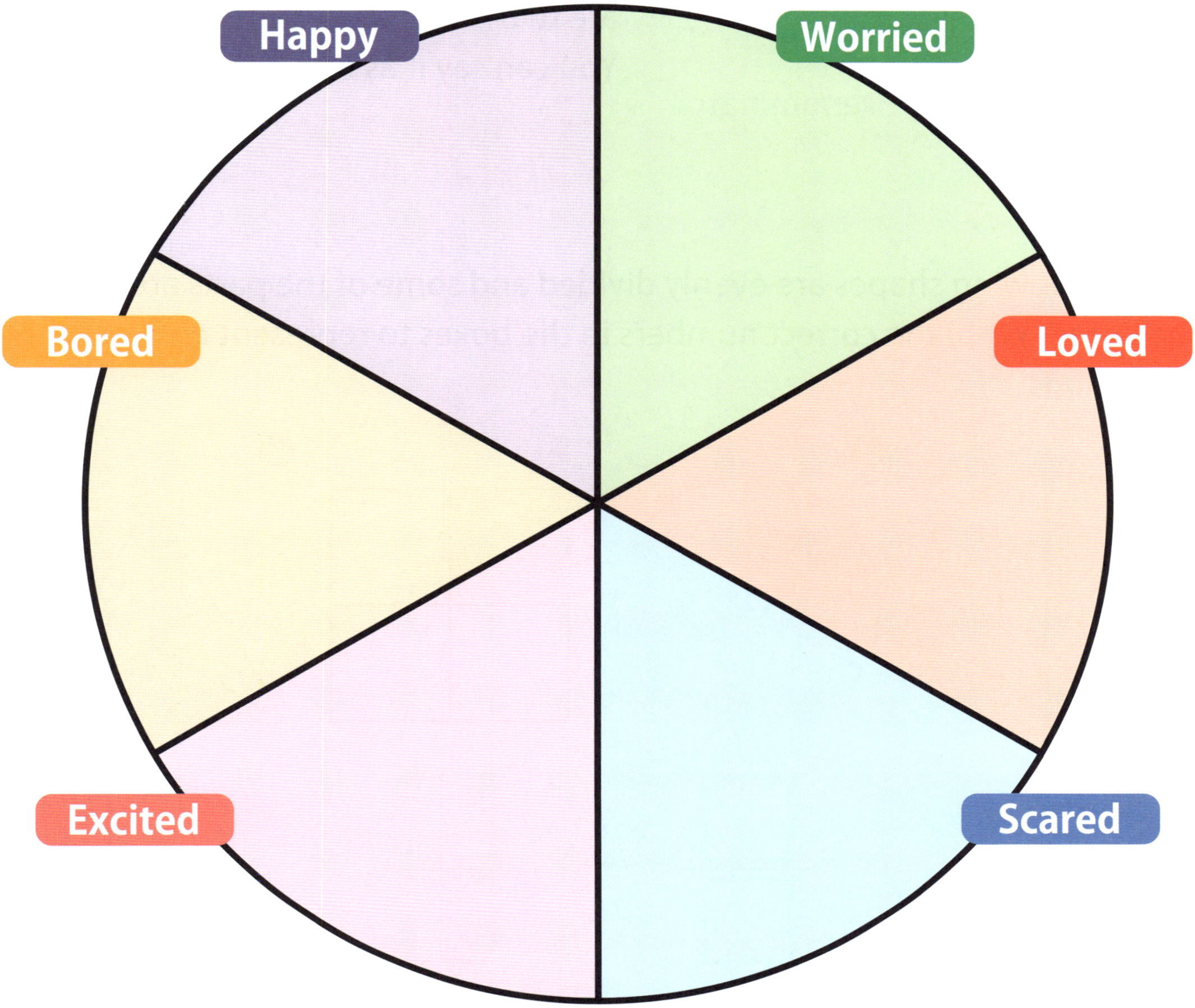

Happy **Worried**

Bored **Loved**

Excited **Scared**

Fractions

KEY POINTS

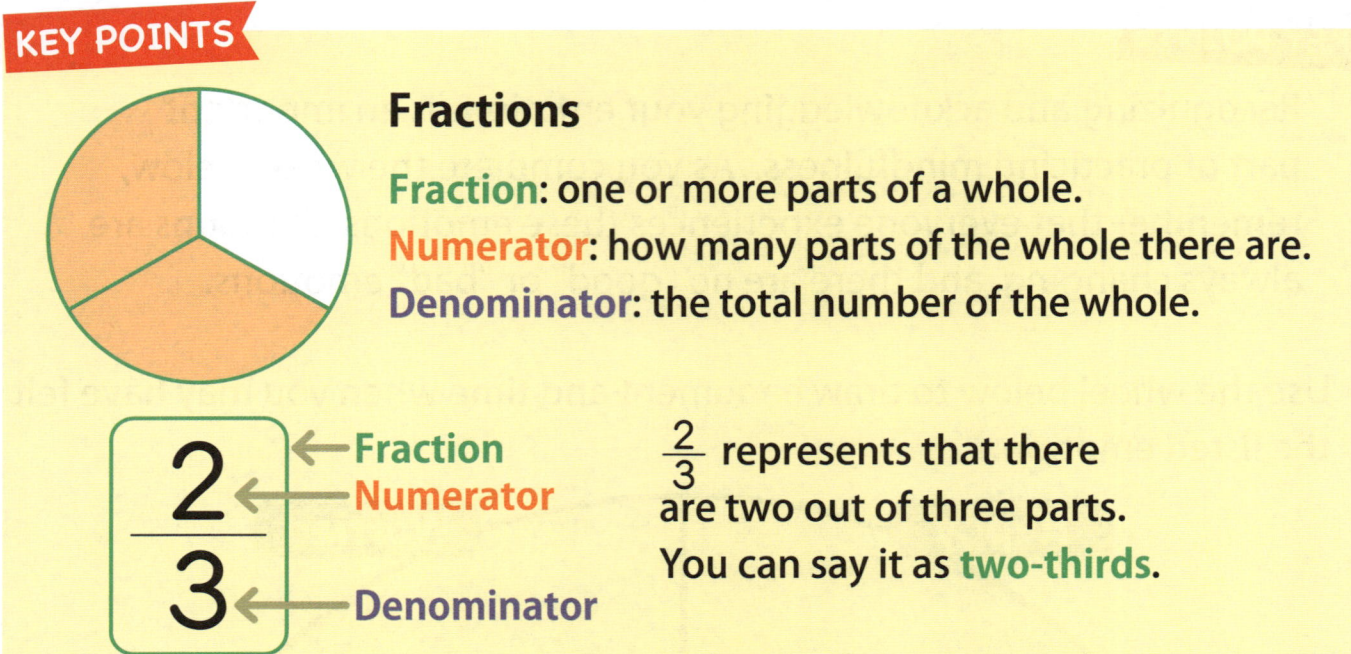

Fractions

Fraction: one or more parts of a whole.
Numerator: how many parts of the whole there are.
Denominator: the total number of the whole.

$\frac{2}{3}$ ← Fraction
2 ← Numerator
3 ← Denominator

$\frac{2}{3}$ represents that there are two out of three parts.
You can say it as **two-thirds**.

■ The following shapes are evenly divided and some of the parts are colored. Write the correct numbers in the boxes to represent them as fractions.

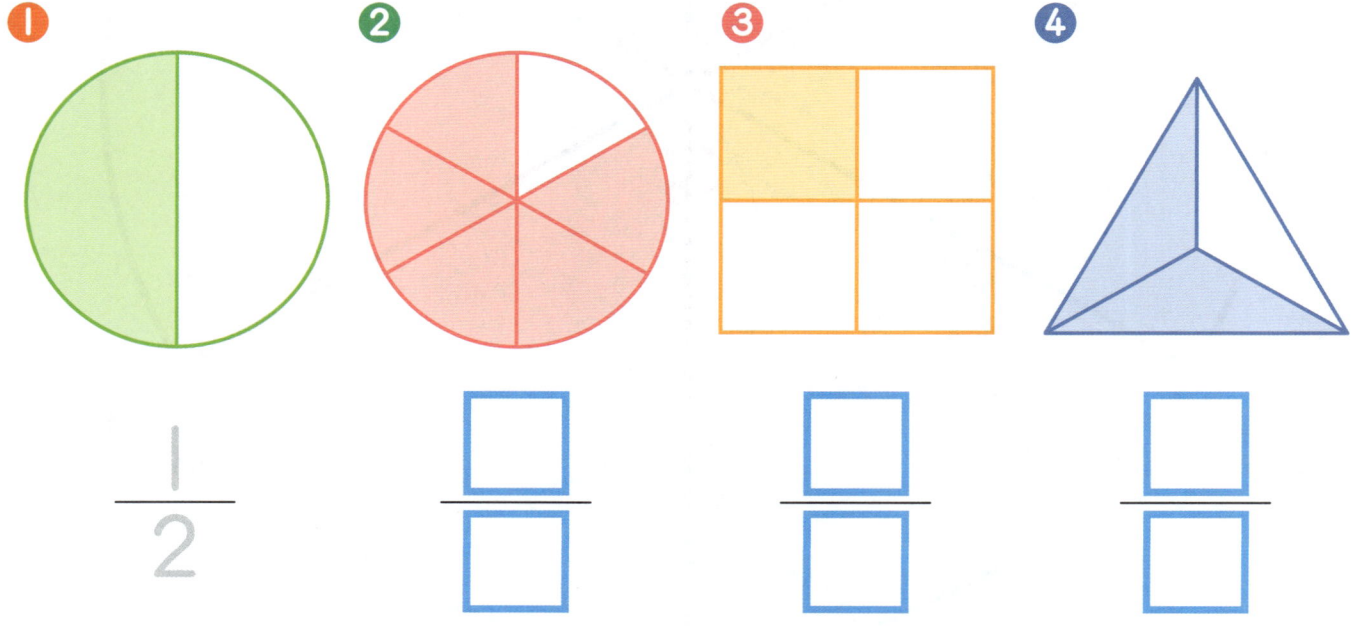

① $\dfrac{1}{2}$ ② ③ ④

■ Color the shapes to represent the fraction below.

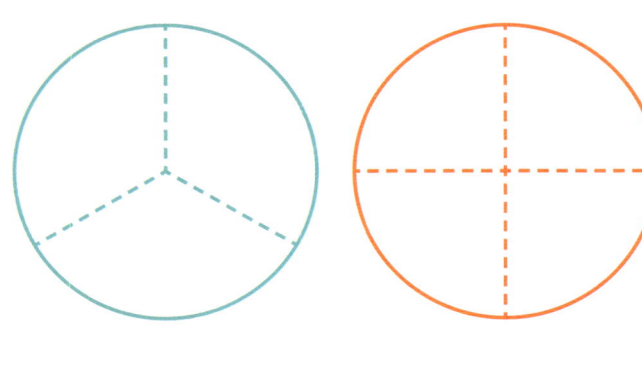

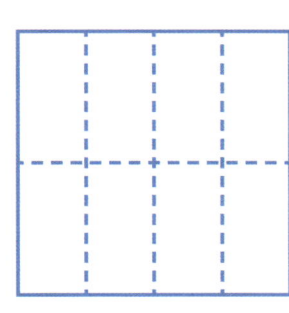

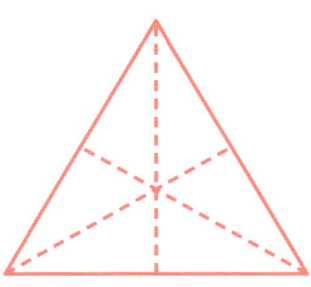

$\dfrac{1}{3}$ $\dfrac{3}{4}$ $\dfrac{1}{8}$ $\dfrac{5}{6}$

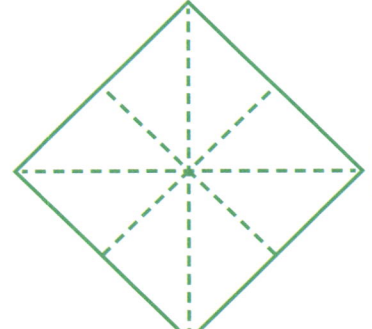

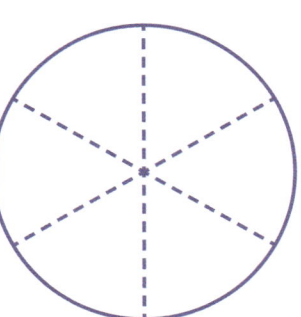

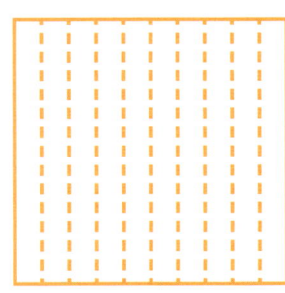

$\dfrac{1}{2}$ $\dfrac{2}{8}$ $\dfrac{4}{6}$ $\dfrac{8}{10}$

Comparing Fractions

■ Write > (greater than), < (less than), or = (equal to) to compare the fractions.

1 $\dfrac{2}{3}$ > $\dfrac{1}{3}$ 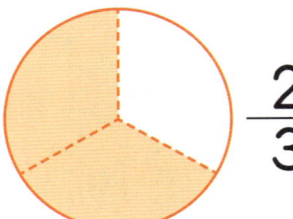 $\dfrac{2}{3}$ 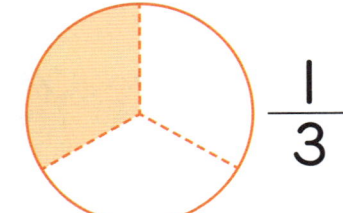 $\dfrac{1}{3}$

2 $\dfrac{1}{4}$ ☐ $\dfrac{3}{4}$ 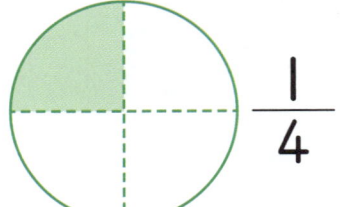 $\dfrac{1}{4}$ 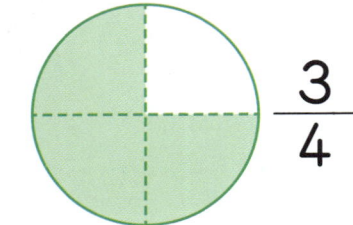 $\dfrac{3}{4}$

3 1 ☐ $\dfrac{2}{2}$ 1 $\dfrac{2}{2}$

4 $\dfrac{2}{5}$ ☐ $\dfrac{4}{5}$  $\dfrac{2}{5}$ $\dfrac{4}{5}$

5 $\dfrac{3}{6}$ ☐ $\dfrac{1}{2}$ 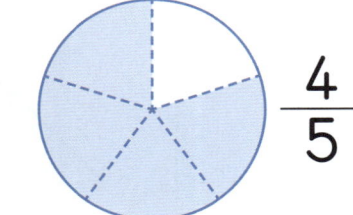 $\dfrac{3}{6}$ $\dfrac{1}{2}$

6 $\dfrac{7}{10}$ ☐ $\dfrac{6}{10}$ 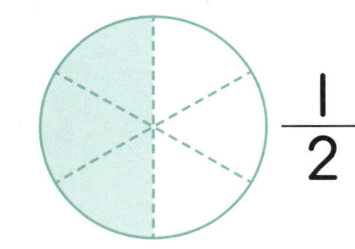 $\dfrac{7}{10}$ $\dfrac{6}{10}$

■ Draw a line to match the fractions that represent the same amount.

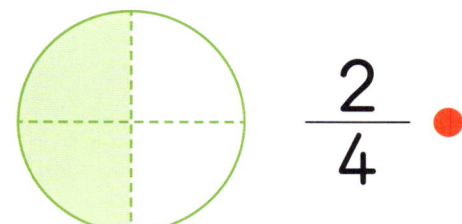 $\dfrac{2}{4}$ ●　　　● $\dfrac{3}{9}$

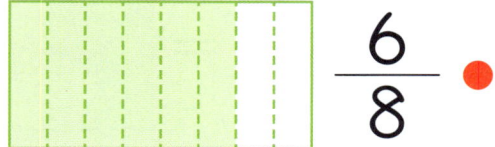 $\dfrac{6}{8}$ ●　　　● $\dfrac{1}{2}$

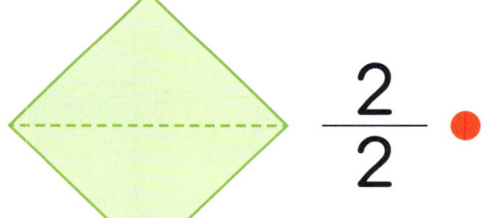 $\dfrac{2}{2}$ ●　　　● $\dfrac{3}{4}$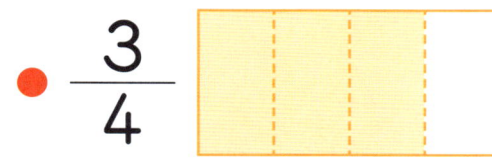

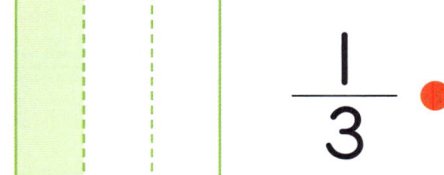 $\dfrac{1}{3}$ ●　　　● $\dfrac{1}{5}$

 $\dfrac{4}{6}$ ●　　　● 1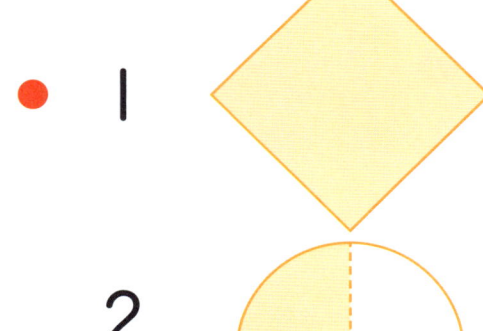

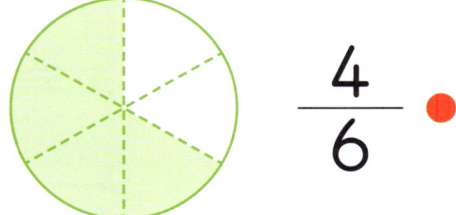 $\dfrac{2}{10}$ ●　　　● $\dfrac{2}{3}$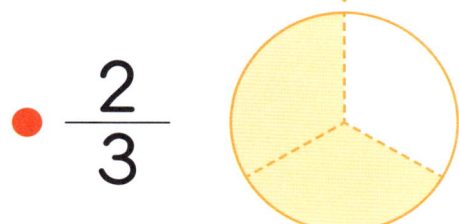

Adding and Subtracting Fractions

■ Add the fractions.

① $\dfrac{1}{3} + \dfrac{1}{3} = \dfrac{2}{3}$

② $\dfrac{2}{9} + \dfrac{3}{9} = \dfrac{\boxed{}}{9}$

③ $\dfrac{1}{4} + \dfrac{2}{4} = \dfrac{\boxed{}}{\boxed{}}$

④ $\dfrac{2}{5} + \dfrac{2}{5} = \dfrac{\boxed{}}{\boxed{}}$

⑤ $\dfrac{3}{7} + \dfrac{1}{7} = \dfrac{\boxed{}}{\boxed{}}$

⑥ $\dfrac{3}{10} + \dfrac{6}{10} = \dfrac{\boxed{}}{\boxed{}}$

⑦ $\dfrac{2}{8} + \dfrac{3}{8} = \dfrac{\boxed{}}{\boxed{}}$

⑧ $\dfrac{1}{6} + \dfrac{4}{6} = \dfrac{\boxed{}}{\boxed{}}$

If the fractions have the same denominator, just add the numerators.

■ Subtract the fractions.

① $\dfrac{2}{3} - \dfrac{1}{3} = \dfrac{1}{3}$

② $\dfrac{4}{5} - \dfrac{1}{5} = \dfrac{\square}{5}$

③ $\dfrac{5}{7} - \dfrac{2}{7} = \dfrac{\square}{\square}$

④ $\dfrac{3}{4} - \dfrac{2}{4} = \dfrac{\square}{\square}$

⑤ $\dfrac{8}{9} - \dfrac{4}{9} = \dfrac{\square}{\square}$

⑥ $\dfrac{4}{6} - \dfrac{3}{6} = \dfrac{\square}{\square}$

⑦ $\dfrac{9}{10} - \dfrac{2}{10} = \dfrac{\square}{\square}$

⑧ $\dfrac{6}{8} - \dfrac{3}{8} = \dfrac{\square}{\square}$

If the fractions have
the same denominator,
just subtract the numerators.

Decimals

KEY POINTS

Decimals

0.3 ← tenths

↑
decimal point

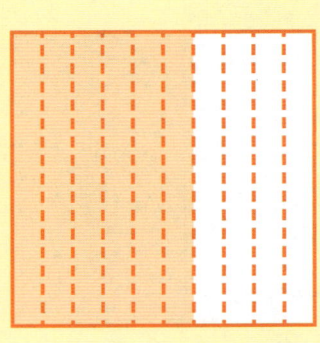

0.6 represents that there are **6 tenths** or $\dfrac{6}{10}$

■ Convert each decimal to a fraction, and each fraction to a decimal.

① $0.6 = \dfrac{\boxed{}}{10}$

② $0.1 = \dfrac{\boxed{}}{10}$

③ $0.3 = \dfrac{\boxed{}}{10}$

④ $0.7 = \dfrac{\boxed{}}{10}$

⑤ $0.4 = \dfrac{\boxed{}}{10}$

⑥ $0.8 = \dfrac{\boxed{}}{10}$

⑦ $\dfrac{9}{10} = \boxed{}$

⑧ $\dfrac{2}{10} = \boxed{}$

⑨ $\dfrac{7}{10} = \boxed{}$

⑩ $\dfrac{3}{10} = \boxed{}$

⑪ $\dfrac{5}{10} = \boxed{}$

⑫ $\dfrac{1}{10} = \boxed{}$

KEY POINTS

Decimals

tenths

0.06

↑
hundredths

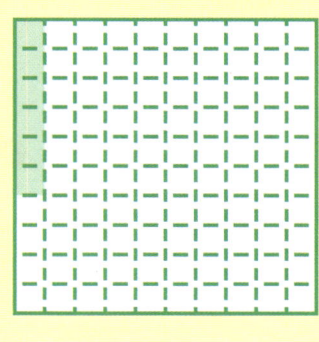

0.06 represents that there
are 6 hundredths or $\dfrac{6}{100}$

■ Convert each decimal to a fraction, and each fraction to a decimal.

① $0.06 = \dfrac{\boxed{}}{100}$

② $0.04 = \dfrac{\boxed{}}{100}$

③ $0.01 = \dfrac{\boxed{}}{100}$

④ $0.08 = \dfrac{\boxed{}}{100}$

⑤ $0.09 = \dfrac{\boxed{}}{100}$

⑥ $0.03 = \dfrac{\boxed{}}{100}$

⑦ $\dfrac{1}{100} = \boxed{}$

⑧ $\dfrac{2}{100} = \boxed{}$

⑨ $\dfrac{5}{100} = \boxed{}$

⑩ $\dfrac{7}{100} = \boxed{}$

⑪ $\dfrac{11}{100} = 0.11$

⑫ $\dfrac{12}{100} = \boxed{}$

Fractions and Decimals

■ Connect each figure, fraction, and decimal that represents the same value.

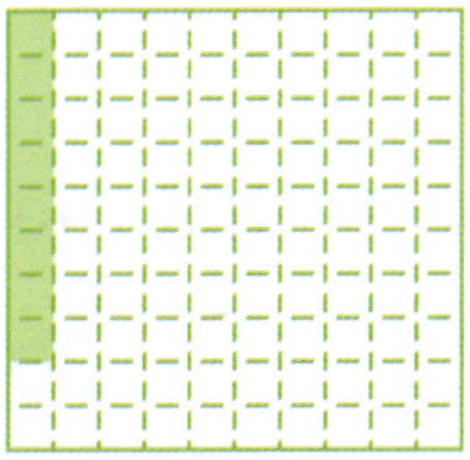

$\dfrac{4}{10}$ 0.1

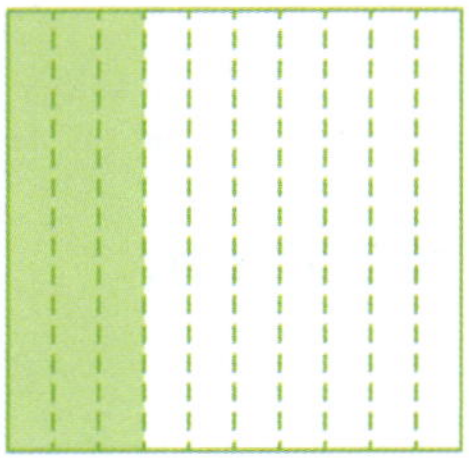

$\dfrac{3}{100}$ 0.4

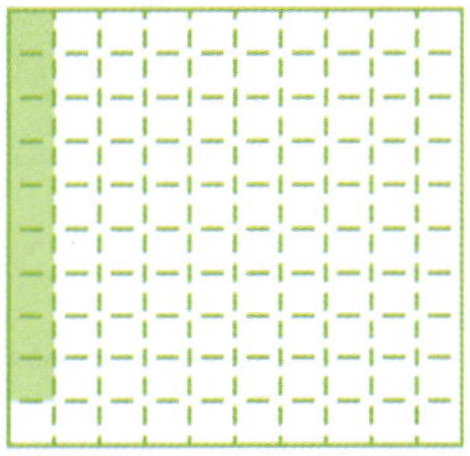

$\dfrac{8}{100}$ 0.03

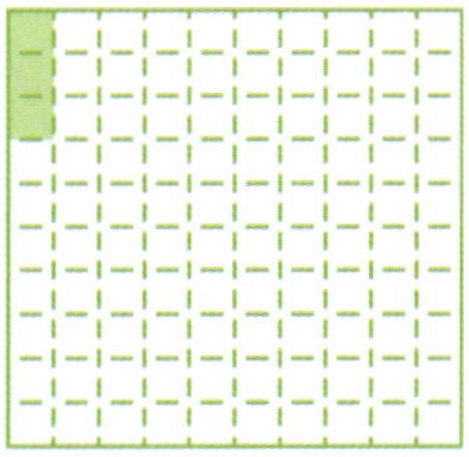

$\dfrac{1}{10}$ 0.3

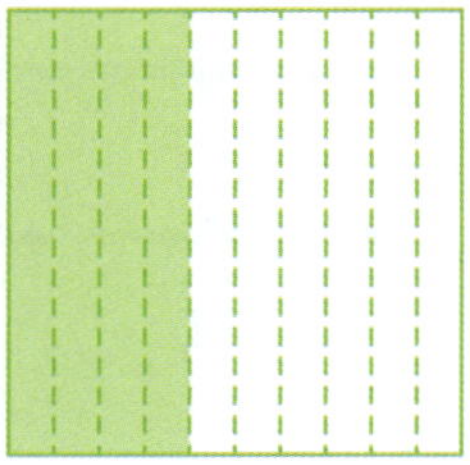

$\dfrac{9}{100}$ 0.08

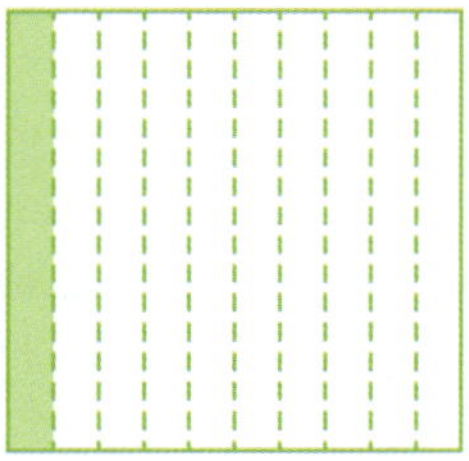

$\dfrac{3}{10}$ 0.09

Date

Great Job Sticker

Connect each figure, fraction, and decimal that represents the same value.

$\frac{2}{10}$	0.04	0.2
0.5	$\frac{6}{100}$	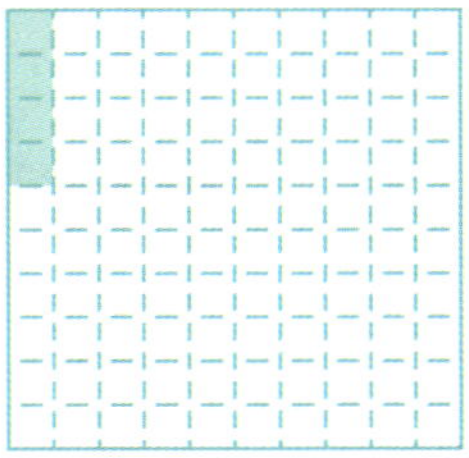
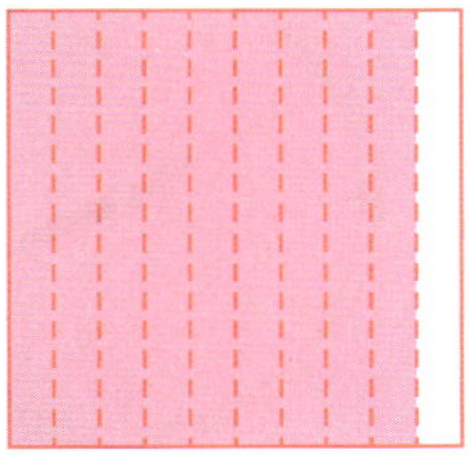	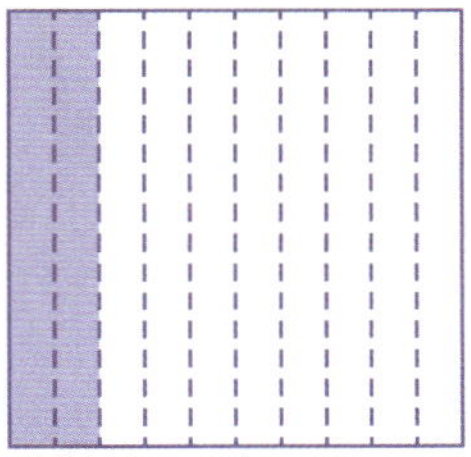	0.9
$\frac{4}{100}$	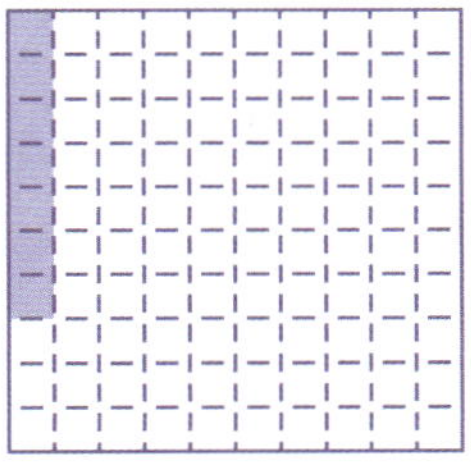	$\frac{7}{100}$
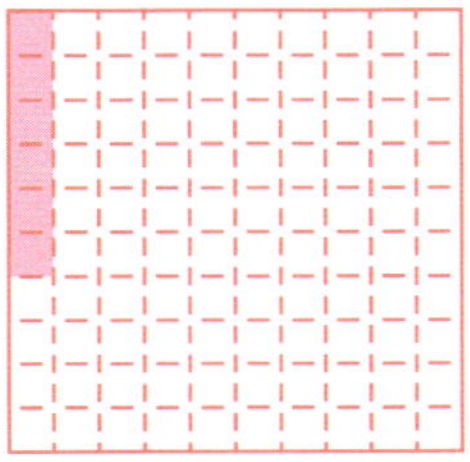	$\frac{5}{10}$	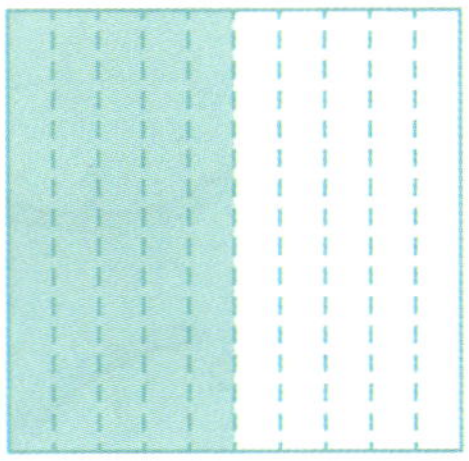
0.07	$\frac{9}{10}$	0.06

Brain Break
Telling Time Quiz

■ Circle five clocks that show the same time as the clock on the right.

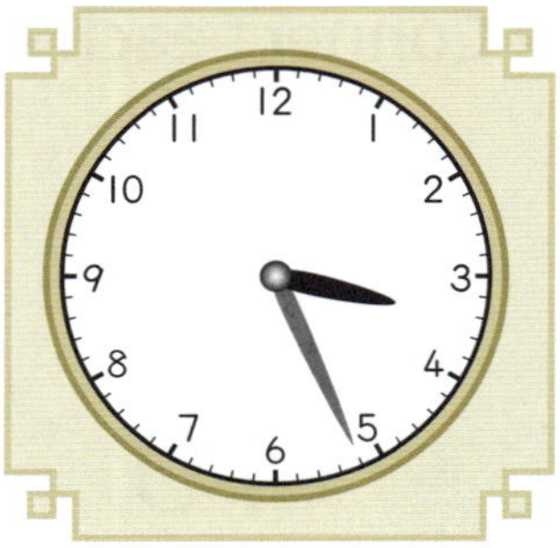

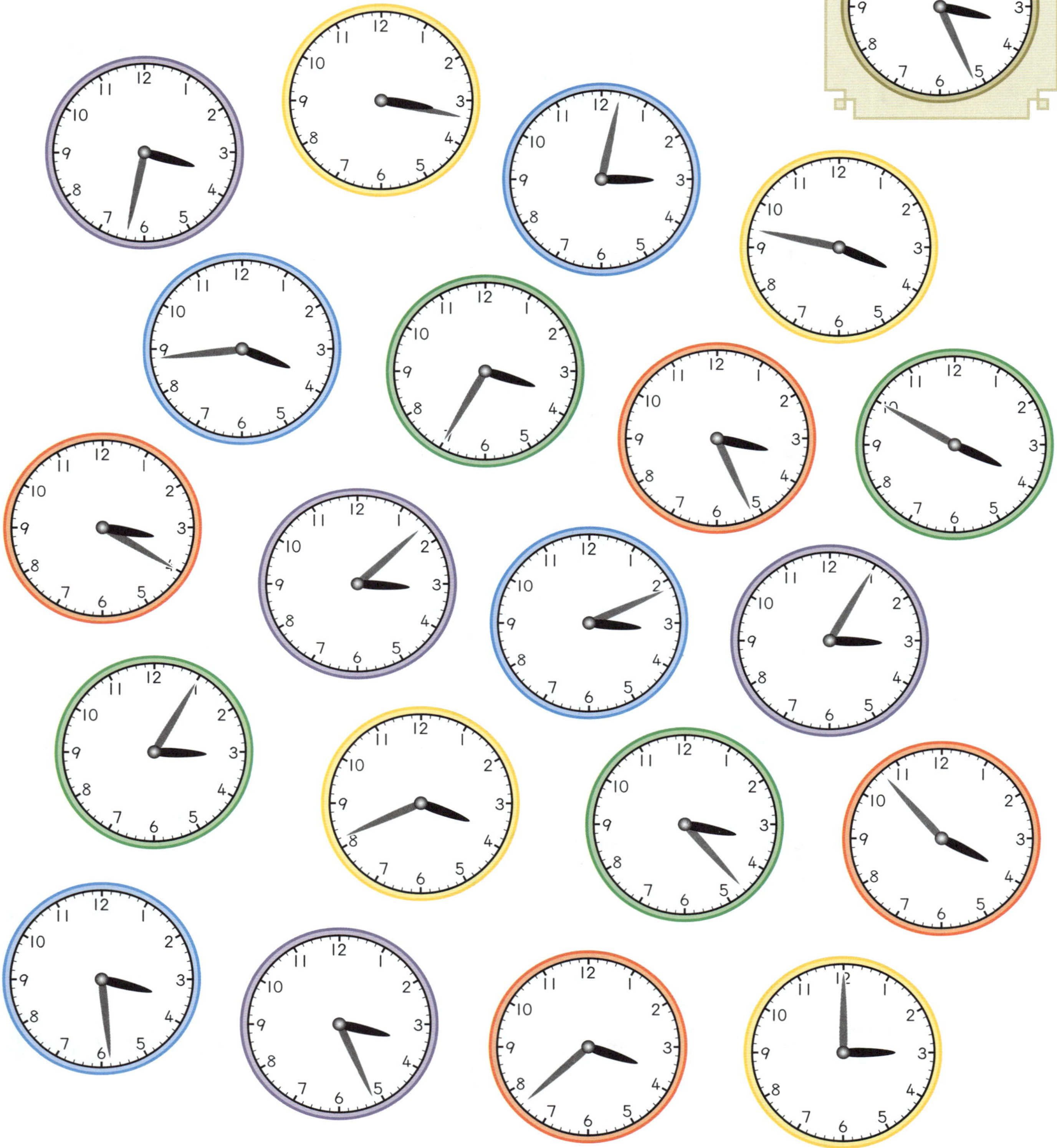

Climate and Weather

KEY POINTS

Weather is the word we use to describe the combination of the temperature, precipitation (rain, snow, sleet, hail), humidity (how much water is in the air), wind speed and direction, and air pressure in a place's lower atmosphere at a certain time. The atmosphere is the air around the earth that protects the earth from getting extremely hot when facing the sun during the day and keeps the air from getting extremely cold at night, when facing away from the sun. Weather can be hot, cold, warm, rainy, windy, stormy, snowy, foggy, humid—we have so many words to talk about the weather! The weather can also change from one minute to the next.

Climate is the word we use to describe what an area's weather conditions are typically like over many years. To determine the climate of a place, you need to observe the weather patterns for a long time—at least thirty years! Scientists observe different weather patterns over many years to determine what the climate is.

Today, Earth's climate is changing. Human activity is causing Earth to get warmer on average. Cold periods might last a few days or a few weeks, but they aren't a major change in the climate. They would need to last for years before they would count as a change in climate.

■ Answer the questions.

❶ What is weather?

_____

❷ What is climate?

_____

❸ What is climate change doing to Earth's weather?

_____

■ **Answer true or false for each statement.**

1 Weather changes from hour to hour and day to day.

2 The atmosphere is the air around Earth.

3 Humidity is how much water is in the air.

4 Climate can be determined by observing the weather.

5 Earth's climate doesn't change and is the same as 100 years ago.

6 Rain, temperature, and humidity are used to describe climate.

Climate and Weather around the World

KEY POINTS

There are many types of climates, but three important ones are tropical, temperate, and arctic climates.

Tropical climates are warm and humid all year. They usually have two seasons: the rainy season and the dry season. The temperature does not change very much throughout the year. Tropical climates are closer to the equator, where the sun shines strongly all year.

Temperate climates have four seasons. Winter is cold and summer is hot. The amount of rain may vary depending on the season. Temperate climates are in between the tropical climates near the equator and the arctic climates at the North and South Poles. They get stronger sun during their summers and weaker sun during their winters because of the way Earth tilts towards or away from the sun.

Arctic climates are cold all year round, but they are less cold during their summers than during their winters. They have long, cold winters and short, cool summers. In the summer, they have very long days and very short nights because they are tilted towards the sun. In the winter, they have very short days and very long nights because they are tilted away from the sun. The North and South Poles and the lands near them have arctic climates.

■ Read the description and write what type of climate each place has.

❶ Alaska, US: The winter lasts from October to April. Temperatures range between 55 F and 70 F in the summer to 20 F to -10 F in the winter! There can be a lot of snow depending on the area. In the summer the sun shines for 18 to 20 hours a day! In the winter the sun only shines a few hours a day. Typical weather is snowy and cold.

❷ Rome, Italy: Typically has four seasons. Weather is warm in the summer and cool in the winter with some snow.

❸ Nassau, The Bahamas: Has high temperatures year round, but is warmest in May to October. It receives large amounts of rain during the summer, up to 55 inches.

❹ Glasgow, Scotland: Typically has warm summers and cool winters. It receives about 200 days of rain a year.

Meteorology

KEY POINTS

Meteorology is the study of weather and climate. Weather scientists are called meteorologists. Meteorologists observe current weather patterns and research weather patterns from the past.

Some meteorologists make weather predictions. They look at weather conditions, like the temperature, wind speed and direction, humidity, air pressure, and more. They use this information and knowledge of past weather to predict what will happen. Especially when there could be hazardous weather, like a blizzard or hurricane, it is important for meteorologists to predict these events and warn people. Even on typical days, it is helpful to know how hot it will be or if it is likely to rain so you know how to dress.

Meteorologists use many tools to help them study the weather. Below are some examples.

Thermometers measure temperature, or how hot or cold something is. Meteorologists measure the temperature of the air and sometimes of the surface of the ocean.

Barometers are used to measure the air pressure in the atmosphere. When air pressure is very low, it is likely that a storm will happen soon. Barometers help meteorologists predict storms.

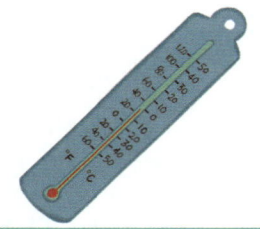

Windsocks are giant, striped, fabric tubes. The way they point tells the direction the wind is blowing. The number of striped sections that are held up by the wind tell how strong the wind is. Meteorologists use windsocks, and so do airplane pilots. It is important for pilots to know the direction and strength of the wind so they can fly their planes safely.

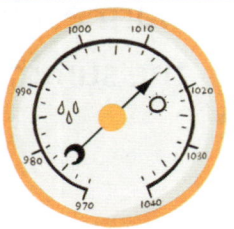

■ **Answer the questions.**

❶ **What is meteorology?**

❷ **What do meteorologists do?**

❸ **Name a few examples of weather conditions.**

■ **Match the meteorology tools with their function.**

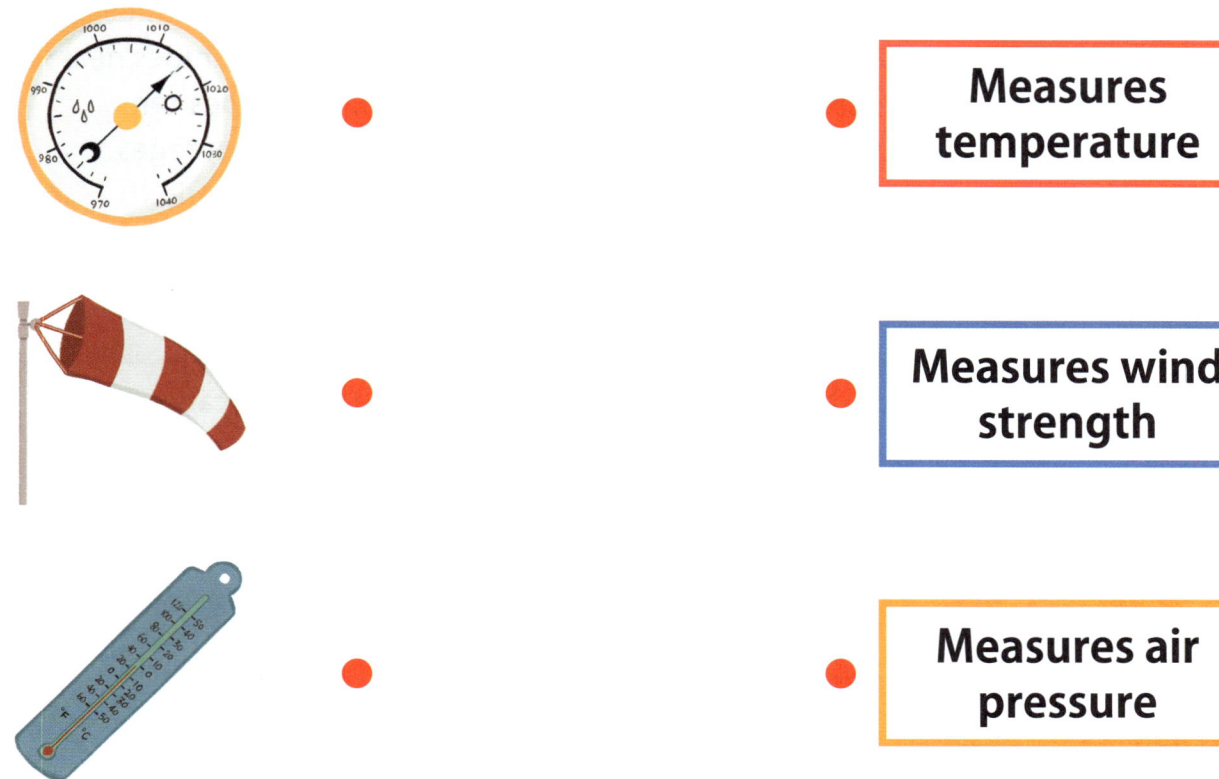

Hazardous Weather

KEY POINTS

Some kinds of weather can be hazardous, or dangerous.

Thunderstorms are rain showers combined with lightning and thunder and sometimes tornadoes or hail. Some thunderstorms are small and others are very big. They usually last for a few hours or less. Thunderstorms can be hazardous because they can come with lightning strikes that can start fires, heavy rains that can lead to flooding, and high speed winds that can knock over trees and power lines. Less often thunderstorms can come with tornadoes and hail which destroy buildings and damage property.

Hurricanes are similar to thunderstorms in some ways. They both involve rain and wind and can include tornadoes and floods. Hurricanes always form over the ocean and are much bigger than most thunderstorms. They have high-speed winds that

move in a spiral shape. They get less powerful when they move away from the ocean, which is why communities near oceans are hurt the most by hurricanes. Hurricanes can cause flooding, destruction of buildings, power outages, and more. If you live near the ocean, you may be told to evacuate, before a predicted hurricane. You should always follow these instructions. Hurricanes can be very serious.

Blizzards are snowstorms with heavy snow and strong winds. They can cause whiteouts, where so much snow is blowing in the wind that you can't see anything. Blizzards make driving very dangerous. The wind can knock down trees and power lines. It can be dangerous to lose power during the winter because it is so cold. Governments prepare for storms by building storm walls to prevent flooding and buying snow plows and fire engines. They prepare shelters that people can go to during storms if their houses are damaged or without power and heat in the cold.

■ Fill in the chart with details about each hazardous weather condition. Place an " ✕ " in the box if the storm has the feature.

Features	Thunderstorm	Hurricane	Blizzard
Heavy Rain			
Strong winds			
People can lose power			
Can cause flooding			
Heavy snow			
Extreme cold temperatures			
Lightning Strikes			
Hail			
Thunder			

Brain Break
Science Journal 4

Fill in the chart with information about your own town. Use the Internet or a book to help you.

My town:

Climate:

Daily Weather:

Normal Winter Temperature:

Normal Summer Temperature:

Natural Disaster Risks:

■ Draw a picture for each prompt.

1 Your favorite thing to do on a sunny day.

2 Your favorite thing to do on a rainy day.

Government and Democracy

KEY POINTS

Democracies are governments ruled by the people. In direct democracies, everyone comes together to decide how the country should be run. Most countries are too big for this to be practical, so most democracies are representative democracies. In representative democracies, people vote for representatives whose views are closest to their own. These representatives should try to make the government do the things the people they represent think are important.

Republics are representative democracies where people also vote for a leader, often a president. Many countries around the world are republics. The United States is a democratic republic because it is a democracy and a republic.

Monarchies are governments with one leader, called a monarch, at the head. This monarch can be a queen, king, empress, or emperor. Monarchs usually keep their position as long as they live. Most monarchies are hereditary. That means that each monarch is related to the monarch before them. When a monarch dies, their child or another relative becomes the new monarch.

In an absolute monarchy, the monarch makes all decisions about what the government does. The monarch may have advisors, but they don't have to listen to them.

Constitutional monarchies, have monarchs but also have elected representatives. The United Kingdom in Europe, Lesotho in Africa, and Japan in Asia are all examples of constitutional monarchies. In constitutional monarchies, elected representatives make all important decisions about how the government is run. The monarchs are mostly symbolic and take part in ceremonies.

■ Answer the questions.

❶ What is a democracy?

_____

❷ What is the different between a direct and a representative democracy?

_____

❸ What is a monarchy?

_____

■ Fill in the blank to complete each statement.

1 Democracies are ⬚ ruled by the people.

2 A ⬚ democracy is one where people vote for a representative to help the government make decisions they agree with.

3 A ⬚ democracy is one where everyone comes together to decide how the country should be run.

4 A ⬚ is a representative democracy where people also vote for a leader, often a president.

5 A monarchy is a government with one leader called a ⬚.

6 An ⬚ monarchy is one where a single monarch makes all the decisions about what a government does.

7 Constitutional monarchs are monarchies that also have elected ⬚, that help the monarch make decisions.

The U.S. Constitution

KEY POINTS

A constitution is a document that states the laws for a country or state. They describe how the government should work and how power should be shared.

The United States Constitution is the oldest constitution in the world that is still in use. It was written 1787 at the Constitutional Convention in Philadelphia. It became the law of the US in 1789 after most of the new country's thirteen states had approved it.

When the founders wrote the US Constitution, they had a few main goals. They wanted a document that would explain how the country's government would work. They wanted to make a democracy, or a government that was controlled not by a monarch but by the people. At first, they only wanted certain kinds of people to be able to vote. Only white men who owned a certain amount of land were allowed to vote. The specific rules for this depended on the state. The founders also wanted states and the federal (whole country) government to share power.

After the Revolutionary War, the thirteen states ratified the Articles of Confederation. This document gave the states a lot of power and the federal government very little power. This made it impossible for the federal government to collect taxes or enforce any laws. This didn't work well, so the founders met again and wrote the US Constitution to replace the Articles of Confederation. The US Constitution gives certain rights to the states and other rights to the federal government.

The US Constitution can be changed, but it is difficult to change it. Three-quarters of states and two-thirds of the Senate and House of Representatives have to approve any changes to the US Constitution. These changes are called amendments. Only twenty-seven amendments have been passed in the more than two hundred years since the Constitution was written. Some of the most important amendments ended slavery, gave Black people full citizenship, gave Black men the right to vote, and gave women the right to vote.

■ **Answer the questions.**

❶ What is the purpose of a constitution?

❷ What is an amendment?

■ Write true or false for each statement.

❶ A constitution is a document that states the laws for a country or state.

❷ A constitution describes how a government should work.

❸ The US Constitution, written in 1787, is no longer in use today.

❹ The US Constitution has always said that everyone could vote and have a say in how the government was run.

❺ The Articles of Confederation were different from the Constitution in that it gave more power to the states and less to the federal government.

❻ Changes to the US Constitution are called amendments.

Checks and Balances

KEY POINTS

The writers of the US Constitution wanted to keep any one person from having all of the power. They had been ruled by the king of England and they did not want to have a king again. In order to keep any part of the government from having too much power, the founders created a system of checks and balances in the US Constitution. They created three branches of government.

The legislative branch is made up of the Senate and the House of Representatives. Senators and representatives are elected by people in each state. Together, the Senate and the House of Representatives are called Congress. Some of the legislative branch's most important powers are to make laws and to declare war. They can also impeach presidents and federal judges if they have broken laws.

The executive branch is made up of the president, the cabinet, and fifteen departments, including the Department of Education and the Department of Defense. The executive branch recommends laws to Congress. It can also veto laws that Congress passes. This means that if the president doesn't agree with a law that Congress passes, the president can stop it from becoming a law unless two-thirds of both the Senate and the House of Representatives vote to make it a law. The president is the commander-in-chief of the US military. The president can send soldiers to fight in wars, but the president cannot declare a war on another country. Only Congress can do that.

The third branch of the US government is the judicial branch. The judicial branch is made up of courts with judges. The president chooses all federal judges, including the judges on the Supreme Court. However, the Senate has to approve judges. Judges decide if people or companies are guilty or if they owe money to others, sometimes with the help of a jury. The Supreme Court can also decide if a law goes against the US Constitution. If a state or federal law contradicts the US Constitution, they can declare it unconstitutional. In that case, it is no longer a law. Federal judges serve until they retire or die, unless they are impeached by Congress.

In this way, the legislative, executive, and judicial branches all have power over each other. The executive branch chooses judges. The legislative branch approves judges. The legislative branch makes laws. The executive branch approves laws. The judicial branch decides if laws are constitutional. The legislative branch can impeach judges or the president if they have broken laws. Through this system of checks and balances, the branches keep each other from getting too powerful.

■ Answer the questions.

① How many branches of government are there in the US?

② Explain the checks and balance system in your own words.

■ Fill in the boxes with help from the Key Points.

Executive Branch

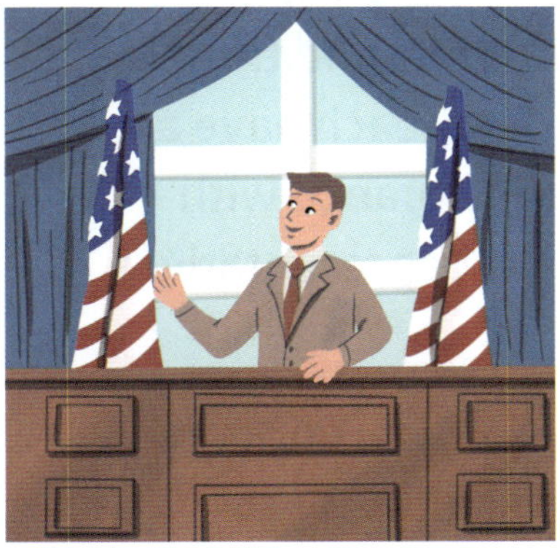

What are the powers?

Who checks them?

Legislative Branch

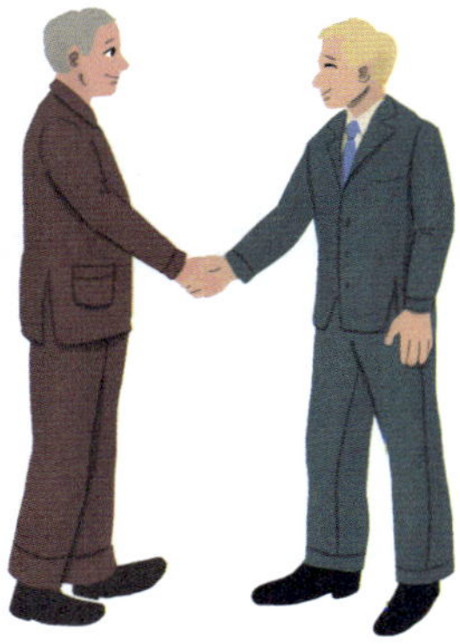

What are the powers?

Who checks them?

Judicial Branch

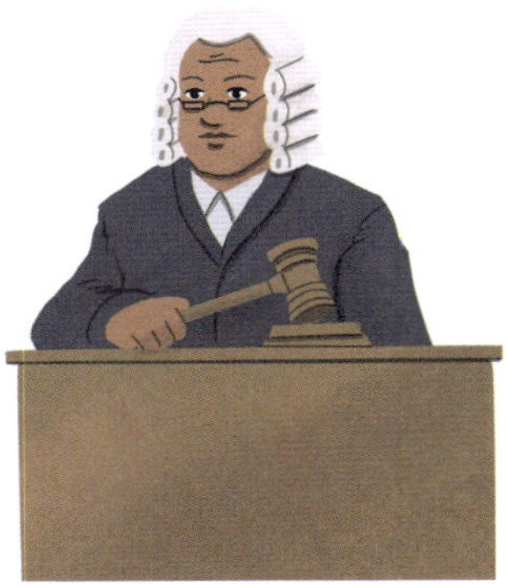

What are the powers?

Who checks them?

US State Governments and Constitutions

KEY POINTS

When the founders wrote the US Constitution, it was important to them that states have the power to make many of their own laws and decisions. It was also important that all of the states follow the US Constitution and respect federal laws. All 50 US states have their own constitutions and three branches of government, just like the federal government. They each have an executive branch with a governor. They each have a legislative branch with representatives. Most have a state senate and a state house of representatives. They each have a judicial branch with state courts.

The tenth amendment to the US Constitution states that any powers not given to the federal government by the Constitution belong to the states. That means that if the Constitution doesn't say that the federal government gets to decide something, the states get to decide. Because of this, laws are different in each state. People might pay different amounts of taxes. Schools might teach different things. Speed limits may be different.

When adults vote, they get to vote for local, state, and federal representation. Local representatives decide local laws and how money is spent in a city or town. State representatives decide state laws and how money is spent in the state. Federal representatives decide laws for the whole country and how money is spent in the whole country.

■ **Answer the questions.**

1 How many US states have their own constitutions?

2 If the Constitution doesn't say that the federal government gets to decide something, who gets to decide?

KEY POINTS

All US states have their own branches of government similar to the federal government. States have an executive branch run by a governor and towns have a mayor. There are state judges for the judicial branch and state representatives for the legislative branch. These people work together to help make laws and decide how states handle different issues. They are also elected officials which means they can change when people vote each year.

■ Ask your parent or guardian to help you fill in the information about your state government.
You can also use the internet with your parent or guardian's help.

❶ My state governor currently is [ ] .

❷ My state representatives are currently [ ]

and [ ] .

❸ My state has this many elected judges or justices: [ ] .

❹ My state senator is [ ] .

❺ My town/city mayor is [ ] .

❻ My town/city trustees are [ ] .

Brain Break
Word Search

■ Find the words below in the word search puzzle.

government	democracy	republic	monarchy
monarch	king	queen	emperor

M	B	K	I	N	G	C	D	E	M
G	Q	Z	X	C	V	B	D	F	O
O	W	V	F	R	J	N	E	G	N
V	R	E	S	H	B	L	M	H	A
E	T	M	C	K	G	K	O	J	R
R	E	P	U	B	L	I	C	K	C
N	Y	E	E	L	F	J	R	L	H
M	U	R	E	P	D	H	A	M	Y
E	I	O	W	Q	S	F	C	N	H
N	O	R	U	I	O	D	Y	B	G
T	P	T	R	E	Q	W	A	V	F
P	A	Y	Q	U	E	E	N	C	D
O	S	D	F	G	H	J	K	X	S
I	M	O	N	A	R	C	H	Z	A

Mindfulness Break!

■ Color the picture. Focus only on coloring and breathing.

Jigsaw Puzzles

■ Write the letter of each missing puzzle piece in the correct box.

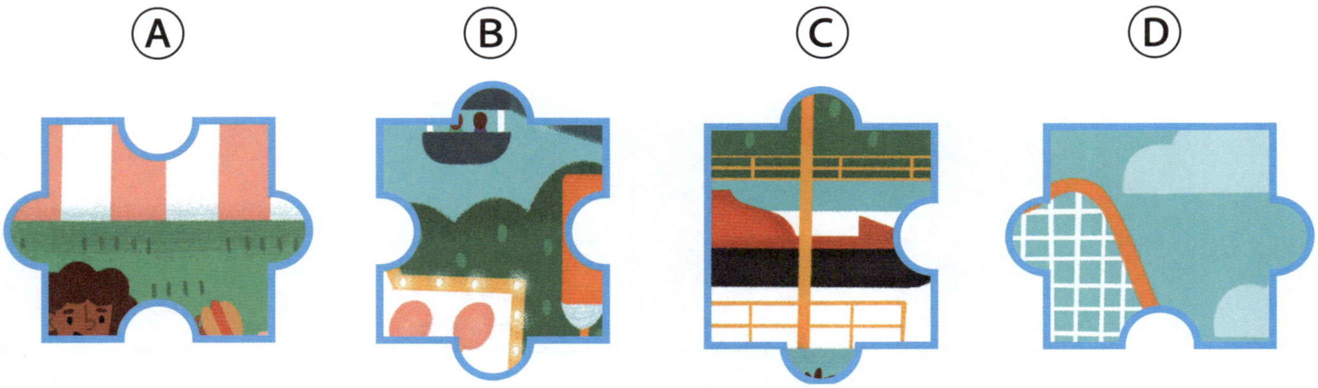

Ⓐ   Ⓑ   Ⓒ   Ⓓ

Ⓐ　　　Ⓑ　　　Ⓒ　　　Ⓓ

Maze Puzzles

■ Which section below completes the maze? Write a check mark (✔) in the box.

1

Ⓐ

Ⓑ

2

Ⓐ

Ⓑ

■ Draw a line to match the objects with their shadows.

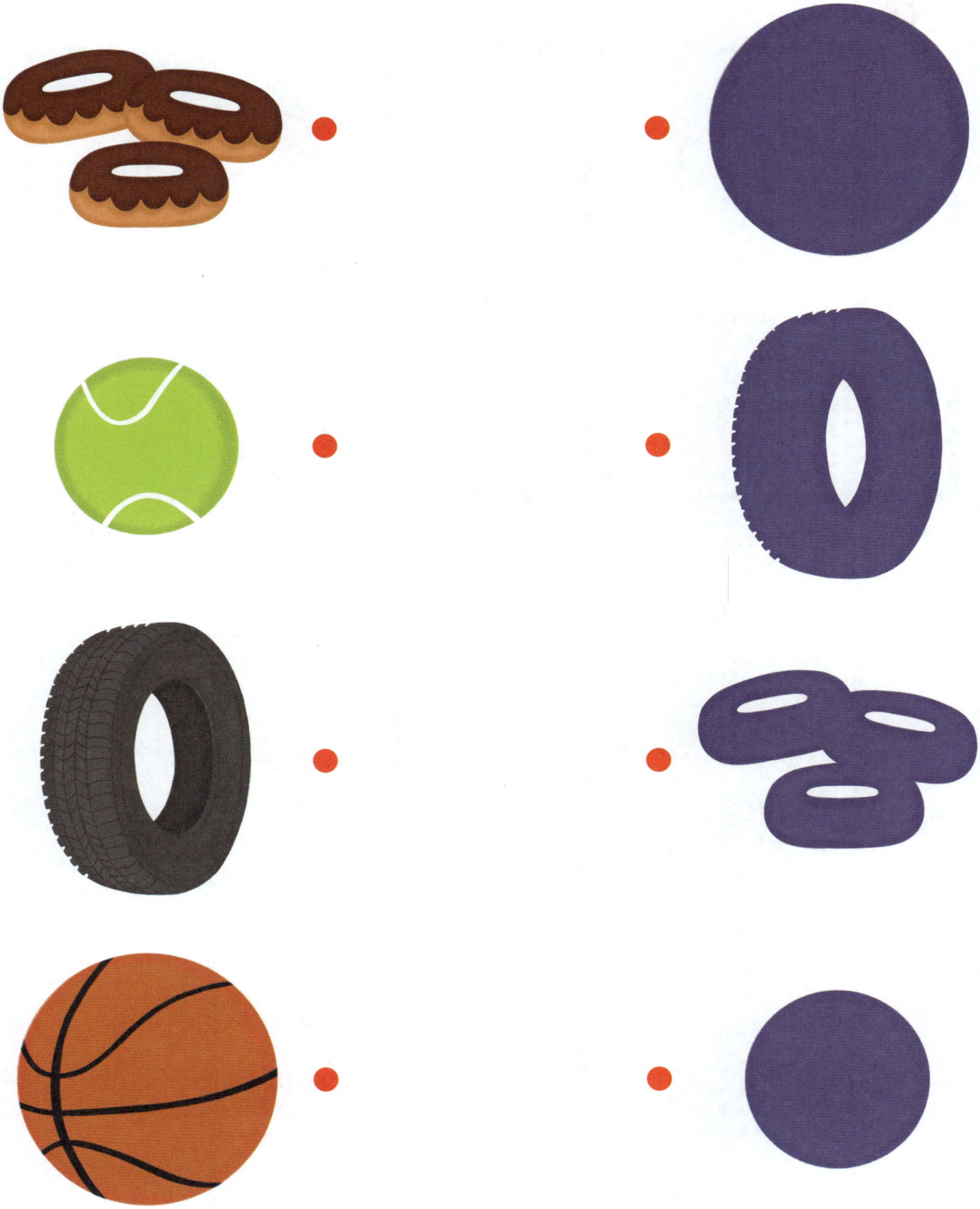

Date

Great Job Sticker

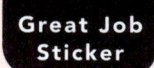

■ Draw a line to match the shadows with with the objects that made them.

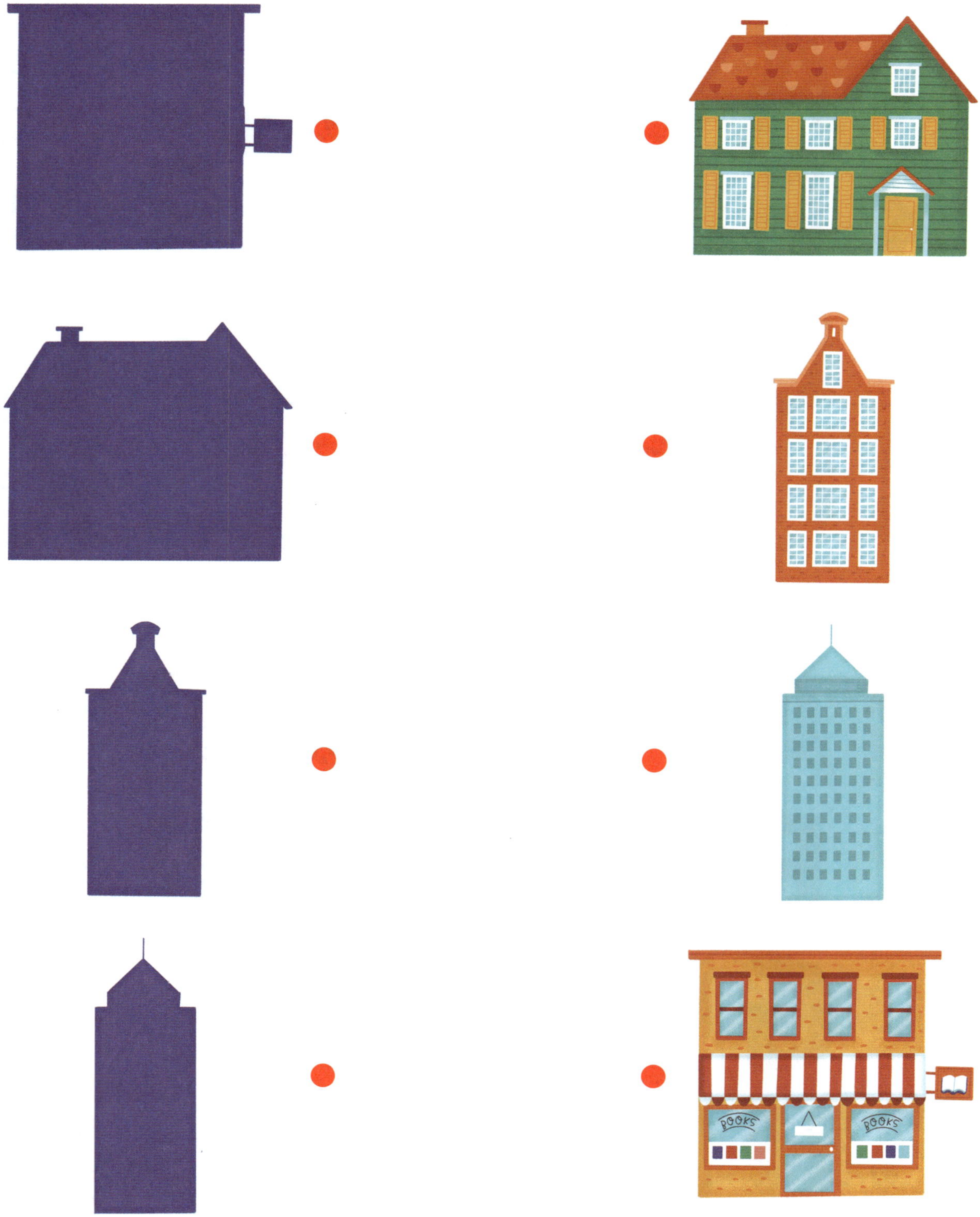

■ There is one letter or number that is different in each pair of images. Find it, and circle it in the lower image.

NAPAJACI
REMAHTRO
NGNIHSIL
BUPNOMUK

. . . .

NAPAJACI
REMAHTRO
NGNIHSIL
BUDNOMUK

6 4 7 3 9 1 4 5 9 7
0 2 6 1 7 3 9 1 6 8
7 1 0 2 8 9 3 3 2 0
8 6 5 0 4 5 3 5 0 2
1 4 8 2 9 8 4 6 7 5

6 4 7 3 9 1 4 5 9 7
0 2 6 1 7 3 9 1 6 8
7 1 0 2 8 9 3 3 2 0
8 6 5 0 4 5 3 5 6 2
1 4 8 2 9 8 4 6 7 5

Physical Education Break!

It's important to move your body and exercise!
Try this fun activity below to break up your studying!

■ Complete the exercise for each letter to spell your name.

Spell Your Name Exercise Game!

A-B-C	D-E-F	G-H-I
10 Jumping Jacks	15 Arm Circles	5 Lunges to the Left

J-K-L	M-N-O	P-Q-R
15 High Knees	Run in Place for 60 Seconds	5 Lunges to the Right

S-T-U	V-W-X	Y-Z
15 Toe Touches	15 Jumping Jacks	5 Sit Ups

Use this page to keep track of your progress throughout the book. Place a check mark in the box when you have completed a section.

Reading

Writing

Math

Science

Social Studies

Thinking Skills

KEY POINTS

Growing your vocabulary is essential for success as a reader and writer.

■ Use the context clues in the passage to determine the meaning of the underlined words.

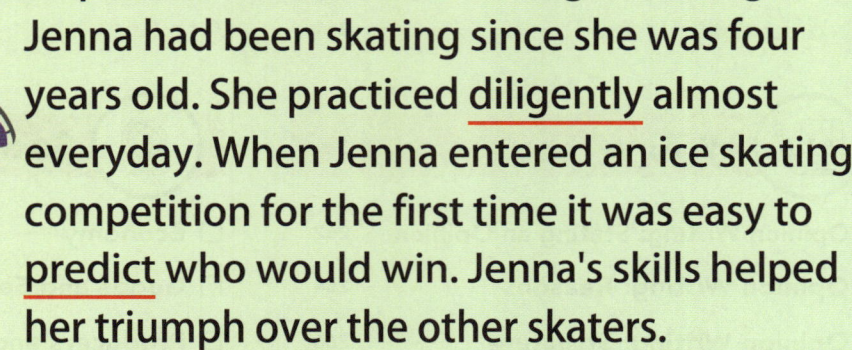

Jenna had a talent for ice skating. She was very good at it. She could easily glide across the ice rink on her skates. She could do quick turns and spins better than the other girls her age. Jenna had been skating since she was four years old. She practiced diligently almost everyday. When Jenna entered an ice skating competition for the first time it was easy to predict who would win. Jenna's skills helped her triumph over the other skaters.

talent → _____
_____

diligent → _____
_____

predict → _____
_____

triumph → _____
_____

■ Fill in the blank with the correct word from the Word Box.

Word Box

talented   diligently   predict   triumphed   competition

1 All the players practiced daily for the gymnastics

.

2 Jeramiah wanted to guess who would win the race.

He tried to _____ the outcome.

3 Miguel _____ at the science fair.

4 Farah _____ practiced her violin every day.

5 The singer was _____ .

She knew every song.

Vocabulary 2

KEY POINTS

Growing your vocabulary is essential for success as a reader and writer.

■ Use the context clues in the passage to determine the meaning of the underlined words.

> David is a careful kid. He avoids the monkey bars because he worries about getting hurt. His brother, Derek, is more bold. He takes risks when climbing and is not as careful. Derek can swiftly climb across the monkey bars. But Derek is a considerate brother. He helps David play safely and have fun.

careful →

bold →

swiftly →

considerate →

■ Fill in the blank with the correct word from the Word Box.

Word Box

careful   bold   swiftly   considerate   avoid

❶ Brandon jumped to [_____] the puddle.

❷ Carina was [_____] as she picked up the delicate vase.

❸ The coach [_____] replaced the injured player.

❹ Maya was [_____] and opened the door for her grandmother.

❺ Alec made a [_____] move and scored a winning goal for his team.

Multiple-meaning Words

KEY POINTS

Some words look and sound the same, but have different meanings.

Fly can be a noun meaning the name of an insect. Or it can be a verb like "a bird can fly."

It is important to pay attention to the other words in a sentence to help find the meaning of multiple-meaning words.

■ Choose the correct meaning of each underlined word.

❶ The <u>pitcher</u> was in his uniform ready to play.

    a a container for liquid

    b a position in a baseball game

❷ The dog's <u>bark</u> was very loud.

    a the sound a dog makes

    b the outside layer of a tree

❸ I <u>hear</u> an ice cream truck down the road!

    a to listen to a sound

    b a place someone is

■ Use the context clues in the passage to determine the meaning of the underlined words.

Casey went for a walk through his neighborhood. He could **hear** birds singing and other kids playing outside. He noticed the **leaves** on the trees were starting to change to red and yellow. Suddenly, he heard a **racket**. A dog had gotten out of the **yard** and was chasing a squirrel! Casey helped chase the dog. He watched the owner take the dog back inside safely. Then Casey walked back home.

❶ hear

   ⓐ to listen

   ⓑ a place someone is

❷ leaves

   ⓐ part of a tree

   ⓑ someone going from a place

❸ racket

   ⓐ an object used to play tennis

   ⓑ a loud noise

❹ yard

   ⓐ a term of measurement

   ⓑ part of a house that is outside

Decoding Words

KEY POINTS

An affix can be added to the beginning of a word to change the meaning. An affix can be a prefix like *dis-* or *un-* that goes at the beginning of a word, or it can be a suffix that goes at the end of a word. The word the affix is added to is often called the root word.

Ex. Connected with the prefix *dis-* becomes disconnected and means not connected.

Adding an affix changes the meaning of a sentence. For example:
We *disconnected* from the internet.
or
We *connected* to the internet.

■ Circle the affix in each word. Remember that some words may have a prefix and a suffix.

disagreeable	**useless**
unremarkable	**useful**
reorganize	**happiness**
reading	**fruitful**

■ **Choose the correct affix to complete each sentence.**

Word Box

un	ful	less	dis	re	s

1 Peter lied to his parents about his text grade.

He was [   ] honest .

2 Greg never showed up to work on time. He was [   ] reliable.

3 Our new puppy loves to fetch. She is very play [   ] .

4 Karen always broke her brother's toys. She was very

care [   ] .

5 Hannah had to [   ] write her essay for class.

6 There were many cow [   ] on the farm.

Brain Break
Trace the Path

■ Trace each path. Write the new words that can be made by combining the root words with each affix.

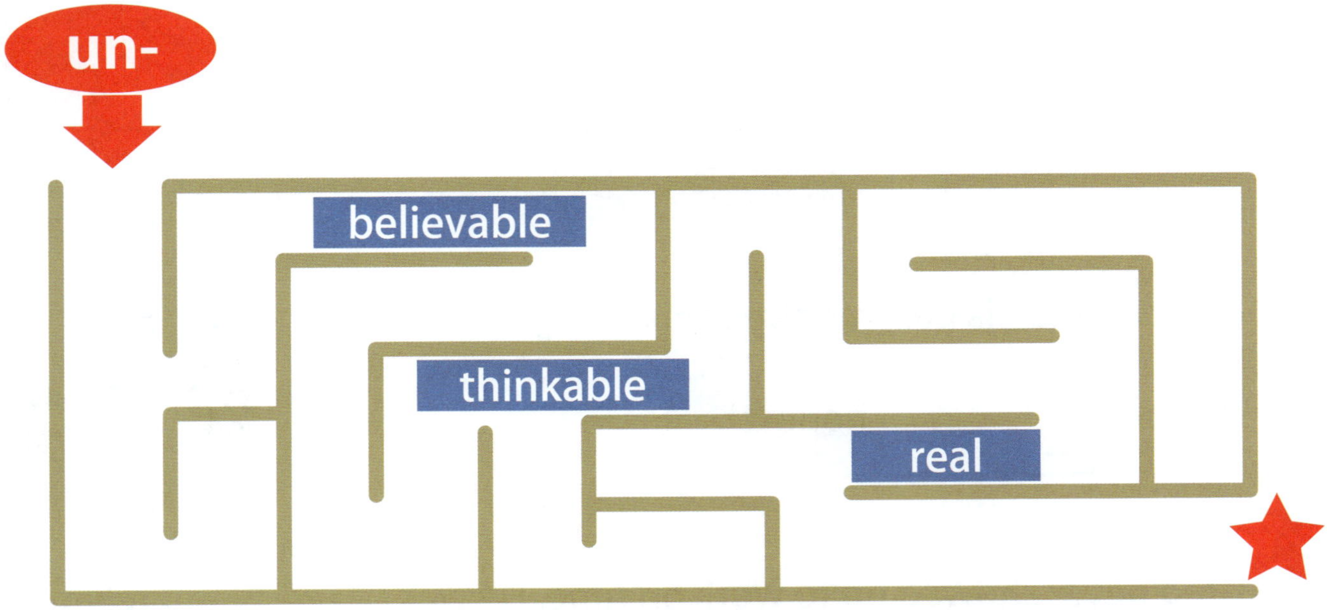

un-

believable

thinkable

real

① [ ]   ② [ ]   ③ [ ]

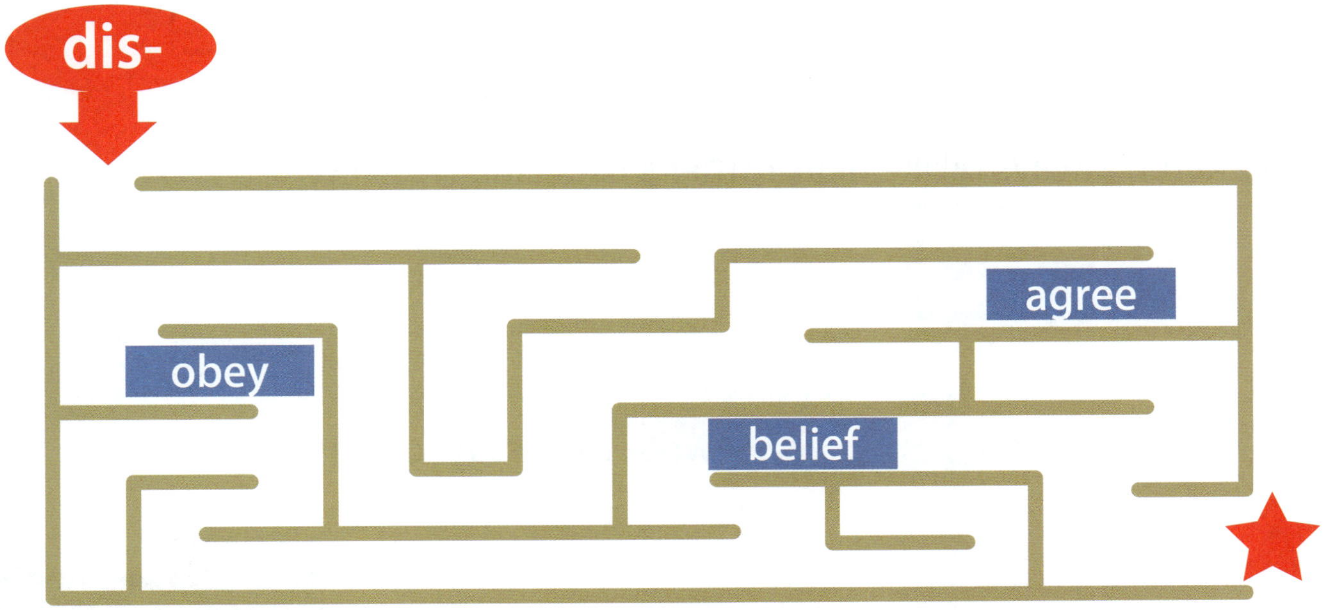

dis-

agree

obey

belief

① [ ]   ② [ ]   ③ [ ]

Mindfulness Break!

KEY POINTS

There are different ways to practice mindfulness. Focusing your attention on one word can help you stay in the moment and be mindful.

■ Choose a word to help you focus your mind. Fill in the answers below.

❶ Choose a word that makes you feel calm and relaxed.

❷ My word is [   ] .

❸ This word makes me feel [   ] .

❹ The color of my word would be [   ] .

❺ How do you feel after spending some time focusing on your mindful word?

[   ]

Opinion Writing: Stating an Opinion

KEY POINTS

Opinion pieces are a chance for a writer to give their opinion about a topic or a text. One of the most important things for a writer to do when they create an opinion piece is to state their opinion clearly! The reader should know exactly what the writer's opinion is on the topic.

■ Read the text below. Then write the author's opinion below.

I believe that we should all stop using plastic as much as possible. We all use plastic cups and bottles sometimes. But what happens to these pieces of plastic at the end of the meal? We may put them in the recycling bin, but that doesn't mean they always get recycled. A lot of plastic winds up in garbage dumps and even in the ocean. So pay attention, and stop using so much plastic!

■ In a few activities, you will write an opinion piece of your own. On this page, you will write several opinion statements about a topic. Then you will choose the opinion you want to write about. You can choose to write about one of the topics below, or a topic of your choice.

Topic ❶ Should kids get homework every night?

Topic ❷ What is the scariest animal?

Topic ❸ How old should you be when you get your first phone?

Topic ❹ What sport is the most difficult to play?

Opinion I will write about:

Opinion Writing: Reasons

KEY POINTS

It's not enough for an opinion text to just have an opinion! Opinion pieces also need to have reasons to back up the opinion. Reasons help the reader understand why the writer feels the way they do. They may also persuade the reader to feel the same way.

■ Underline the reasons in the text below:

Citizens of a community should help keep their streets clean by picking up litter. Having garbage around is not nice to look at. It can also cause rats and other pests to come out. Picking up garbage helps make your community look nicer and more pleasant. And, if you go out and pick up garbage, your neighbors will probably be interested in what you're doing. They may even want to help!

Date

Great Job Sticker

- When you write your opinion piece, you will need reasons to support your opinion. List at least four reasons here:

1

2

3

4

Opinion Writing: Structure

KEY POINTS

Usually an opinion piece has a introduction that hooks the reader or explains the topic. Then it has an opinion statement. The opinion is followed by reasons. Finally, it ends with a conclusion that gives a sense of closure.

■ Read the text below. Write an I above the introduction. Underline the opinion statement. Circle each reason. Write a C below the conclusion.

When you look around the supermarket, you probably think most of the food you see will eventually get eaten, right? Unfortunately, not all of it will. A surprising amount of food gets thrown out every day. We should all be careful to avoid wasting food. Food waste is bad for the environment, because it is a waste of resources. It's also a waste of money, since people pay for food that they wind up not using. And all of that wasted food goes into garbage dumps where it takes up lots of space! For all of these reasons, we should all take care not to buy more than we need.

Date

Great Job Sticker

Fill out the outline below to plan your opinion piece.

Introduction

Opinion Statement

Reasons

1

2

3

4

Conclusion

Writing an Opinion Piece

■ Use your outline to write your full opinion piece. Don't forget to include an introduction, opinion statement, reasons, and a conclusion.

Brain Break
Your Favorite Book

■ Write about your favorite book below. Why is it your favorite? Who would you recommend it to?

Mindfulness Break!

■ Meditation can be an important mindfulness tool. Read the steps below and try meditation!

Let's Start!

❶ Pick a quiet place and get comfortable!

❷ Sit up straight, but stay relaxed.

❹ Close your eyes and take a deep breath in and then let it out.

❸ Think about what your arms and legs are doing. Try and keep them relaxed.

❺ Focus on breathing, in and out.

❻ Notice when your mind starts to wander and try to bring it back to your breathing. Focusing on breathing in and out.

Bonus: You can also try a "mantra" to focus on while breathing like, "Today will be a good day!"

❼ When finished, open your eyes and bring your mind back to the present and what's around you.

Measurement 1

KEY POINTS

1 foot (ft.) = 12 inches (in.)
1 yard (yd.) = 3 feet (ft.) = 36 inches (in.)
1 mile (mi.) = 1,760 yards (yd.) = 5,280 feet (ft.)

■ Write the appropriate number in each box.

❶ 2 yards = ☐ feet

❷ 6 feet = ☐ inches

❸ 9 feet = ☐ yards

❹ 5,280 feet = ☐ mile

❺ 52,800 feet = ☐ miles

❻ 1,760 yards = ☐ mile

❼ 17,600 yards = ☐ miles

❽ ☐ inches = 9 feet

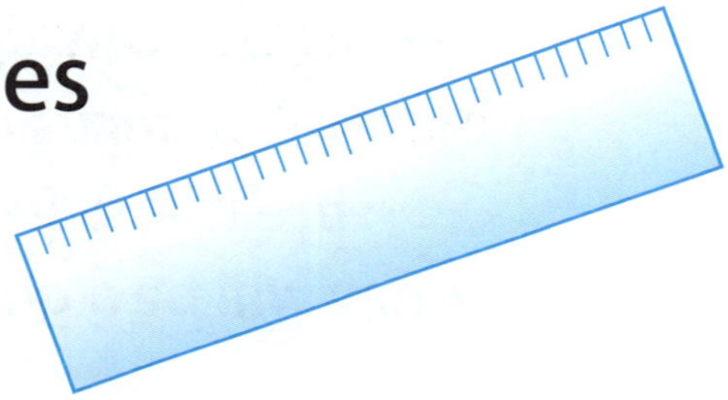

■ Circle the answer that gives the best estimate.

❶ the length of a spoon

> 5 inches   5 feet   5 yards

❷ the height of a basketball hoop

> 10 inches   10 miles   10 feet

❸ the width of a garden

> 15 inches   15 miles   15 yards

❹ the distance of a running trail

> 3 feet   3 inches   3 miles

Measurement 2

KEY POINTS

10 millimeters (mm) = 1 centimeter (cm)
100 centimeters (cm) = 1 meter (m)
1,000 meters (m) = 1 kilometer (km)

■ Write the appropriate number in each box.

1 100 mm = ☐ cm

2 3 cm = ☐ mm

3 500 cm = ☐ m

4 10 m = ☐ cm

5 2,000 m = ☐ km

6 5 km = ☐ m

7 1,000 mm = ☐ m

8 2,000 cm = ☐ m

■ Circle the answer that gives the best estimate.

❶ the length of a smartphone

15 centimeters   15 meters   15 millimeters

❷ the distance between two cities

20 centimeters   20 meters   20 kilometers

❸ the width of a bus

12 kilometers   12 meters   12 centimeters

❹ the distance of a marathon race

42 kilometers   42 meters   42 centimeters

Measuring Liquids

KEY POINTS

1 cup (c) = 8 ounces (oz.)   1 pint (pt.) = 2 cups (c)
1 quart (qt.) = 2 pints (pt.)   1 gallon (gal.) = 4 quarts (qt.)
1 liter (L) = 1,000 milliliters (mL)

■ Write the appropriate number in each box.

1 2 pints = ☐ cups

2 5 quarts = ☐ pints

3 ☐ gallons = 12 quarts

4 ☐ ounces = 4 cups

5 2,000 milliliters = ☐ liters

6 5 liters = ☐ milliliters

7 ☐ quarts = 8 pints

8 7 gallons = ☐ quarts

■ Circle the unit that would be good to measure each item.

❶ the size of an ice cream container

quart   inch   meter

❷ the size of a bottle of milk

millimeter   gallon   yard

❸ the size of a refrigerator

ounce   pint   liter

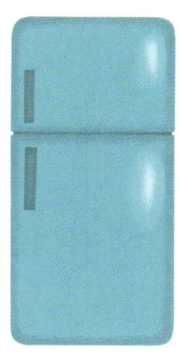

❹ the size of a can of juice

quart   milliliter   gallon

Measuring Weight

KEY POINTS

I pound (lb.) = 16 ounces (oz.)   I ton (t) = 2,000 pounds (lb.)

I kilogram (kg) = 1,000 grams (g)

I ton (t) = 1,000 kilograms (kg)

■ Write the appropriate number in each box.

❶ 2 pounds = [ ] ounces

❷ 160 ounces = [ ] pounds

❸ [ ] tons = 6,000 pounds

❹ [ ] pounds = 1 ton

❺ 4 kilograms = [ ] grams

❻ 8,000 grams = [ ] kilograms

❼ [ ] tons = 3,000 kilograms

❽ 7 tons = [ ] kilograms

■ Circle the unit that would be good to measure each item.

❶ the weight of flour to bake a small cake

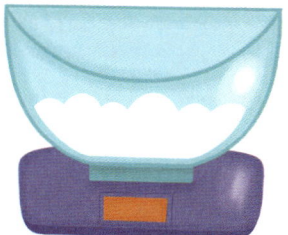

> pound   kilogram   ton

❷ the weight of a zipper bag

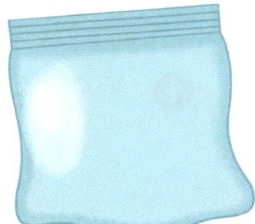

> pound   kilogram   gram

❸ the weight of a medium-sized cat

> ton   ounce   kilogram

❹ the weight of a whale

> ton   gram   pound

Measuring Perimeter

KEY POINTS

Perimeter

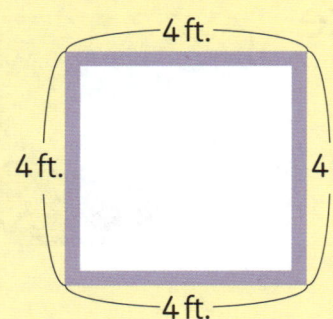

4 ft.

4 ft. 4 ft.

4 ft.

The **perimeter** is the total distance around a shape. You can find the perimeter by adding up the lengths of all the sides.

$$4 + 4 + 4 + 4 = 16 \text{ feet}$$

■ **Find the perimeter of each shape.**

1

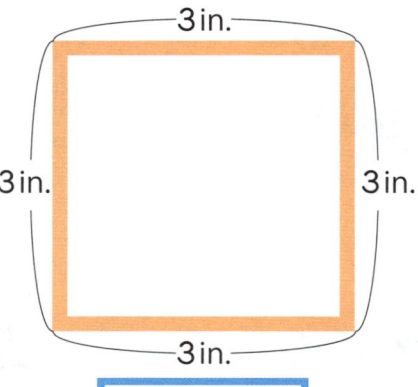

3 in.

3 in. 3 in.

3 in.

[   ] inches

2

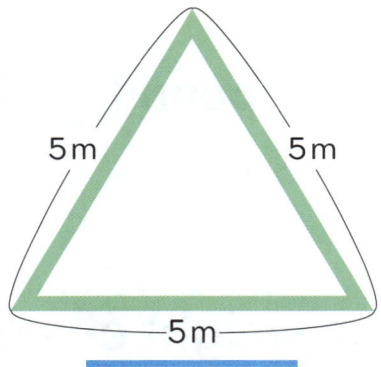

5 m 5 m

5 m

[   ] meters

3

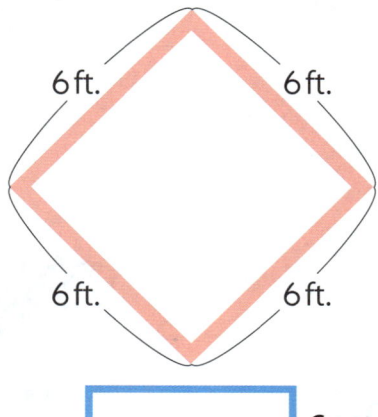

6 ft. 6 ft.

6 ft. 6 ft.

[   ] feet

4

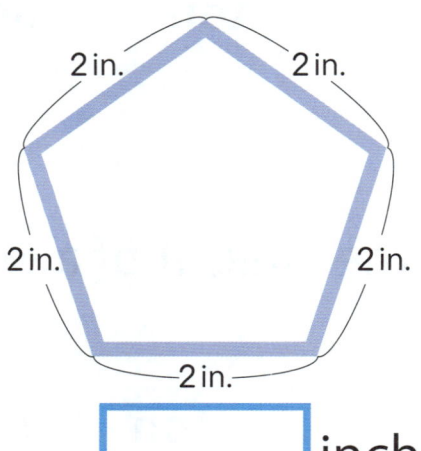

2 in. 2 in.

2 in. 2 in.

2 in.

[   ] inches

■ **Find the perimeter of each shape.**

①

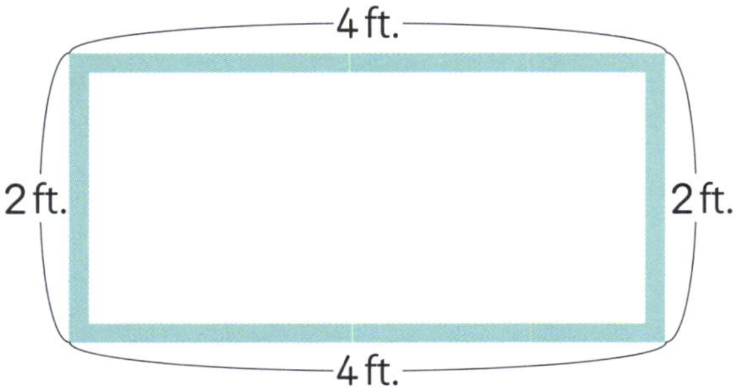

4 ft.

2 ft.   2 ft.

4 ft.

[ ] feet

②

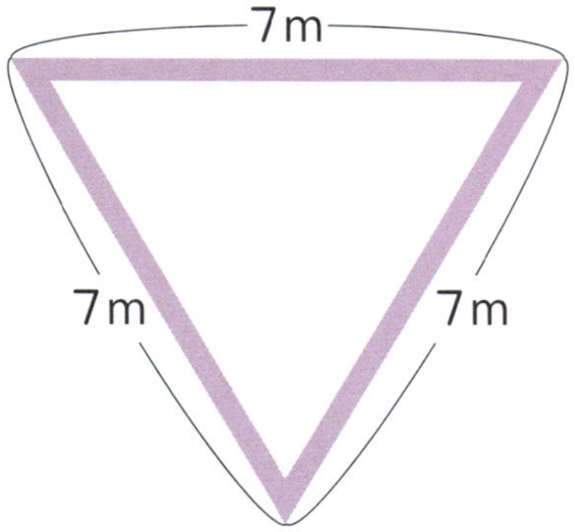

7 m

7 m   7 m

[ ] meters

③

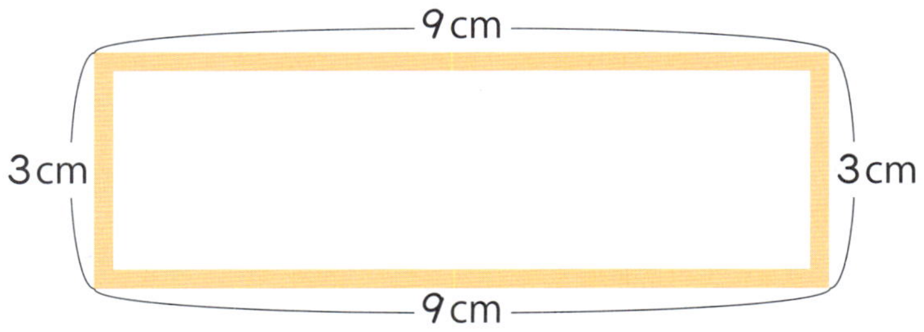

9 cm

3 cm   3 cm

9 cm

[ ] centimeters

④

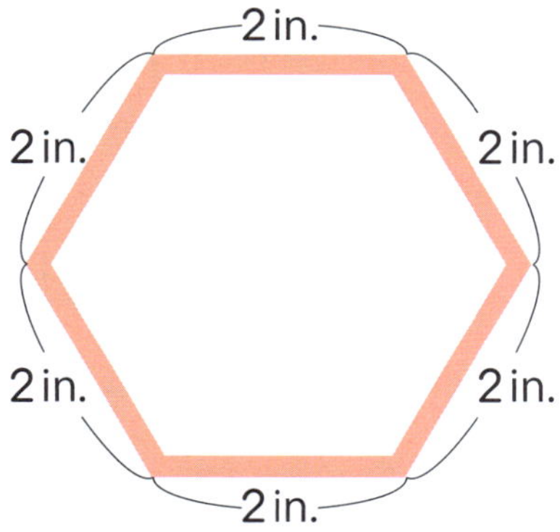

2 in.

2 in.   2 in.

2 in.   2 in.

2 in.

[ ] inches

⑤

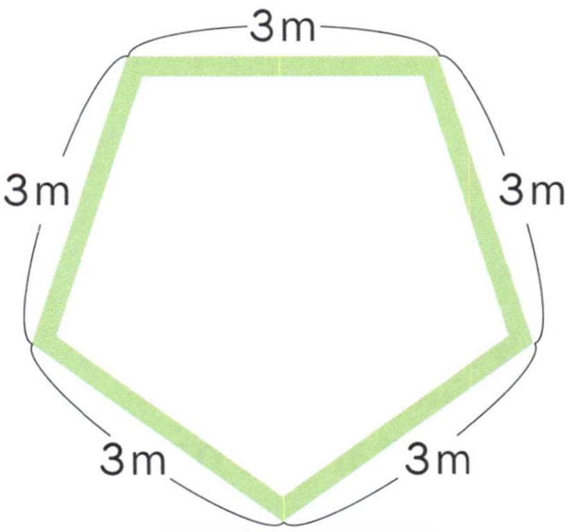

3 m

3 m   3 m

3 m   3 m

[ ] meters

⑥

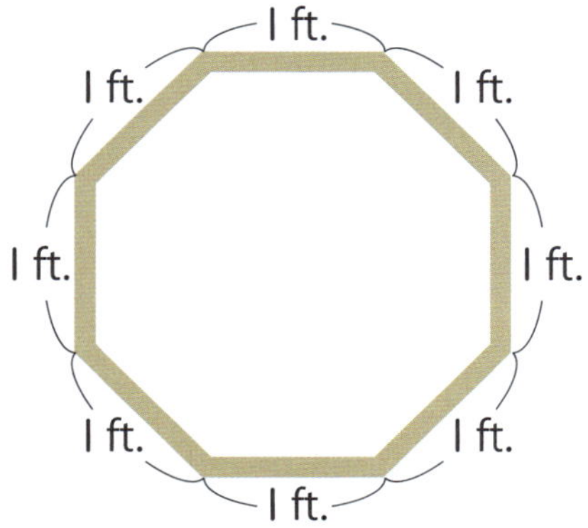

1 ft.

1 ft.   1 ft.

1 ft.   1 ft.

1 ft.   1 ft.

1 ft.

[ ] feet

Brain Break
Area and Square Unit Quiz

■ How many square units are in each rectangle? Write the number in the box.

1

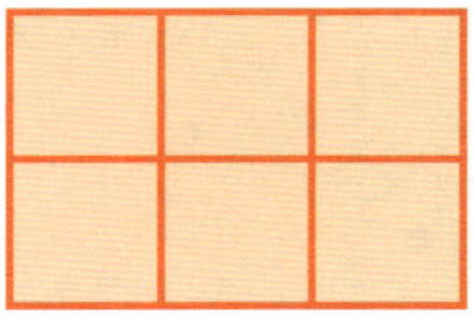

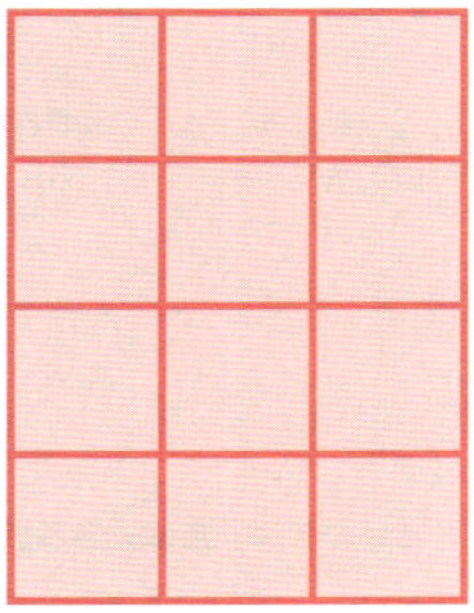

| | square units

2

| | square units

3

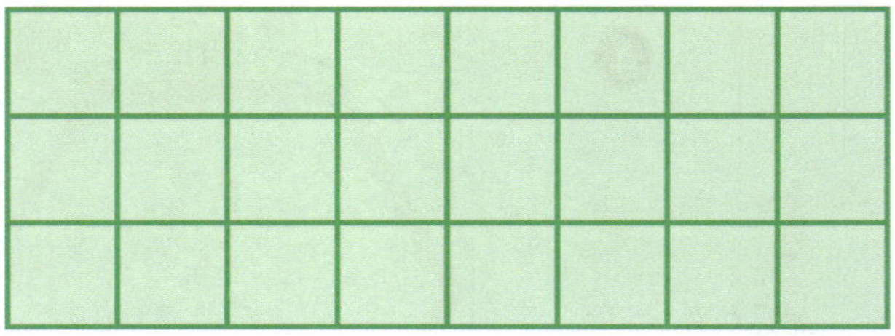

| | square units

4

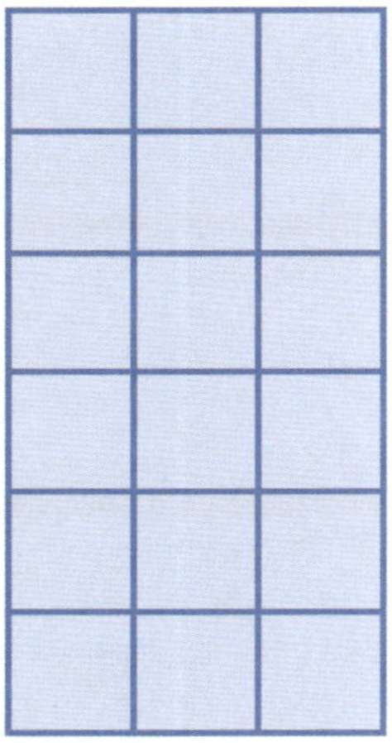

| | square units

| Remember |

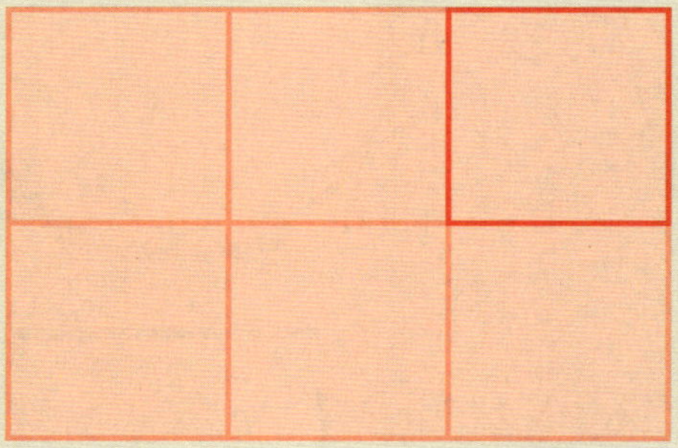

← **1 square unit**

This rectangle has 6 square units. So the area of the rectangle is 6 square units.

■ **Write a check mark (✓) for any pair of rectangles that have the same area.**

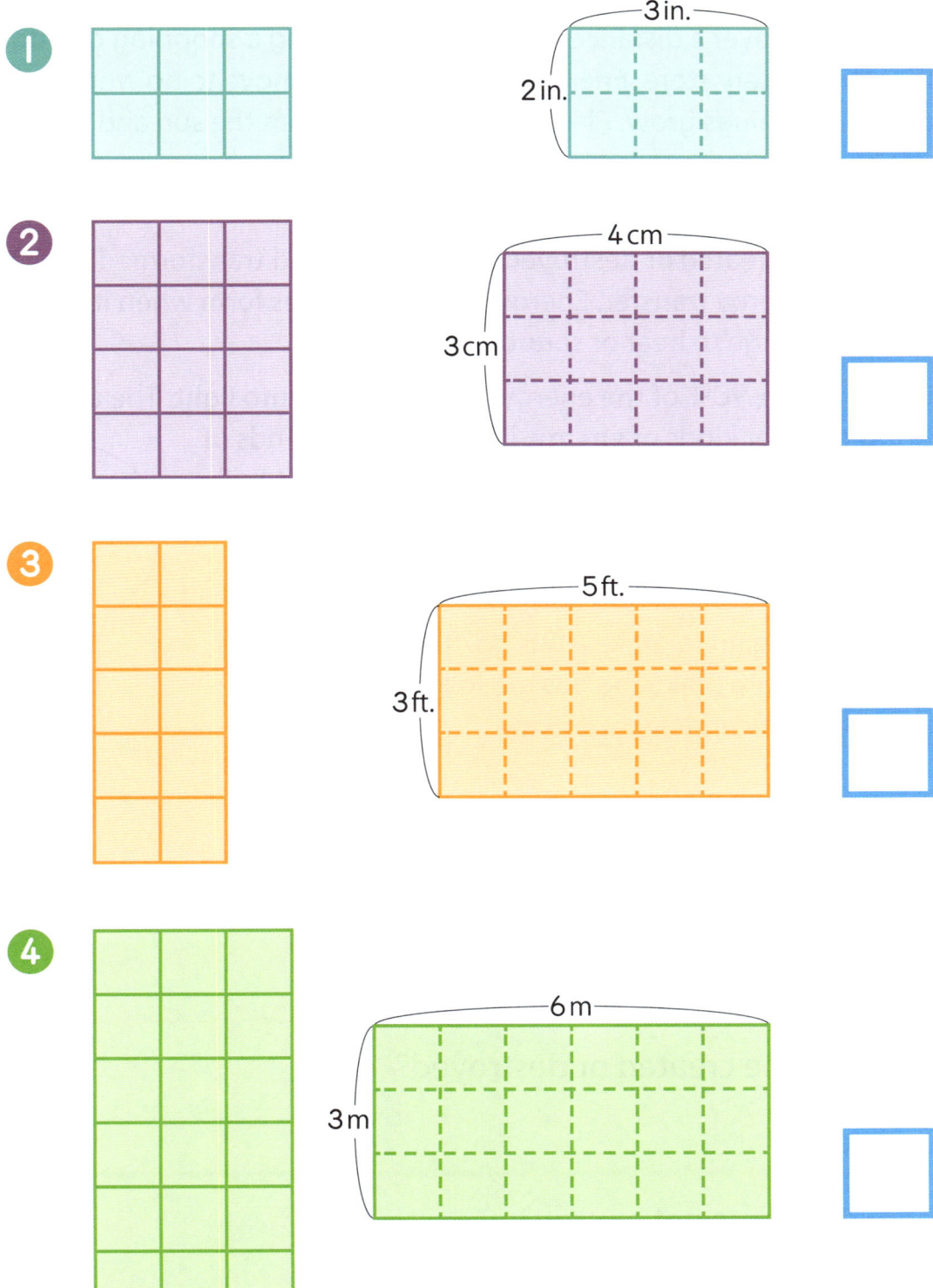

KEY POINTS

In science, energy is defined as the ability to do work. In this definition, work means using force over a distance–for example, pushing a shopping cart down the aisle at the grocery store. Energy makes machines move to do work. Energy also makes living things grow. Plants gather energy from the sun and turn it into food through photosynthesis. Animals eat plants or other animals and get energy from them.

Energy cannot be created or destroyed, only moved and transformed. Moving energy is called energy transfer. Energy is often changes form when it is used. Some of it can change to heat or sound energy.

In an LED light bulb, 90% of the energy used is turned into light. The other 10% is converted to other kinds of energy, like heat. Older kinds of light bulbs are much less efficient. That's why older light bulbs feel so hot if you accidentally touch them! So, even though energy cannot be destroyed, it can stop being available for us to use in the same way. If you burn gas to make a bus go, it cannot be used again to make a bus go. It has been turned into motion energy to make the bus move and into heat energy, which is why engines are so hot.

■ Answer the questions.

❶ What is the scientific definition of energy?

_____

❷ Can energy be created or destroyed?

_____

❸ Where do plants get energy?

_____

■ Answer true or false for each statement.

1 Energy is the ability to do work.

2 Energy helps living things grow.

3 Animals get energy from the sun.

4 Energy is destroyed when it is used.

5 When energy is transferred it can change form.

6 A bus uses the energy from fuel to move.

Forms of Energy 1

KEY POINTS

Energy has many forms. It can transform from one kind of energy to another.

Light is a kind of radiant energy. Radiant energy travels in waves. Other kinds of radiant energy, like x-rays and radio waves, are invisible to us. We can see light energy. It can travel across empty spaces. The Sun gives off radiant energy, including light. Light bulbs and burning candles also give off light energy.

Sound energy is moving energy that is produced by the back and forth vibration of an object. Drums, trains, people's voices, and thunder all give off sound energy.

Heat, or thermal energy, is produced when molecules and atoms (the tiny particles that make up an object) move. The faster they move, the more heat they give off. Fires, radiators, and boiling water give off thermal heat.

Motion energy is the energy stored in a moving object. An object needs energy to move. Before it stops moving, it releases that energy. For example, if you kick a soccer ball, you are transferring motion energy to the soccer ball. If the ball accidentally hits a window and breaks it, the energy from the ball is transferred to the window. Wind is another kind of motion energy. Its power can be captured using wind turbines. The wind makes the turbines turn and the energy is stored to be used as electrical energy.

■ **Answer the questions.**

1 What is motion energy?

_____

2 Which is not an example of a form of energy?

Ⓐ **light**   Ⓑ **sound**   Ⓒ **motion**   Ⓓ **house**

■ **Match the energy source.**

   •

   •

   •

   •

•    **Light**

•    **Sound**

•    **Thermal**

•   **Motion**

Forms of Energy 2

KEY POINTS

Other forms of energy can be more complex.

Mechanical energy is energy stored through tension. If you stretch out a rubber band, you are using energy to do that. That energy is stored as mechanical energy in the rubber band. When you let it go and it flies through the air, it releases the energy, probably as sound and heat.

Chemical energy is energy that is stored in the bonds of molecules and atoms. It holds the molecules together. Chemical energy can be transformed into heat through burning. For example, burning wood turns its stored chemical energy into thermal energy, or heat. Our bodies transform the stored chemical energy in food into mechanical energy and thermal energy to allow us to move and to keep our bodies warm.

Electrical energy is energy that moves in tiny particles called electrons. Lightning is an example of electrical energy in nature. Humans have learned how to use electrical energy to power things that we use, like computers and refrigerators.

Gravitational energy is stored in an object's height and weight. The higher up and the heavier an object is, the more gravitational energy it has. If you skateboard down a hill, gravitational energy will make you go quickly down the hill. If you drop a stone from a bridge over a river, gravitational energy will make the stone fall down into the water. Hydropower captures the gravitational energy stored in water and stores it so we can use it to produce electricity.

■ **Answer the questions.**

1 Where is chemical energy stored?

2 Where is gravitational energy stored?

■ Identify the type of the energy that is used in each case.

1 When riding a bike, you move your legs to move the pedals and make the bike move.

2 You have a sandwich for lunch so you have energy to swim after school.

3 You plug in your computer to charge it.

4 You are riding a skateboard down a hill and picking up speed as you go.

Potential vs Kinetic Energy

KEY POINTS

Potential energy is stored energy. Kinetic energy is moving energy. Energy can change from potential energy to kinetic energy. Chemical, gravitational, and mechanical energy are all forms of potential energy. An example of chemical potential energy is coal, which can be burned to make heat. Before it is burned, the energy in the coal is potential. Once it is burning, the energy is transformed into heat and light energy, which are kinetic energy. If a sled is at the top of a snowy hill, it has stored gravitational energy, which is potential energy. If the sled starts to go down the hill, the energy changes to motion energy, which is kinetic energy.

Mechanical energy is energy stored through tension. For example, the coiled spring in a jack-in-the-box toy stores potential energy. When it changes into motion energy, the jack-in-the-box pops up. Heat, light, sound, and electrical energy are all forms of kinetic energy. Kinetic energy moves. Heat, or thermal energy is the movement of the molecules in an object. The faster they move, the more heat they give off. Light moves across spaces in light waves. Sound moves in sound waves. It is produced by objects vibrating back and forth. Electrical energy is the movement of tiny particles called electrons and protons. This moves electricity from one place to another.

■ **Answer the questions.**

1 What is potential energy?

_____

2 What is kinetic energy?

_____

3 Is the heat energy from burning wood potential or kinetic energy?

_____

■ **Write whether the situation has potential or kinetic energy.**

❶ An apple hanging on a tree.

❷ An apple falling from a tree.

❸ A child winding up to throw a ball.

❹ A ball moving through the air after being thrown.

❺ A rollercoaster stopped at the top of the hill track.

❻ A rollercoaster going down the hill on a track.

❼ An arrow flying towards a target.

❽ An arrow pulled back in a bow.

Brain Break
Science Journal 5

Rubber bands hold potential energy. Find a rubber band or a hair tie. Follow the steps below to see how the energy from stretching the rubber band changes to motion energy.

Step 1: Stretch the rubber band one or two inches between your fingers.

Step 2: Let it go and see how far it travels. Make sure to point the rubber band away from yourself when you let go.

Step 3: Take the rubber band and stretch it as far as possible.

Step 4: Let it go and see how far it goes.

Step 5: Repeat the process, stretching the rubber band different lengths each time.

Questions:

❶ Do the rubber bands travel farthest when they are stretched more or less?

❷ Is the distance the rubber band flies the same or different for each stretch?

❸ What forces act on the rubber band as it flies through the air?

■ Color the picture.

Economy

KEY POINTS

Economics is the study of the economy. The economy is the part of society that creates wealth. Wealth is money and things that are worth money, like land, food, cars, and labor. Labor is the work that a person does to create value. You can also say that the economy is how people make, use, buy, and sell stuff. You might have heard people talk about the economy being "good" or "bad." When people say this, they are often talking about the economy of the country where they live. Each country has its own economy, but there is also a world economy. Countries buy and sell things to each other, so their economies affect each other.

There are a lot of factors that make an economy "good" or "bad." In general, when the economy is doing well, unemployment is low. That means that almost everyone who wants to have a job can find a job. In a good economy, most people earn enough money to buy the things they need and the things they want. Businesses make money, hire more workers, and pay them well.

In a bad economy, unemployment is high. Lots of people who want jobs can't find them, or they have to take jobs that pay badly and don't use their skills. Many businesses lay people off, which means they take away their jobs because they can't or don't want to pay them anymore. Many businesses close. Some people don't have enough money to pay for the things they need, like a place to live, food to eat, medical care, and clothes. Even people who have enough money for these essential things feel worried that they could lose their jobs. They try to save more money in case of an emergency. Because they are spending less money, this makes it harder for businesses to earn enough money to hire more people again.

■ Answer the questions.

❶ **What is the economy?**

❷ **What happens in a good economy?**

❸ **What happens in a bad economy?**

■ Fill in the blanks to complete each statement.

❶ [ ] is the study of the economy.

❷ The economy is the part of the society that creates

[ ].

❸ [ ] is the work a person does to create value.

❹ A country's economy can be [ ] or

[ ].

❺ When an economy is good, [ ] is low. When an

economy is bad, [ ] is high.

❻ High unemployment means there are not enough

[ ] in an economy.

Goods and Services

KEY POINTS

Countries, companies, and people earn money by selling goods and services. Goods and services are both things that have value. People want them and are willing to pay for them.

Goods are physical things that you can touch. Carrots and loaves of bread are goods. Soccer balls, winter coats, backpacks, cars, bicycles, and houses are all goods. Some goods cost a little bit of money and others cost a lot. For example, a banana costs around twenty-five cents. A house usually costs hundreds of thousands of dollars!

Services are things that people do for others, often in exchange for money. Babysitters provide childcare. Doctors provide medical care. Hairdressers cut and dye people's hair. Car mechanics fix cars. People with these jobs might also charge for some goods, like if a mechanic has to buy a new part in order to fix the car. When people are paid for services, they are paid for their time, work, and expertise. People who provide services often have to study at school to learn how to do their jobs well. Others learn on the job and from people with more experience.

The economy is based on people, companies, and countries creating, selling, and buying goods and services from each other.

■ **Answer the questions.**

❶ What is a good?

_____

❷ What is a service?

_____

❸ Name three kinds of goods that you or your family buy.

_____

■ Determine if the items are goods or services.

1 You buy a new book from a bookstore.

| Good | Service |

2 You pay for a haircut.

| Good | Service |

3 Nathan's mom bought him a new bike.

| Good | Service |

4 Samantha bought her brother an ice cream.

| Good | Service |

5 Thomas took his dog to the vet for a shot.

| Good | Service |

6 Jeanette is a math tutor.

| Good | Service |

7 Liu's dad fixes cars.

| Good | Service |

8 Xavier and Kyle made lemonade to sell at their lemonade stand.

| Good | Service |

Producers and Consumers

KEY POINTS

Economies have producers and consumers. Producers make goods and/or services and sell them. Consumers buy and use goods and services. Most people are both producers and consumers.

A producer could be an individual person or a company. A farmer might grow and sell tomatoes. They are a producer of tomatoes. The people who buy them are consumers. A nail artist sells the service of doing other people's nails. The people who pay the nail artist to do their nails are consumers. A clothing company could employ designers, sewers, and others to design and make clothing. The company and the people who work for it are producers. People who buy and wear the clothes are consumers.

Imagine if your family had to produce all of the things you use yourself. You would not have as many things. For example, it would be impossible to make your own computer. Even if you know how to put the pieces together to make a computer, you probably don't have your own mines where you can find your own copper, lead, zinc, aluminum, and more. And you probably don't have your own processing centers to turn those minerals into computer parts. Even if you just had to grow your own food, you would have much less variety. For example, if you live somewhere where rice can be grown, it's probably too wet and warm to grow wheat.

Because we live in a big economy where consumers can buy from producers in different parts of the world, we can have a much wider variety of products than if we had to produce everything ourselves or could only buy things produced by the people we know.

■ **Answer the questions.**

1 What do producers do?

2 What do consumers do?

3 What is an advantage of having a big economy where consumers can buy from producers in different parts of the world?

■ Write true or false for each statement.

❶ Producers make goods.

❷ Consumers buy goods and services.

❸ A farmer growing tomatoes is a consumer.

❹ Economies need producers and consumers.

❺ We have a variety of products because we consume goods from all over the world.

❻ If you had to make everything you own, you would own fewer products.

Earning, Saving, and Spending

KEY POINTS

People earn money by working. Many people work for companies, organizations, or governments that pay them for their work. Other people have their own businesses and are paid directly by their customers. For example, if someone has a house-painting business, customers will pay the owner of the business. If the business owner has employees who help with the painting, the owner will pay the employees for their work. Some money goes to pay for the supplies like paint and ladders, some goes to pay taxes to the government, and the rest of the money is profit for the business owner.

People save money for several reasons. They save for retirement so that when they are older and stop working, they will still have money to live on. They save in case of an emergency when they will need a lot of money at once. They save up for big expenses, like buying a new car, sending a child to college, or going on an exciting trip.

When people spend the money they earn or save, they spend it on needs and wants. Needs are goods and services like groceries and doctors visits Wants are more fun items like a trip to an amusement park or a new video game. People need to be careful of overspending on wants and not having enough money for their needs. This is why it is important to understand earning, saving, and spending.

Kids can earn, save, and spend, too. You can ask your family if there are extra chores you can do for money. You can also ask your family to tell neighbors and friends that you are looking for opportunities to earn money. Maybe you like gardening and could weed someone's garden or rake someone's yard. Maybe you love animals and could feed someone's fish when they're away. Some kids receive allowances from their families or are given money for birthdays or holidays. In some families, all money belongs to the family as a unit.

■ **Answer the questions.**

❶ Define earning in your own words.

❷ Name two examples of wants when it comes to spending money.

❸ Name two reasons why people save money.

■ Write if the statement is about earning, saving, or spending money.

1 Francis buys new clothes for school.

2 Pauline makes her first paycheck at the café where she works.

3 Joan makes money by working as an assistant vice principal.

4 Gaston put his allowance in a piggybank. He wants to buy a new video game.

5 Mei keeps her birthday money from her grandparents.

6 Arjan buys himself and his sister candy at the movies.

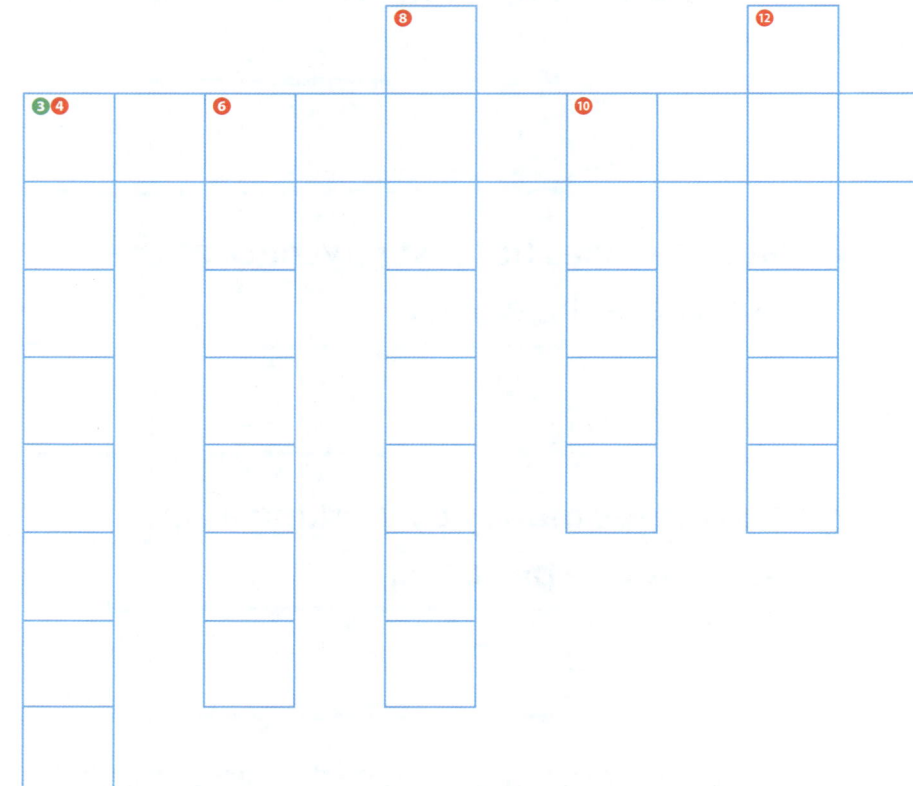

Brain Break
Crossword Puzzle

■ Use the clues to complete the crossword puzzle.

goods
employment
labor
economics
product
consumer
money
income

Across

❶ Items you can buy and consume.
❸ Having a job.

Down

❷ Performing work for a wage.
❹ The study of the economy.
❻ An item than can be bought or consumed.
❽ The person who buys and uses a product.
❿ Form of payment used to pay for and buy items or services.
⓬ The money you make from having a job.

Mindfulness Break!

KEY POINTS

Praise is expressing admiration or approval of something or someone's actions. It is important to praise ourselves, but also to praise people around us for their good actions. Praise is important, but how we praise each other and even ourselves makes all the difference!

■ Read each situation and write what you would say to praise each person.

1 You aced your test.

> **How would you praise yourself?**

2 Your best friend didn't make the soccer team they tried out for.

> **How would you praise them?**

3 Your younger sibling is afraid to go down the slide, but they try anyway.

> **How would you praise them?**

4 Your mom made your favorite dinner.

> **How would you praise her?**

5 Your pet dog learned a new trick on the first try!

> **How would you praise them?**

■ Write a check mark (✓) below the picture that comes next in the pattern.

①

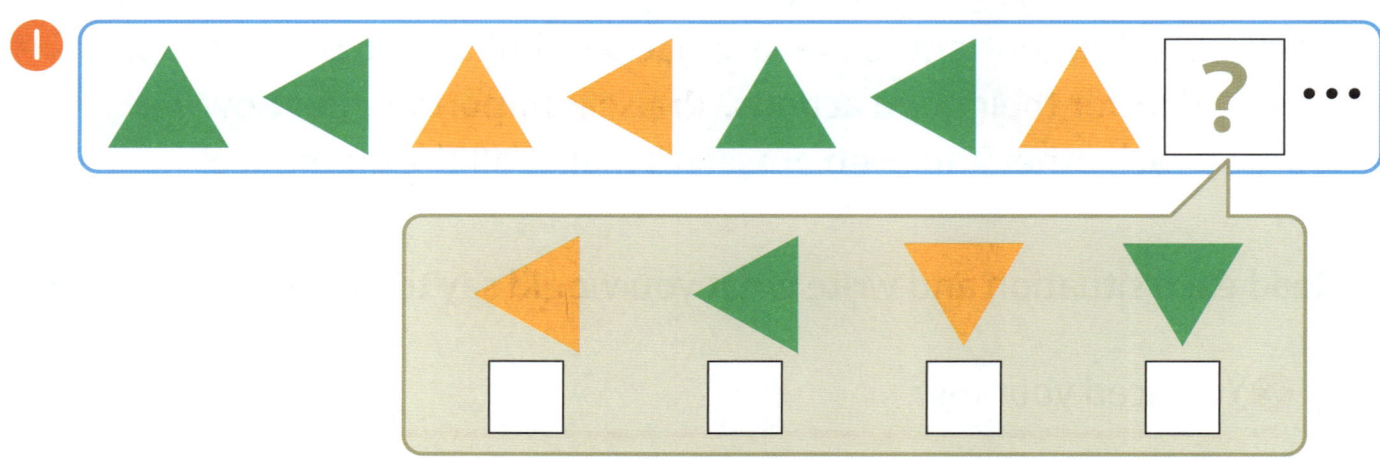

②

③

Date

Great Job Sticker

Use the pattern to complete the blank area.

1

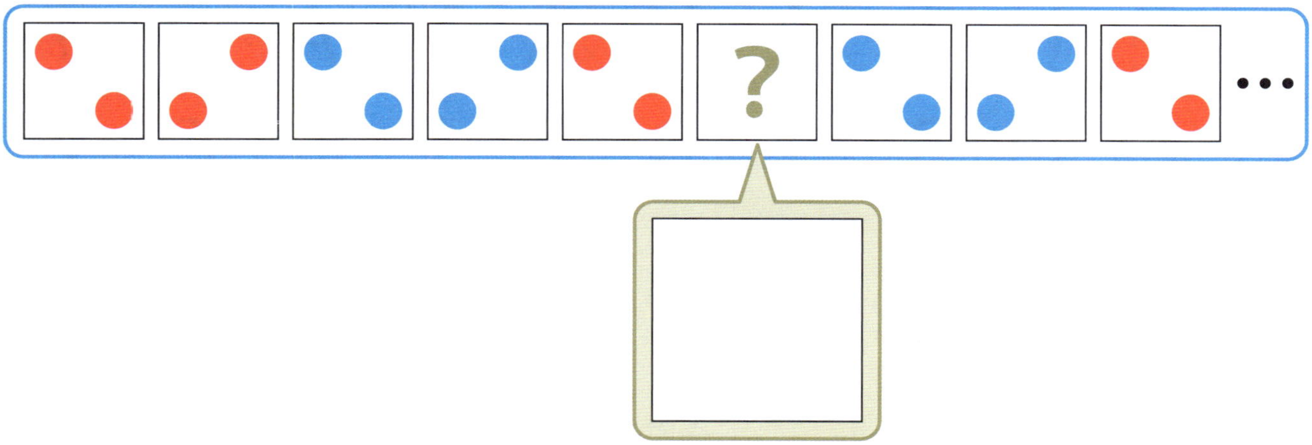

2

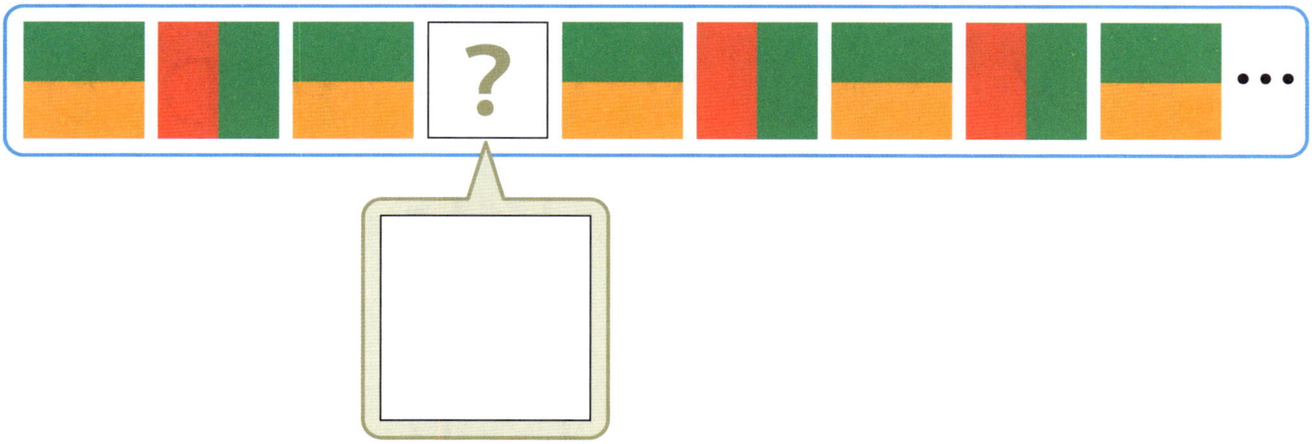

3

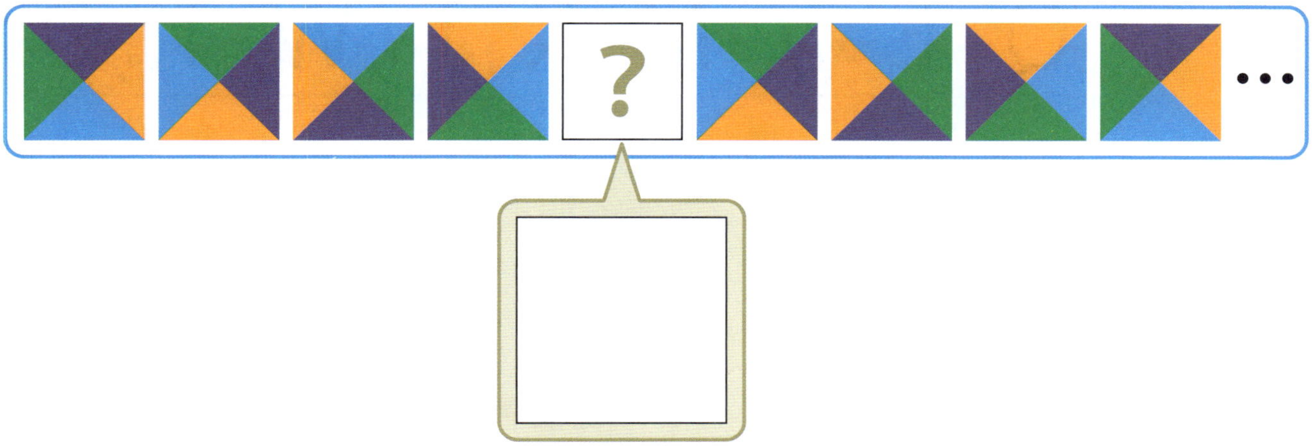

Word Search

■ Find and circle the fruit words pictured below.

G	U	B	A	N	A	N	A	P	J
W	H	T	I	B	Z	S	M	C	Y
A	V	Z	N	A	B	X	E	S	R
W	A	T	E	R	M	E	L	O	N
O	L	X	G	S	W	Q	P	T	M
R	Y	I	B	N	O	V	P	D	U
A	R	F	L	Z	J	G	A	X	B
N	C	W	J	O	T	R	Q	E	V
G	K	T	Y	S	E	P	A	R	G
E	Q	E	V	M	K	F	W	T	O

■ **Find and circle the vegetable words pictured below.**

F	P	J	B	H	G	O	A	K	N
A	O	R	E	L	V	E	J	U	O
M	T	I	K	D	P	G	T	B	I
H	A	F	Q	B	W	A	G	O	N
I	T	X	C	A	Y	B	Z	C	O
V	O	D	A	Z	L	B	F	J	E
K	Z	T	R	H	Y	A	M	G	R
F	W	B	R	O	C	C	O	L	I
O	B	K	O	Q	D	S	I	C	Y
C	G	X	T	J	P	E	H	M	A

Creative Drawing

■ Create an image using each circle below as a starting point. What can you imagine the circle will be?

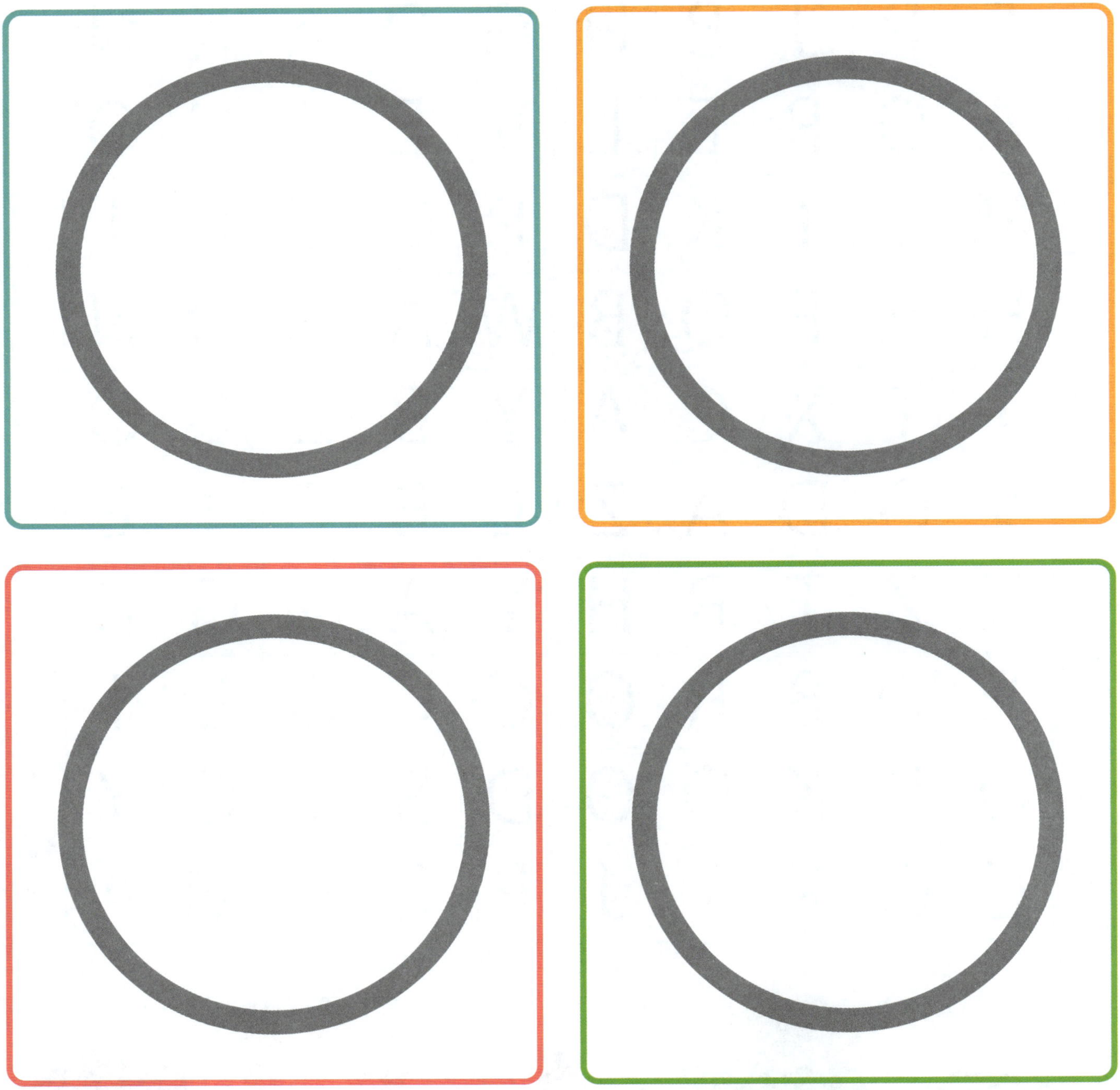

■ What does the shape below remind you of? Draw your own image starting with the shape below.

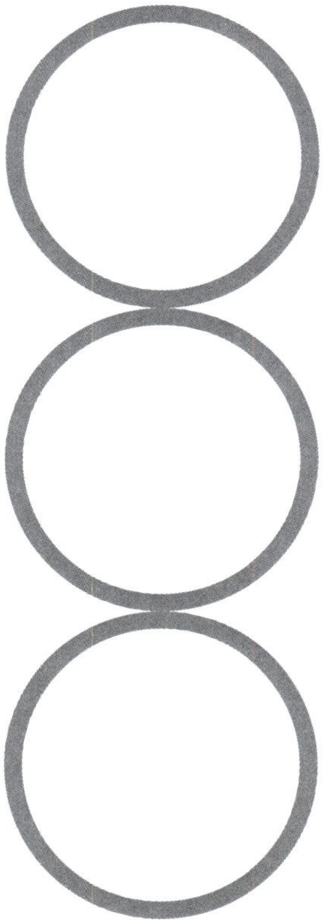

Problem Solving

■ Draw a solution to help Andy round up all the chickens and prevent them from escaping again.

■ Draw a solution to help Ramone get the piano inside the school.

SCHOOL

Physical Education Break!

It's important to move your body and exercise!
Try this fun activity below to break up your studying!

- Pick 5 exercises from the list and try to do them daily!
  Record your progress in the chart!

10 jumping jacks	5 sit ups	5 squats
1 minute run in place	10 frog hops	
1 minute yoga pose	30 seconds high knees	
30 seconds marching in place	10 star jumps	

Daily Exercise Plan

Exercise	❶	❷	❸	❹	❺
Monday					
Tuesday					
Wednesday					
Thursday					
Friday					
Saturday					
Sunday					

Ace Third Grade
Answer Key

Unit 1 Language Arts

p. 4

Anna	they
Lee and Maude	it
Bicycle	she
Mike	he

p. 5

On Tuesday, I went over to Mindy's house. She has a backyard. We played outside. Mindy's family has a dog named Rover. He likes to play fetch in the backyard. We had a great time.

p. 6

❶squeaks ❷writes ❸play

p. 7

❶☒ We walk to the library.
❷☑
❸☒ Susan washes her hands.
❹☒ My dad cooks dinner.
❺☒ We draw pictures.
❻☑

p. 8

❶tall / taller / tallest
❷big / bigger / biggest
❸long / longer / longest

p. 9

❶longer / longest
❷quieter / quietest
❸softer /softest
❹happier / happiest
❺shinier / shiniest
❻quicker / quickest
❼slower / slowest
❽heavier / heaviest

p. 10

❶because ❷but
❸Although

p. 11

(Answers will vary.)

p. 12

(Answers will vary.)

Unit 1 Reading

p. 14

❶The runner is fast like a cheetah on the track.
❷Jamie was as strong as an ox.
❸The teacher was as busy as a bee.
❹She could swim like a fish.

p. 15

(Answers will vary.)

p. 16

❶He is a night owl.
❷Laura is an angel.
❸His head was always in the clouds.
❹The tiger's teeth were knives.

p. 17

(Answers will vary.)
❶Life goes up and down like a rollercoaster.
❷I felt nervous.
❸The baby's cry was so loud and irritating like a truck siren.
❹Paul's room was messy.

p. 18

wake, lake, snowflakes
quickly, prickly, thickly

p. 19

fro, day, measure, longer, regret, good-bye

p. 20

At the zoo, the lions roar like thunder,
monkeys swing playfully through the trees,
and zebras wear their stripes,
like puzzles in black and white.

Giraffes stand as tall as skyscrapers,
eating leaves from the tallest trees.
And elephants look like big grey ships,
Passing slowly through the sea.

p. 21

(Answers will vary.)

p. 22

(Answers will vary.)

Unit 1 Math

p. 24

❶60 ❷83 ❸83 ❹78
❺284 ❻396 ❼581 ❽782
❾895 ❿686 ⓫799 ⓬978
⓭82 ⓮484 ⓯680 ⓰477

p. 25

❶531 ❷634 ❸736 ❹780
❺908 ❻900 ❼532 ❽723

p. 26

❶24 ❷19 ❸45 ❹45
❺148 ❻257 ❼608 ❽959
❾253 ❿221 ⓫301 ⓬226
⓭36 ⓮243 ⓯808 ⓰339

p. 27

❶184 ❷347 ❸267 ❹293
❺69 ❻63 ❼79 ❽57

p. 28

❶20 ❷30 ❸60
❹10 ❺40 ❻60
❼30 ❽30 ❾90
❿80 ⓫40 ⓬90

p. 29

❶200 ❷300 ❸700
❹100 ❺300 ❻800
❼500 ❽800 ❾900
❿700 ⓫700 ⓬500

p. 30

❶70+20=90 ❷50−30=20
❸40+40=80 ❹70+30=100
❺80−20=60 ❻80−60=20
❼40+20=60 ❽50−20=30

p. 31

❶700+100=800
❷400−200=200
❸300+500=800
❹200+700=900
❺600−100=500
❻300−200=100
❼200+400=600
❽900−500=400

p. 32

❶174+286=460 (books)
❷349+329=($) 678
❸448+264=712 (animals)
❹156+165=321 (pages)

p. 33

❶243−125=118 (stickers)
❷631−147=484 (students)
❸463−285=178 (apples)
❹764−389=375 (pennies)

pp. 34-35

D

Unit 1 Science

p. 36

❶B
❷(Answers will vary.)
❸It can slow it down or speed it up.

p. 37

❶Motion ❷speed
❸force ❹direction

A train going 75 miles per hour.

A girl riding a bike going 5 miles per hour.

A racecar going 150 miles per hour.

p. 38

❶Unbalanced
❷Balanced
❸(Answers will vary.)

p. 39

❶Unbalanced ❷Unbalanced
❸Unbalanced ❹Balanced

p. 40

❶More force will make the ball move faster.
❷The ball would not move as fast because of friction.

p. 41

❶true ❷true ❸true
❹false ❺true

p. 42

❶Magnets are made of metal.
❷Magnetism
❸Magnets are used to hang things on the fridge and in many electronics.

p. 43

p. 44

(Answers will vary.)

Unit 1 Social Studies

p. 46

❶The first people came to America by crossing a land bridge from Asia.
❷France and Spain
❸Christopher Columbus

p. 47

❶North America
❷Indigenous people
❸Christopher Columbus
❹Indians
❺France and Spain

p. 48

❶Unhappiness with British rule and similar government systems.
❷Connecticut, Rhode Island, Massachusetts, and New Hampshire
❸The southern colonies

p. 49

❶true ❷true ❸false
❹true ❺true ❻false

p. 50

❶They made decisions about how the thirteen colonies would fight the British together.
❷France

p. 51

❶1765 ❷1775 ❸1776
❹1778 ❺1781

p. 53

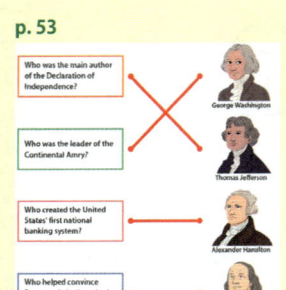

p. 54

Across
1. Hamilton
3. Washington
5. England
7. colony
9. Franklin

Down
2. Revolution
4. thirteen
6. Jefferson

Unit 1 Technology

p. 56

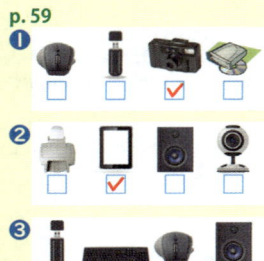

p. 57

1. screen
2. mouse
3. webcam
4. printer
5. speaker
6. keyboard

p. 58

p. 59

p. 60

(keyboard diagrams)

p. 61

(keyboard diagram)

p. 62

1. 519
2. 0843
3. 84651
4. 273709

p. 63

1. (4) 1 9 9 7
2. E b (r R) E e
3. I R 4 (I 4 R) R 4 I
4. R 9 r 7 9 e I R (B 4 E 7)

Unit 2 Language Arts

p. 66

1. Laura's
2. class'
3. cat's
4. houses'

p. 67

1. dinosaur's
2. door's
3. Molly's
4. Douglas'
5. cars'
6. goose's
7. Jess'
8. principal's

p. 68

1. trotting
2. sleepiness
3. strutting
4. creaminess

p. 69

1. dries
2. pries
3. shies
4. denies

p. 70

1. Goodnight Moon
2. The Hungry Caterpillar
3. Romeo and Juliet
4. Charlie and the Chocolate Factory

p. 71

1. ✓
2. ✗ The Great Gatsby
3. ✓
4. ✗ The Lion, the Witch, and the Wardrobe
5. ✗ Pride and Prejudice
6. ✗ Of Mice and Men

p. 72

1. ,   2. .   3. !   4. .

p. 73

. / , / ! / ? / . / ! / .

p. 74

(Answers will vary.)

Unit 2 Reading

p. 76

1. Jared was excited to learn to swim, but he was scared at first.
2. Coach Megan's encouragement and a kickboard.

p. 77

1. Samantha was excited for her first day of school.
2. She was less worried about making friends after sitting down near a girl who introduced herself.
3. She was looking forward to making new friends.

p. 78

1. The moral of the fable is even a small person can help a big one in some situations.
2. When the mouse says, "But as you can see, sometimes even a mouse can help a lion."

p. 79

1. The moral of the fable is a good plan is nothing if you can't complete it.
2. When the old mouse says "It is a good plan, but who will put the bell on the cat."
3. (Answers will vary.)

p. 80

(Answers will vary.)

p. 81

1. Long brown hair and shorter than her classmates.
2. She is happy and optimistic.
3. (Answers will vary.)

p. 82

1. Red
2. She is extremely happy.

p. 83

1. Ballerina
2. Because he was a zombie.
3. A piñata

p. 84

(Answers will vary.)

Unit 2 Math

p. 86

1×Table
1 2 3 4 5 6 7 8 9 10
1. 4
2. 7
3. 5
4. 10
5. 2
6. 6
7. 9
8. 8

p. 87

2×Table
2 4 6 8 10 12 14 16 18 20
1. 2
2. 8
3. 16
4. 10
5. 20
6. 6
7. 12
8. 4

p. 88

3×Table
3 6 9 12 15 18 21 24 27 30
1. 9
2. 15
3. 21
4. 27
5. 12
6. 24
7. 18
8. 6

p. 89

4×Table
4 8 12 16 20 24 28 32 36 40
1. 12
2. 40
3. 36
4. 4
5. 20
6. 32
7. 16
8. 8

p. 90

5×Table
5 10 15 20 25 30 35 40 45 50
1. 20
2. 30
3. 35
4. 10
5. 40
6. 15
7. 45
8. 5

p. 91

6×Table
6 12 18 24 30 36 42 48 54 60
1. 12
2. 42
3. 36
4. 24
5. 60
6. 48
7. 18
8. 30

p. 92

7×Table
7 14 21 28 35 42 49 56 63 70
1. 35
2. 14
3. 42
4. 63
5. 21
6. 49
7. 7
8. 70

p. 93

8×Table
8 16 24 32 40 48 56 64 72 80
1. 32
2. 24
3. 40
4. 64
5. 56
6. 16
7. 80
8. 48

p. 94

9×Table
9 18 27 36 45 54 63 72 81 90
1. 27
2. 63
3. 45
4. 54
5. 36
6. 81
7. 9
8. 18

p. 95

10×Table
10 20 30 40 50 60 70 80 90 100
1. 90
2. 30
3. 10
4. 70
5. 100
6. 20
7. 60
8. 50

pp. 96-97

All the multiplication facts are True.

Unit 2 Science

p. 98

1. Plants, animals, and fungi.
2. Living things can move on their own and breathe.
3. By wind, water or people.

p. 99

1. Living things
2. Non-living things
3. Energy
4. feel
5. Plants

p. 100

1. A life cycle is a series of changes that living things go through to grow.
2. Birds, fish, and reptiles lay eggs.
3. Marsupials raise babies in pouches.

p. 101

1. Tadpole
2. Froglet
3. Adult frog

p. 103

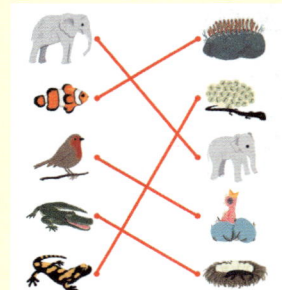

p. 104
1 Adaptations are traits living things develop to survive.
2 They help living things reproduce and survive.
3 Birds having different beaks.

p. 105
1 behavioral
2 physical
3 behavioral
4 physical

p. 106
(Answers will vary.)

Unit 2 Social Studies

p. 108
1 the government
2 Anyone can create rules for anything.
3 (Answers will vary.)

p. 109
1 safe
2 the government
3 rules
4 Federal
5 elected representatives

p. 110
1 Rules are for some people and laws are for everyone to follow.
2 stealing money

p. 111
1 true 2 true 3 true
4 false 5 true 6 true

p. 113
1 West Virgina 2 Arizona
3 North Dakota 4 Indiana
5 Georgia 6 Pennsylvania

p. 115
1 Right and Responsibility
2 Right
3 Right and Responsibility
4 Responsibility 5 Right
6 Right 7 Right

p. 116

```
G O V E R N M E N T
W F C G T E O P M Q
E G Z D F R H B O A
R J A I L B W T I S
G T S A C V E Q U E
J Y G H O M R C T U
K U R U L E G R I O
L I A K P N C I H I
O M W R L K X M B P
P U N I S H M E N T
B W S B T Z D D K M
Y C F C A X Q P O L
R I G H T Z Y U I A
C V A S E D H J L W
```

Unit 2 Technology

pp. 118-119

pp. 120-121

pp. 122-123
1 ✓ repeat 6 times / repeat 4 times / repeat 3 times
2 repeat 2 times / repeat 2 times / ✓ repeat 2 times
3 repeat 2 times / ✓ repeat 3 times / repeat 2 times

pp. 124-125

Unit 3 Reading

p. 128
1 Tall trees and a sparkling lake.
2 Liam was less afraid because he had his flashlight and teddy bear.

p. 129
1 A volcano
2 Yes, she did.
3 Winning the science fair made Sophie more excited about doing future science projects.

p. 130
1 The main topic of the passage is platypuses. "The platypus is a very unique animal that lives in Australia."
2 It is a mammal that lays eggs.

p. 131
1 Give the reader information about the sport of cricket.
2 "Cricket is a popular sport played in many countries" and there are details about how it is played.
3 He is a famous cricket player.

p. 132
1 "who lived in the 1800's," "In 1881,"
2 Clara Barton and the start of the American Red Cross.

p. 133
1 How to plant a vegetable garden.
2 First, next, after, and finally
3 Because the steps are important for the vegetable garden to come out right. If not, the plants might not grow.

p. 135
1 Red pandas
2 To teach people about red pandas in text one, and to persuade people that red pandas are amazing in text two.
3 The informational text
4 Informational texts are based on facts and not opinions, so they have more truth.
(Facts: May vary.)
• Red pandas are special animals.
• Red pandas are endangered.

p. 136
First / Next / After / Then / Finally

Unit 3 Writing

p. 138
Circle: three pigs / wolf
1 The pigs decided to build houses.
2 The wolf came.
3 He blew down all the house but the brick house.

p. 139
(Answers will vary.)

p. 140
1 Underline: "Lucy?" / "Are you there?"
2 She runs into the hall.
3 "I thought I had heard my sister coming up the stairs."
4 "I started to worry."

p. 141
(Answers will vary.)

p. 142
1 Before bed, I brush my teeth.
2 After, breakfast I wash my plate.
3 First, I put on my socks and then my shoes.
4 Later, Sam had dance practice.
5 Yesterday, we went to the movies.
6 Tomorrow, Johnny has a soccer game.

p. 143
(Answers will vary.)

pp. 144-145
(Answers will vary.)

p. 146
(Answers will vary.)

Unit 3 Math

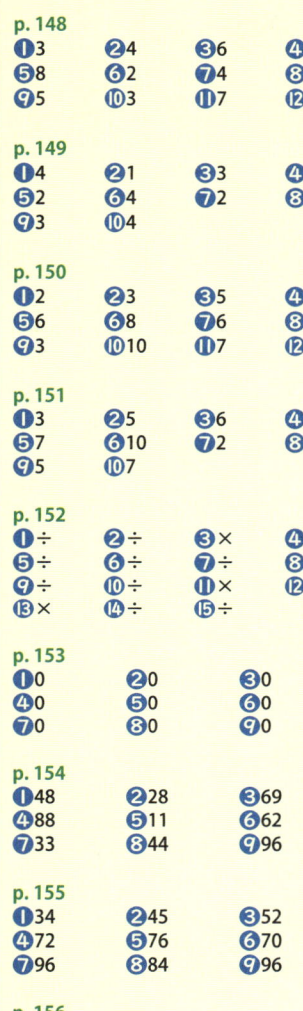

p. 148
1 3 2 4 3 6 4 9
5 8 6 2 7 4 8 10
9 5 10 3 11 7 12 4

p. 149
1 4 2 1 3 3 4 5
5 2 6 4 7 2 8 5
9 3 10 4

p. 150
1 2 2 3 3 5 4 7
5 6 6 8 7 6 8 9
9 3 10 10 11 7 12 9

p. 151
1 3 2 5 3 6 4 8
5 7 6 10 7 2 8 8
9 5 10 7

p. 152
1 ÷ 2 ÷ 3 × 4 ×
5 ÷ 6 ÷ 7 ÷ 8 ×
9 ÷ 10 ÷ 11 × 12 ÷
13 × 14 ÷ 15 ÷

p. 153
1 0 2 0 3 0
4 0 5 0 6 0
7 0 8 0 9 0

p. 154
1 48 2 28 3 69
4 88 5 11 6 62
7 33 8 44 9 96

p. 155
1 34 2 45 3 52
4 72 5 76 6 70
7 96 8 84 9 96

p. 156
1 4×2=8 (people)
2 7×5=35 (chairs)
3 3×9=27 (marbles)
4 8×6=48 (buttons)

p. 157
1 9÷3=3 (groups)
2 24÷6=4 (treats)
3 56÷8=7 (rows)
4 40÷5=8 (bricks)

p. 158
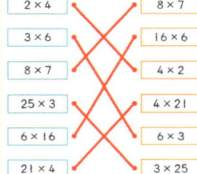

2 × 4	8 × 7
3 × 6	16 × 6
8 × 7	4 × 2
25 × 3	4 × 21
6 × 16	6 × 3
21 × 4	3 × 25

p. 159

8	×	9	=	36	×	2	=	24	×	3
4	×	7	=	7	×	4	=	14	×	2
81	÷	9	=	45	÷	5	=	3	×	3
54	÷	9	=	48	÷	8	=	42	÷	7
8	×	7	=	14	×	4	=	28	×	2
5	×	2	=	80	÷	8	=	20	÷	2

Unit 3 Science

p. 160
❶An ecosystem is made up of living and non-living things in one area.
❷Parts of an ecosystem affect each other. It something changes it effects others.
❸The ecosystem would be affected and can be damaged.

p. 161
❶If all the eagles left the ecosystem there would be so many mice that they would eat all the grass and the ecosystem would be out of balance.
❷There would be so many mice they would eat all the berries and the berry bushes would die out.
❸Humans could help breed more eagles in captivity and release them into the ecosystem to help rebalance it.

p. 162
❶energy
❷A food chain is the transfer of energy in an ecosystem.
❸A

p. 163
❶A or D ❷B ❸C

p. 165
❶true ❷false ❸false
❹true ❺true ❻false

p. 166
❶Humans can cause a lot of damage to an ecosystem like pollution and deforestation.
❷People can help stop climate change by reforesting areas and limiting pollution.

p. 167

p. 168
(Answers will vary.)

Unit 3 Social Studies

p. 171
❶Mountains ❷plains
❸islands ❹Plateaus
❺Valleys ❻hills

p. 173
❶true ❷true ❸true
❹true ❺true ❻true
❼false

p. 175
❶topographical map
❷town map
❸political map
❹town map
❺topographical map

p. 176
❶A map scale is a scale on a map to show distance.
❷A compass rose is used on a map to show the four main directions.

p. 177
❶about 7 miles
❷about 9 miles
❸about 10 miles
❹about 8 miles
❺about 6 miles

p. 178

P	L	A	I	N	Q	W	L	E	V
R	T	Y	U	I	O	P	A	A	A
G	H	I	L	L	F	D	K	S	L
H	J	K	L	M	P	N	E	B	L
D	P	S	A	Z	L	X	C	V	E
M	O	U	N	T	A	I	N	O	Y
F	N	G	H	J	T	K	L	P	O
T	D	Y	O	C	E	A	N	U	P
R	E	W	Q	Z	A	X	C	V	B
J	H	G	F	D	U	S	A	M	E
I	S	L	A	N	D	C	O	I	E
K	L	W	T	Y	R	I	V	E	R

Unit 3 Personal Finance

p. 180
❶1.30 ❷2.52
❸0.39 ❹3.26

p. 181

p. 182

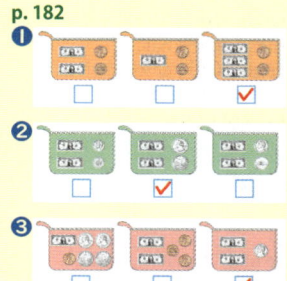

p. 183
(Answers will vary.)

pp. 184-185
❶0.30 ❷0.05
❸0.10 ❹0.05

p. 186

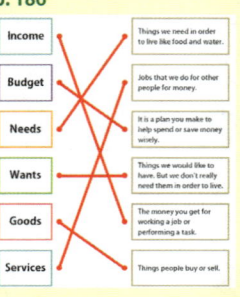

p. 187
❶Service ❷Good ❸Good
❹Good ❺Service ❻Service

Unit 4 Reading

p. 190
Box: "I believe that cats are better than dogs."
Underline: "First…"; "Cats are also…"; "Cats are playful too."; "Cats are good…"
Circle: "They don't need…"; "Dogs have more…"; "You can play…"

p. 191
❶The writer's main opinion is that chores are good for teaching kids responsibility.
❷It teaches them that their actions matter and they can be helpful in their own families. That kids learn to manage their time and learn other helpful skills for the future.
❸(Answers will vary.)

pp. 192-193
❶Children playing video games.
❷Passage 1 has a positive opinion.
❸(Answers will vary.)
❹Passage 2 has a negative opinion.
❺❻❼(Answers will vary.)

p. 194
❶The main argument of this text is that homework is good for kids.
❷It helps students practice what they learned in school and it helps them do better on tests.

p. 195
❶It is important to eat breakfast.
❷It helps your body and brain start the day strong. It gives you energy. It can keep you healthy by keeping you full and stop you from eating unhealthy snacks.
❸❹(Answers will vary.)

p. 196
❶That kids should have longer recess time in schools.
❷It would help kids get fresh air and let their energy out which can make them more focused in class.

p. 197
❶That reading is better than watching movies.
❷You get to picture the book in your mind, and you can read wherever you want.
❸❹(Answers will vary.)

p. 198
(Answers will vary.)

Unit 4 Writing

p. 200
❶Frogs make funny noises.
❷Frogs live in and around bodies of water.
❸Frogs are great at jumping.

p. 201
(Answers will vary.)

pp. 202-203
(Answers will vary.)

p. 204
Circle: Hermit crabs work together in a fascinating way.
Underline: Then they will keep trading shells down the line, so each crab gets a slightly bigger shell.

p. 205
(Answers will vary.)

pp. 206–207
(Answers will vary.)

p. 208
(Answers will vary.)

Unit 4 Math

p. 210
❶$\frac{1}{2}$ ❷$\frac{5}{6}$ ❸$\frac{1}{4}$ ❹$\frac{2}{3}$

p. 211
Example

p. 212
❶> ❷< ❸=
❹< ❺= ❻>

p. 213

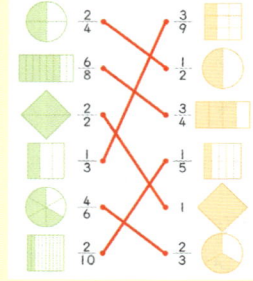

p. 214
❶$\frac{2}{3}$ ❷$\frac{5}{9}$ ❸$\frac{3}{4}$ ❹$\frac{4}{5}$
❺$\frac{4}{7}$ ❻$\frac{9}{10}$ ❼$\frac{5}{8}$ ❽$\frac{5}{6}$

p. 215
❶$\frac{1}{3}$ ❷$\frac{3}{5}$ ❸$\frac{3}{7}$ ❹$\frac{1}{4}$
❺$\frac{4}{9}$ ❻$\frac{1}{6}$ ❼$\frac{7}{10}$ ❽$\frac{3}{8}$

p. 216
❶6 ❷1 ❸3 ❹7
❺4 ❻8 ❼0.9 ❽0.2
❾0.7 ❿0.3 ⓫0.5 ⓬0.1

p. 217
❶6 ❷4 ❸1 ❹8
❺9 ❻3 ❼0.01 ❽0.02
❾0.05 ❿0.07 ⓫0.11 ⓬0.12

p. 218
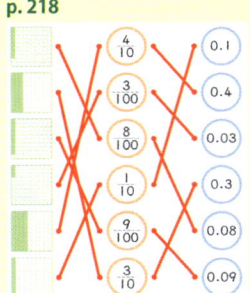

p. 219
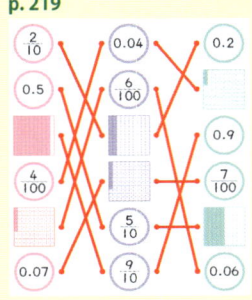

p. 220

p. 221

Unit 4 Science

p. 222
❶Weather is the combination of temperature, precipitation, wind speed and air pressure in an area at a certain time.
❷Climate is an area's weather over a certain period of time.
❸Climate change is making Earth's weather warmer and unpredictable.

p. 223
❶true ❷true ❸true
❹true ❺false ❻true

p. 225
❶arctic ❷temperate
❸tropical ❹temperate

p. 227
❶Meteorology is the study of the earth's weather.
❷Meteorologists study and predict the weather based on patterns and climate in an area.
❸Rain, snow, and wind.

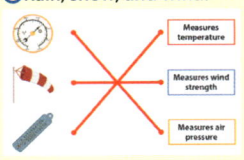

p. 229

Features	Thunderstorm	Hurricane	Blizzard
Heavy Rain	✕	✕	
Strong winds	✕	✕	✕
People can lose power	✕	✕	✕
Can cause flooding	✕	✕	
Heavy snow			✕
Extreme cold temperatures			✕
Lightning Strikes	✕	✕	
Hail	✕	✕	✕
Thunder	✕	✕	

p. 230
(Answers will vary.)

Unit 4 Social Studies

p. 232
❶A democracy is a government run by the people.
❷A direct democracy is when everyone comes together to decide how the country should be run. But a representative democracy elects representatives to make decisions for the people.
❸A monarchy is a government with one leader.

p. 233
❶governments ❷representative
❸direct ❹republic
❺monarch ❻absolute
❼representatives

p. 234
❶A constitution is a document that states the laws of a country or state.
❷An amendment is a change to a constitution that is approved by the government.

p. 235
❶true ❷true ❸false
❹false ❺true ❻true

p. 236
❶There are three branches of government.
❷(Answers will vary.)

p. 237
Executive Branch
Power to recommend laws, veto new laws, send soldiers to war.
Checked by – Judicial and Legislative

Legislative Branch
Power to make laws and declare war, impeach presidents and judges.
Checked by – Executive Branch

Judicial Branch
Power to choose judges, decide if people are guilty or not guilty and decide if a law goes against the constitution.
Checked by – Executive and Legislative

p. 238
❶All 50 states
❷The states decide by themselves.

p. 239
(Answers will vary.)

p. 240

```
M B K I N G C D E M
G Q Z X C V J B D O
V W R F R J N E N
E T E S H B L M O A
R E M C K G K O J R
R P U B L I C K C
N Y E E L F J R L H
M U R E P D H A M Y
E O O W Q S F C N H
N I R U I O D Y V G
T P T Y Q W A B C F
P A S Q U E E N C D
O S D F G H J K X Z
I M O N A R C H Z A
```

Unit 4 Thinking Skills

pp. 242–243
❶C ❷D ❸A ❹B
❺C ❻B ❼D ❽A

pp. 244–245
❶A ❷B

p. 246

p. 247

p. 248
```
N A P A J A C I
R E M A H T R O
N G N I H S I L
B U D N O M U K
```

p. 249
```
6 4 7 3 9 1 4 5 9 7
0 2 6 1 7 3 9 1 6 8
7 1 0 2 8 9 3 3 2 0
8 6 5 0 4 5 3 5 6 2
1 4 8 2 9 8 4 6 7 5
```

Unit 5 Reading

p. 252
❶something someone does well
❷to practice consistently
❸guess the correct outcome
❹to win or succeed at something

p. 253
❶competition ❷predict
❸triumphed ❹diligently
❺talented

p. 254
❶to be cautious
❷to do something brave or risky
❸quick and agile
❹to be thoughtful of someone else's experience or situation

p. 255
❶avoid ❷careful
❸swiftly ❹considerate
❺bold

p. 256
❶b ❷a ❸a

p. 257
❶a ❷a ❸b ❹b

p. 258
dis agree able	use less
un remark able	use ful
re organ ize	happi ness
read ing	fruit ful

p. 259
❶dis ❷un ❸ful
❹less ❺re ❻s

p. 260
❶ unbelievable ❷ unthinkable
❸ unreal ❹ disagree
❺ disobey ❻ disbelief

Unit 5 Writing

p. 262
That people should stop using plastic.

p. 263
(Answers will vary.)

p. 264
Underline: Having garbage around is not nice to look at. It can also cause rats and other pests to come out.

helps make your community look nicer and more pleasant.

p. 265
(Answers will vary.)

p. 266

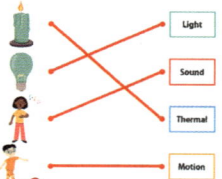

p. 267
(Answers will vary.)

pp. 268–269
(Answers will vary.)

p. 270
(Answers will vary.)

Unit 5 Math

p. 272
❶ 6 ❷ 72 ❸ 3 ❹ 1
❺ 10 ❻ 1 ❼ 10 ❽ 108

p. 273
❶ 5 inches ❷ 10 feet
❸ 15 yards ❹ 3 miles

p. 274
❶ 10 ❷ 30 ❸ 5 ❹ 1,000
❺ 2 ❻ 5,000 ❼ 1 ❽ 20

p. 275
❶ 15 centimeters
❷ 20 kilometers
❸ 12 meters
❹ 42 kilometers

p. 276
❶ 4 ❷ 10 ❸ 3 ❹ 32
❺ 2 ❻ 5,000 ❼ 4 ❽ 28

p. 277
❶ quart ❷ gallon
❸ liter ❹ milliliter

p. 278
❶ 32 ❷ 10 ❸ 3 ❹ 2,000
❺ 4,000 ❻ 8 ❼ 3 ❽ 7,000

p. 279
❶ pound ❷ gram
❸ kilogram ❹ ton

p. 280
❶ 3+3+3+3=12 (inches)
❷ 5+5+5=15 (meters)
❸ 6+6+6+6=24 (feet)
❹ 2+2+2+2+2=10 (inches)

p. 281
❶ 4+4+2+2=12 (feet)
❷ 7+7+7=21 (meters)
❸ 9+9+3+3=24 (centimeters)
❹ 2+2+2+2+2=12 (inches)
❺ 3+3+3+3+3=15 (meters)
❻ 1+1+1+1+1+1+1+1=8 (feet)

p. 282
❶ 6 ❷ 12 ❸ 24 ❹ 18

p. 283
Place a check mark on ❶ ❷ ❹.

Unit 5 Science

p. 284
❶ Energy is the ability to do work.
❷ Energy cannot be created or destroyed.
❸ From the sun.

p. 285
❶ true ❷ true ❸ false
❹ false ❺ true ❻ true

p. 287
❶ Motion energy is energy stored in a moving object.
❷ D

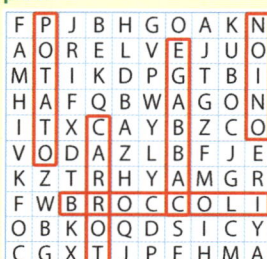

p. 288
❶ Chemical energy is stored in the bonds of molecules and atoms.
❷ Gravitational energy is stored in an object's height and weight.

p. 289
❶ Mechanical energy
❷ Chemical energy
❸ Electrical energy
❹ Gravitational energy

p. 290
❶ Potential energy is stored energy.
❷ Kinetic energy is moving energy.
❸ kinetic energy

p. 291
❶ potential ❷ kinetic
❸ potential ❹ kinetic
❺ potential ❻ kinetic
❼ kinetic ❽ potential

p. 292
(Answers will vary.)

Unit 5 Social Studies

p. 294
❶ The economy is the part of a society that creates wealth.
❷ In a good economy people have jobs and money to spend on needs and wants.
❸ In a bad economy, there are not enough jobs and people don't spend their money enough to help it improve.

p. 295
❶ Economics
❷ wealth
❸ Labor
❹ good / bad
❺ unemployment / unemployment
❻ jobs

p. 296
❶ A good is a product or object people buy.
❷ A service is an act someone performs for money.
❸ Answers will vary. Ex. Milk, eggs, bread.

p. 297
❶ Good ❷ Service
❸ Good ❹ Good
❺ Service ❻ Service
❼ Service ❽ Good

p. 298
❶ Producers make goods and perform services.
❷ Consumers use and pay for goods and services.
❸ There are more options and people can spend more making the economy stronger.

p. 299
❶ true ❷ true ❸ false
❹ true ❺ true ❻ true

p. 300
❶ Earning is working for money.
❷ Candy and toys.
❸ People save money for bills and expensive things like cars.

p. 301
❶ spending ❷ earning
❸ earning ❹ saving
❺ saving ❻ spending

p. 302
Across
❶ goods ❸ employment
Down
❷ labor ❹ economics
❻ product ❽ consumer
❿ money ⓬ income

Unit 5 Thinking Skills

p. 304
❶
❷
❸

p. 305
❶ ❷ ❸

p. 306

G	U	B	A	N	A	N	A	P	J
W	H	T	I	B	Z	S	M	C	Y
A	V	Z	N	A	B	X	E	S	R
W	A	T	E	R	M	E	L	O	N
O	L	X	G	S	W	Q	P	T	M
R	Y	I	B	N	O	V	P	D	U
A	R	F	L	Z	J	G	A	X	B
N	C	W	J	O	T	R	Q	E	V
G	K	T	Y	S	E	P	A	R	G
E	Q	E	V	M	K	F	W	T	O

p. 307

F	P	J	B	H	G	O	A	K	N
A	O	R	E	L	V	E	J	U	O
M	T	I	K	D	P	G	T	B	I
H	A	F	Q	B	W	A	G	O	N
I	T	X	C	A	Y	B	Z	C	O
V	O	D	A	Z	L	B	F	J	E
K	Z	T	R	H	Y	A	M	G	R
F	W	B	R	O	C	C	O	L	I
O	B	K	O	Q	D	S	I	C	Y
C	G	X	T	J	P	E	H	M	A

pp. 308–309
(Answers will vary.)

pp. 310–311
(Answers will vary.)

CERTIFICATE

OF ACHIEVEMENT

─────────────────────────────────

is hereby congratulated on completing

Kumon Ace Third Grade

_____   _____

Date   **Parent or Guardian**

Ace Third Grade

Unit 1
COMPLETED!

Unit 2
COMPLETED!

Unit 3
COMPLETED!

Unit 4
COMPLETED!

Unit 5
COMPLETED!

All Pages Completed!

Excellent Work!